Reluctant Reformers

Also by Robert L. Allen
Black Awakening in Capitalist America

Reluctant Reformers

Racism and Social Reform Movements in the United States

by **Robert L. Allen**

with the collaboration of
Pamela P. Allen

HOWARD UNIVERSITY PRESS

Washington, D.C. ● *1983*

Printed in the United States of America.

Library of Congress Cataloging in Publication Data

Allen, Robert L., 1942–
  Reluctant reformers.

  Includes bibliographical references and index.
    1. United States—Social conditions—1960-1970.
  2. United States—Race question.   3. Social movements—
  United States.   I. Allen, Pamela P.   II. Title.
  HN59.A554   1982   303.4′84   82-23197
  ISBN 0-88258-002-7
  ISBN 0-88258-026-4 (pbk.)

In memory of my father,
Robert L. Allen, Sr.

Contents

Reluctant Reformers

Preface

The idea for this book arose in the course of teaching the history of racism in the United States. I was teaching in the Black Studies Department and New College at San Jose State College, and Pamela Allen was leading study classes on institutional racism for women's movement groups. The classes we were teaching and our own involvement in social change movements made both of us acutely aware of the problems confronting social reformism. As a result, in discussions between ourselves and with students and friends, we were led to ask how American social reform movements in the past had met the challenge of racism. Many friends encouraged us to undertake a study that might offer some insights into this question.

In the spring of 1971 I led a seminar on "Race and Reform" in the New College. Pam participated in the seminar, and we presented in rough form much of the material in this book. To the members of this seminar we owe many thanks for their comments, criticisms and unflagging encouragement. The students in the seminar were: Michael AuClair, Marge Bernard, Guadalupe Hernandez, Frederick Douglass Perry, Carrie Starr, Stephen Takakuwa, Melvin Terry and Howard L. Walker.

I must also express my gratitude to colleagues in the Black Studies Department, Dr. Leonard Jeffries and Dr. Carlene Young, who were kind enough to review parts of the manuscript. In addition, special thanks are extended to Harry Chang, a friend whose knowledgeable comments did much to help bring nebulous ideas into sharper focus.

I wish there were more editors like Paula Giddings at Howard University Press. She took the project very seriously and worked diligently with us in the final editing stages, making many valuable criticisms and suggestions.

Gaby Hughes worked long hours deciphering rough drafts and typing the final manuscript, a grueling task which never dampened her good spirits.

Finally, I must acknowledge my great debt to Pamela Allen. This project could not have been completed without her aid. Pam contributed to the research and writing of every chapter, and she assumed primary responsibility for preparing the chapter on the woman suffrage movement. In this task she was aided by several friends and co-workers, especially Judy Syfers and Kathy Barrett.

Parts of chapters VII and VIII have been published in different form in the *International Socialist Review* (October, 1971) and *The Black Scholar* (February, 1972).

—R.L.A.

San Francisco
August, 1973

CHAPTER I:

Introduction

In the United States in recent years it has become acceptable, even fashionable in some quarters, to assert that the source of racism is to be found in white society. This assertion represents a sharp reversal of earlier opinion which tended to conceptualize the matter in terms of a "Negro Problem," a "Chinese Question," and so on. This change in viewpoint, although certainly not as widespread as some observers have suggested, indicates a growing awareness of the historical origins and contemporary functioning of racism. Black people and other racial minorities have been the victims of this historical process, but they are not its cause. To contend otherwise would be like arguing that the existence of crime is to be understood in terms of the behavior of the victims. Thus it is that we now find whites from all social strata, from prominent government officials to anonymous survey respondents, affirming, at least verbally, their opposition to *white* racism.

Of course, if the locus of racism is white society then one must conclude that some kind of basic change must be made in that society if racism is to be eliminated. This is not to suggest that white society is somehow monolithic or static; on the contrary, numerous strata and competing interest groups exist, and changes of greater or lesser extent are almost constantly occurring. Indeed, it is difficult to identify decades in white America's history when change was not taking place. Not only has change occurred but social reformers have continuously attempted to influence the direction of change by establishing organizations and movements for this purpose. The reformers usually explained their activities in terms of advancing democratic ideals and social justice. There can be no doubt that the overwhelming majority of reformers sincerely believed that what they were doing was for the social good, and in this sense they can be thought of as the more progressive elements of white society.

Yet the question immediately arises: What have white reformers done to abate racism, especially before the racial militancy of the 1950's and 1960's made opposition to segregation and discrimination popular "causes"? As part of their battle for social justice, did early white reformers carry the message of racial equality to their more bigoted brothers and sisters? Did they oppose segregationist and exclusionist movements organized by racists? Did they open their own organizations to participation by nonwhites? In short, if white society is in need of basic changes to purge it of racism, can we say that progressive whites, enlightened social reformers, historically have been a source of such anti-racist thinking and development? This is a central question to be explored in the present study.

The history of the United States is marked by a series of social reform movements, each aimed at correcting some perceived major injustice. Included among these are the militant abolitionist movement, which sought to end slavery; the Populist movement, a radical agrarian alliance of small and poor farmers who opposed exploitation of the farmer by large corporate interests; the turn-of-the-century progressive campaign of middle-class citizens who decried the dangerously growing power of economic monopolies; the woman's rights movement, which fought for the ballot and equality for women; the labor movement, which aimed to protect and improve the lot of the ordinary workingman; and the socialist and communist movements, which professed to seek a totally new society of equality and freedom from all forms of exploitation. Each of these movements sought to transform and improve American society. Accepting their ideals at face value, one would have expected these movements to break down racism, even if only indirectly. Instead, as will be seen, their actual courses were marred by confusion, evasion and opportunism, stemming from varied external and internal causes.

We have chosen these six reform campaigns for study because they were major, national movements that touched all classes and social groups in the nation.[1] Hence, they provide us with a broad view of social reformism. At the same time, the reforms demanded by these movements were also needed by nonwhites, who suffered excruciatingly from the stresses of a rapidly changing social system. Therefore, the question of relations between the races was a subject of more than incidental concern in these movements. This question was given added urgency by the attempts of black reformers to take part in the reform movements, which they believed could benefit black people.

This book is particularly concerned with the ideological impact of racism on predominantly white social reform movements. We will examine how racist ideologies affected both the thinking and the practices of reformers. Racism is both an ideology (but not a static ideology) and a set of social institutions. Although our primary focus here is on ideology, this in no way depreciates the fundamental role played by institutions as the channels through which concrete social behavior operates. On the contrary, ideology, as the term will be used in this study, refers to a coherent, systematic set of social ideas associated with particular institutions, social strata or interest groupings. Thus we take the materialist position that ideology is an outgrowth of social structure. At the same time, however, the reader should be aware that we seek to avoid a narrowly mechanistic view of ideology: Once an ideology is formed it is perfectly capable of playing at least a semi-independent role in subsequent social developments.[2] These statements are put forward here as assumptions, but efforts will be made to assess their usefulness throughout the study.

That racism is an ideology, not a scientific theory, should be obvious to most people today. Virtually all attempts at scientific classification of races and racial characteristics have ended in failure. This is because "race" is not a concept that arose from scientific investigation; rather it developed historically among whites as a social idea to "explain" the inferior status assigned to nonwhites. Thus, when we discuss racism we are dealing with a set of social ideas that reflect established social relations. If we want to know how these social relations originally came to be established, we must look beyond the ideology. Once racism began developing as an ideology, however, there was no lack of scientific "experts" who sought to lay upon it the mantle of scientific objectivity.

In the chapters which follow we will approach the relationship between racism and social reformism from two different viewpoints. On the one hand we will examine each movement in turn, discussing its nature, leadership, and internal dynamics. Our purpose here is to gain a factual appreciation of the complexity of the movements, and their similarities and differences. On the other hand, in the concluding chapter we will attempt a synthesis through discussing the place and role of these movements in the larger flow of American—and world—history. Necessarily this concluding discussion will be more theoretical and panoramic in sweep. Our purpose in the last chapter is not simply to compare and contrast the movements but to understand them from a materialist developmental perspective; that is, to grasp the social forces that motivated their growth and movement and, consequently, their relationship to racism. This requires that we also at that point give some attention to the historical development of racist ideology as a phenomenon in itself.

By taking this twofold approach—individual case studies combined with historical synthesis—we hope to arrive at a broader and deeper appreciation of social reformism and racism, and the significance of their interaction. Just as society is more than a simple sum of individual actions, history is more than a chronology of social events. In effect, the case studies provide factual data for theoretical synthesis; while the synthesis, flowing from a larger and different framework, explains and gives meaning to the particular instances. Both frameworks are necessary and contribute to each other, and each must be measured against the other to determine their overall correctness and value. As with all natural and social phenomena, knowledge is advanced through examining the individual manifestations while also attempting to perceive and understand the whole of which they are part.

The time span of this study begins with the first reform movement after the war of independence and the political formation of the nation. Starting with abolitionism early in the nineteenth century we examine various movements, ending with those that lasted into the middle of the twentieth century. The movements are discussed chronologically—according to when they ended—with those which endured into the twentieth century presented last. Elsewhere I have discussed the struggle against racism since the 1950's in detail.[3]

In compiling the material in this volume we have referred to standard studies of the various reform movements. Where possible we have also relied upon reports by black participants. We were particularly interested in black accounts of social reformism because blacks were the only nonwhite group participating to a significant degree in all six movements.

In sum, this book is a study of the ideological impact of racism on six social reform movements—how racism affected the movements' thinking and action, and thus their role in contributing to changes in general social thought and institutions.

CHAPTER II:

Black Militancy Confronts Militant Abolitionism

Compromise and expediency were themes which characterized the birth of the United States as an independent nation. This was especially true of the question that was later to split the young nation into warring sections: the question of slavery. Slavery was an integral part of the colonial economy, especially in the Southern colonies, and with few exceptions the slave system was generally accepted by the colonists. By the mid-eighteenth century the slave-plantation system of the North American colonies was more than a century old, and its permanency seemed assured.

But problems were beginning to manifest themselves sharply. Soaring production by the tobacco growers had glutted the market, lowering prices and causing severe economic difficulties for many plantations. Some slave owners turned to other crops, such as cotton, but the slow and laborious work required to separate the seeds made commercial cotton-growing largely unfeasible. In the latter half of the eighteenth century, these economic difficulties led many, including numerous slaveholders, to believe that the slave-plantation system was doomed to gradual extinction. Moreover, the new philosophical and political ideas associated with the Industrial Revolution in Europe stimulated the growth of anti-slavery sentiment. Quakers and others condemned slavery as sinful and called for its gradual abolition. Finally, some independence advocates among the colonists also opposed slavery; they felt it was hypocritical to demand freedom from England while still holding black people in slavery. Thus, on the eve of the independence struggle, slavery had become an issue throughout the colonies.

The American Revolution emancipated the colonies but left the slaves in bondage. The original draft of the Declaration of Independence in June, 1776, had included an attack on the slave trade as a "cruel war against human nature itself," but in the interest of compromise and expediency it was eliminated. Although the slave system was in trouble, powerful forces opposed its willful destruction. Northern merchants had long been active in the profitable slave trade, and Southern planters, dependent on slavery, had no intention of becoming accomplices in what was in effect a move to abolish their class.

Again at the Constitutional Convention in 1787, anti-slavery forces tried to have an article written into the Constitution prohibiting the slave trade. This ran into sharp opposition from the pro-slavery forces. Instead, a compromise was reached which imposed an import duty on slaves but prohibited Congress from outlawing the trade before 1808.

With slavery left intact, its political role in the new nation had to be clarified. Again a compromise was worked out. Northern delegates to the Constitutional Convention sought to enhance the political power of the Northern states and insisted that the slaves (who were mainly found in the South) should not be counted for purposes of apportioning representatives to the new Congress. Of course, the Southerners felt otherwise and insisted that the slaves be counted along with the white people. The compromise, written into the United States Constitution, was that each slave would be counted as 3/5 of a person.

In subsequent years, the power of the pro-slavery forces was greatly increased. The invention of the cotton gin, the growth of textile industries in England and New England, and the general agricultural recovery that followed the American Revolution, gave new life to the slave plantation economy of the South. The hope that slavery would gradually disappear was itself abolished by the reinvigoration of that peculiar institution. The slave system was further strengthened by the flourishing slave trade and the enactment of repressive measures designed to keep an increasingly rebellious slave population in check. The ideology of white superiority was buttressed as never before. Preachers, politicians, plantation owners, historians and ethnologists marshalled voluminous arguments asserting the inherent superiority of whites and the inborn, irreversible inferiority of blacks. This tide of racism swept throughout the white population, North as well as South. No doubt could be tolerated as to the legitimacy of an increasingly aggressive and expansionist slave system. The conservative voices of gradual abolition were inexorably drowned out and silenced. It would take a new breed of abolitionists to meet the renewed energy of the slave system.

To some degree the truculent opposition of slaveholders to even gradualist reforms impelled sincere white abolitionists to assume a more militant and uncompromising posture.[1] However, it was black people, slave and free, who were most immediately affected by the entrenchment of slavery and racism, and it was they who spurred the militant campaign against these twin evils.

Black Influences on Militant Abolitionism

The year 1817 makes a convenient starting point for examining black abolitionism, for it marks the beginning of what may be called the organized black abolitionist movement. Participation in the underground railroad and scattered abolitionist activities had been taking place among black people since the eighteenth century, but these activities did not converge and unite in an organized movement until the 1817 conventions in Richmond, Virginia, and Philadelphia, Pennsylvania. These conventions were the first in what was to be a long series of black gatherings which eventually were to be known as the Negro Convention Movement.

This was also the year that Frederick Douglass was born a slave in Talbot County, Maryland. Douglass was to become a leading figure in the development of the militant abolitionist movement, equalled in significance only by William Lloyd Garrison, who in 1817 was a young boy living in Massachusetts.

What prompted these early black meetings of the Convention Movement was the organization in 1816 of the American Colonization Society, which had the avowed purpose of deporting free blacks to areas outside the United States. The society was a strange mixture of white abolitionists and slaveholders bound together by their common agreement that free blacks must be expatriated. For their part, the slaveholders sought the removal of free blacks because they considered them a dangerous element whose presence might incite the slaves to revolt. The abolitionists based their endorsement of the colonization plan on the belief that slavery could never be ended until slaveholders felt assured that the freed blacks would have someplace to go, preferably far away.

It required vigorous protests by free blacks to begin to break down this peculiar and racist alliance between white abolitionists and white slave owners. The 3,000 blacks, including such prominent figures as James Forten and Richard Allen, who convened at Bethel Church in Philadelphia less than a month after the formation of the Colonization Society, loudly decried the society's efforts "to exile us from the land of our nativity."

The significance of the 1817 conventions and those that followed in subsequent years was their dramatization of free Negroes' opposition to expatriation and colonization schemes—an opposition which affected the development of militant abolitionism among whites. White abolitionist Louis Tappan remarked that "it was their united and strenuous opposition to the expatriation scheme that first induced Garrison and others to oppose it." Garrison originally favored colonization, but his attendance at the 1831 National Negro Convention and his growing familiarity with free blacks' opinions moved him to reverse his stand. Black historian Benjamin Quarles notes that Garrison's 1832 pamphlet, *Thoughts on African Colonization,* "was the sharpest and most sustained attack on the American Colonization Society up to that time. Significantly, the entire second half of the small book is devoted to portraying the negative attitude of Negroes toward emigration to Liberia."[2] This small pamphlet succeeded in discrediting colonization plans in the eyes of many heretofore uncertain white abolitionists.

No discussion of black forerunners of militant abolitionism can ignore David Walker's *Appeal.* Originally published in 1829, this document has been described by historian Herbert Aptheker as the first sustained written assault on slavery and racism by a black man.[3] Walker was a free black who operated a small business in Boston, and in his spare time acted as a local agent for *Freedom's Journal,* a black anti-slavery newspaper. The gist of his appeal was a call for the destruction of slavery combined with an argument that slaves were men just as whites. "We are the most degraded, wretched, and abject set of beings that ever lived since the world began," Walker wrote.[4] The source of this degradation he attributed to the slave system built by Christian Americans. He was particularly enraged by those liberal racists, such as Thomas Jefferson, who, although opposing slavery in the abstract, were nevertheless themselves slaveholders and firm believers in the inferiority of black people. "We, and the world wish to see the charges of Mr. Jefferson refuted by the blacks *themselves,*" Walker asserted, "for we must remember that what the whites have written respecting this subject, is other men's labours, and did not emanate from the blacks."[5] He denounced colonization, and went on in apocalyptic fashion to suggest that a "God of justice and armies" would bring about the destruction of the whole slave system.

Actually, Walker was not altogether clear on how slavery was to be eliminated. Some historians have interpreted his *Appeal* as an all-out call to rebellion on the part of the slaves. However, Walker, like many black spokesmen, was ambiguous on the question of violence. He was well aware of the superior armaments of the white slave owners, and their evident willingness to use them. In the religious tradition of the day, he entreated the masters to repent in the name of God and voluntarily relinquish the slave system. At the same time, however, he cautioned the slaves that *if* a rebellion were launched then "make sure work—do not trifle, for they will not trifle with you—they want us for their slaves, and think nothing of murdering us in order to subject us to that wretched condition—therefore, if there is an attempt made by us, kill or be killed."[6] Thus Walker was no proponent of pacifism, but at the same time he recognized that violence could be helpful to the slaves only if undertaken in propitious circumstances and with great seriousness. Perhaps his position can best be summed up in his own words: "Remember Americans, that we must and shall be free. . . , will you wait until we shall, under God, obtain our liberty by the crushing arm of power? Will it not be dreadful for you? Throw away your fears and prejudices then, and enlighten us and treat us like men, and we will like you more than we do now hate you."[7]

Walker, although ambiguous, raised the question of violent rebellion and thereby clashed directly with the pacifism of many white abolitionists. Benjamin Lundy, a Quaker abolitionist and mentor of Garrison, "set the broadest seal of condemnation" on the *Appeal* in the April, 1830, issue of his paper, *The Genius of Universal Emancipation.* Garrison, who was then Lundy's editorial assistant, wrote an article opposing the circulation of the *Appeal.* Later, writing in his own paper, *The Liberator,* Garrison continued to express disapproval of Walker's pamphlet but he noted that it contained "many valuable truths and seasonable warnings."

Walker's *Appeal* was also to be echoed by black abolitionists in subsequent years. At the 1843 National Negro Convention, Henry Highland Garnet, a young minister, delivered a resoundingly militant speech in which he called upon the slaves to rise up and demand their freedom. If the slave owners attempt violently to suppress the revolt, he said, then "they, and not you, will be responsible for the consequences." Garnet advised: "If you would be free in this generation, here is your only hope. However much you and all of us may desire it, there is not much hope of redemption without the shedding of blood. If you must bleed, let it all come at once—rather die freemen than live to be slaves."[8] This fiery oration created an excited stir at the convention. Frederick Douglass, who was then still committed to Garrisonian pacifism, opposed it, and by a vote of 19 to 18 the delegates refused to endorse Garnet's address. Interestingly, six years later Garnet's address and Walker's *Appeal* appeared together in a pamphlet—reportedly printed at the expense of an obscure farmer named John Brown—when both arguments were more widely accepted in the free black community.[9]

Another issue raised by Walker proved to be a foreshadowing of later developments: his attitude toward American whites. Although he was clear that slave owners were the chief oppressors, Walker took the position that white Americans were the "natural enemies" of black people because of the horrors of racism they had inflicted (or been accomplices to).[10] About the only whites he regarded as genuine friends were the English, because of their abolition of the slave trade in 1807. In fact he advised that if any blacks wanted to emigrate they should "go to those who have been for many years, and are now our greatest earthly friends and benefactors—the English."[11] Beginning in the late 1830's black abolitionists were to debate hotly the question of the extent to which all whites, including abolitionists, were indeed "natural enemies" of black people. The white abolitionists would be accused of approving abolition and equality as abstract intellectual issues, while simultaneously being racist in their everyday practices and attitudes toward blacks.

Walker's *Appeal* was widely circulated in the South as well as in the North. Southern politicians tried to have the pamphlet suppressed and white mobs attacked anyone caught with copies of it. Fearing the spread of Walker's views, Southern legislatures passed laws prohibiting the dissemination of anti-slavery literature and the teaching of reading and writing to slaves and free blacks. A bounty of $3,000 was reportedly offered to anyone who would kill Walker. His death in 1830 under mysterious circumstances remains unexplained to this day.

Still another event that shaped the rise of militant abolitionism was the Nat Turner revolt of 1831. Turner was a Virginia slave who organized and led an insurrection of more than 70 slaves. Some 60 whites were killed. The revolt failed, however, and Turner and his rebel band were all captured or killed. In the ensuing terrorist reaction, at least 120 slaves were killed and hundreds more were arrested. Although the revolt failed, it dispelled all illusions about the submissiveness of black slaves. The white South was terrorized and clamped down even harder on the slaves in a frantic effort to

stave off more revolts. In some areas there was the added fear that
insurgent blacks and Indians might ally against the whites.[12]

In the North a new note of urgency was injected into the anti-
slavery movement. Garrison, who had launched the *Liberator* in
January of that year, was moved by the Turner revolt to begin organizing his New England Anti-Slavery Society.[13] The group held
its first meeting in January, 1832, and in 1833 militant abolitionism
was given a national focus with the organizing, by both black and
white abolitionists, of the American Anti-Slavery Society (AASS)
in Philadelphia.

The New England Society has been described by Truman Nelson
as "the first organized group in the United States to press for the
immediate emancipation of the slaves without compensation to the
slave-owners."[14] The available evidence appears to support this
statement, but it should be noted that the immediatism issue had
been a recurring, although relatively minor, theme among white
anti-slavery writers for a number of years.[15] Immediate emancipation was also urged by *Freedom's Journal* in 1827.[16] Moreover, pri-
or to the early 1830's there existed about fifty black anti-slavery
organizations. Little has been written about these societies, but such
as is known of their activities tends to suggest that they favored
the immediate overthrow of slavery without compensation to the
owners.[17]

Through their activities militant blacks, both slave and free,
raised key issues that were to affect the evolution of militant abolitionism and the debates that would engage black and white abolitionists in subsequent decades. The vocal opposition to colonization
schemes; the raising of the question of violent rebellion by the
slaves; the advocacy of immediate abolition of slavery; the view that
all whites, including white abolitionists, were implicated in racism
and sought to limit the freedom of blacks—all were issues that had
been avoided by the old conservative abolitionist movement but now
confronted the new movement.

The birth of the militant abolitionist groups in New England and
Philadelphia was strongly encouraged and supported by black abolitionists. Most of the existing black anti-slavery groups threw their

support behind the Garrisonian organizations. In addition, blacks were the chief subscribers to Garrison's newspaper. In 1831 of some 450 *Liberator* subscribers fully 400 were black; and by 1834 out of more than 2,000 subscribers only about one-fourth were white. Other anti-slavery papers enjoyed similar Negro support.

Of the 63 original signers of the Declaration of Sentiments of the American Anti-Slavery Society, three were blacks. Six blacks sat on the board of managers of the society. Black abolitionists were also highly active in organizing and guiding affiliates of the new parent society, including groups in Massachusetts, New York, Pennsylvania and Ohio. This kind of black involvement presented quite a contrast to the earlier conservative abolitionist movement. As late as 1826, for example, some 143 white-controlled anti-slavery societies excluded blacks and women from membership.

Black Abolitionists and the Negro Convention Movement

The Negro Convention Movement of the 1830's and 1840's provided the chief vehicle for the expression of black militancy. Six national conventions were held in the 1830's and three in the 1840's, along with a host of state and local gatherings. Although many black abolitionists worked with the predominantly white anti-slavery societies, they maintained close ties with the Negro Conventions. The conventions supplied an independent organizational base for blacks to raise issues and develop programs. In fact, many of the issues which were exposed by the Douglass-Garrison split of the 1850's were already being debated years earlier in the Negro Conventions.

The leadership of the black conventions was drawn primarily from among Negro ministers. The ministry, the only profession easily accessible to blacks, was a natural training ground for black leaders not only for the churches but for all other spheres of black social life. From the church a black activist might go into publishing and editing, the lecture circuit, or business. For generations the black church was a wellspring of articulate spokesmen for black freedom, producing leaders such as Richard Allen and Henry Highland Garnet. Even black leaders who did not have a ministerial background, such as David Walker and Frederick Douglass, were strongly influenced by the teachings of the church and the oratorical style of black preachers.

The 1830 meeting, which is considered the first of the National Negro Conventions, was called specifically to organize aid for a group of blacks emigrating to Canada in order to escape racial strife in Cincinnati, Ohio.[18] Some 40 delegates representing seven states met in Philadelphia's historic Bethel Church from September 20th through 24th.[19] The delegates implored free blacks to "devise and pursue all legal means for the speedy elevation of ourselves and brethren to the scale and standing of men."[20] The convention drew up a constitution which suggested that blacks themselves must assume primary responsibility in organizing economic, social and educational activities aimed at improving their conditions.

The emigration question prompted much agonized discussion in the Negro Conventions. In keeping with its announced purpose, the 1830 meeting voted to help those forced to seek refuge in Canada, but it rapped the American Colonization Society's efforts to expatriate blacks en masse to Liberia. Subsequent meetings witnessed a reappraisal of the emigration issue, especially the proposal to establish a permanent settlement in Canada. Some delegates disapproved of emigration in principle. Others favored it only as a last resort for those forced to flee persecution. There was a growing feeling among the black leaders that any kind of massive emigration by free blacks was in effect a betrayal of their brothers and sisters still held in bondage, since it would perforce remove a section of the population most outspokenly hostile to slavery. This, of course, is precisely what the slaveholders in the Colonization Society hoped to accomplish with their expatriation schemes, and this explains the Negro Conventions' consistent opposition to the Colonization Society. Nevertheless, some blacks were forced to emigrate and the conventions continued to aid these refugees, although the idea of an officially sponsored settlement in Canada was apparently dropped.[21]

Despite this compromise solution, the emigration question remained a source of disquiet, and in the 1850's it assumed a new dimension. A group of pro-emigrationists under the leadership of Martin R. Delaney, an early black nationalist, reflected the growing alienation of many blacks brought on by the passage of the 1850 Fugitive Slave Law. These emigrationists contended that (1) white abolitionists promised a miracle they couldn't deliver, and in the process they robbed blacks of their independence;[22] and (2) the U.S. Constitution was a pro-slavery instrument, as demonstrated by the Fugitive Law, which made a mockery of hopes of emancipation.[23] Consequently, emigration was proposed as the only reasonable option left open to blacks. Delaney, a former co-editor of Douglass' *North Star,* wrote a book discussing emigration and he helped organize an emigration convention in 1854.

Another matter that agitated the Negro Conventions was the dispute over the propriety of separate, all-black organizations. The Garrisonians and some black abolitionists believed that separate organizations perpetuated prejudice and discrimination. Other blacks stressed the need for blacks to act independently of even their so-called friends. This dispute contributed to a split in the Negro Convention Movement in 1835, with Philadelphia Negroes forming an integrationist, pro-Garrisonian group known as the American Moral Reform Society, while New York blacks rallied around the *Colored American,* a black abolitionist newspaper that was becoming increasingly critical of the Garrisonian faith.[24] The split resulted in the discontinuance of the annual black conventions.

The revival of the National Negro Conventions had to await the emergence of the abolitionist Liberty Party in the 1840's.[25] The Liberty Party, in proposing political action against slavery, offered an alternative to the moral suasion tactics of the Garrisonians. This appealed to politically minded New York blacks who called a convention in 1843 with the hope of securing endorsement for the Liberty Party.[26] The endorsement was secured, but over the strenuous objections of a small group of moral suasionists led by Frederick Douglass.

For some, however, even political action was not enough. It was at this convention that Henry Highland Garnet issued his famous call for slave rebellions, and it was Douglass, then still a Garrisonian pacifist, who was partly responsible for the rejection of Garnet's address.[27]

Character of the White Abolitionist Movement

While black people were instrumental in shaping the contours of militant abolitionism, there were serious strains within the white abolitionist movement which in turn were to affect its black counterpart. Basically, the white abolitionists were divided into conservative and militant camps, with the militants being further divided between reformers and radicals. The conservative viewpoint, which characterized most of the earlier abolitionists, had a religious orientation, a low-keyed and conciliatory tone, and favored colonization. A strong sense that slavery was a sin which God would eventually punish provided the religious impulse that guided these early antislavery workers, as well as the later militants. A substantial proportion of the early workers were Quaker pacifists. Many Southern whites were also active in the early movement since they, like many people at the end of the eighteenth century, firmly believed that the plantation system and slavery were doomed to die of their own accord. These Southerners may have inspired the racial and sexual discrimination practiced by the early societies, but as will be shown, the Northern militants of later years were far from agreed on these matters.

A distinguishing feature of the early conservative abolitionists is that almost all were gradualists, that is, they believed that emancipation should be a slow and gradual process spread over many years. This meant, of course, that they counseled the slaves to be passive and patient. Gradualism reflected the view that any precipitous emancipation of the slaves would disrupt Southern institutions and economic life. Describing the conservatives, Quarles

wrote: "Conciliatory to the core, the earlier generation of abolitionists seemed to go out of their way to win the love and esteem
of the South. [They] gave constant and, positive assurance to Southerners that they had no intention of interfering with the rights
of property. Hence slave emancipation was not to be achieved without compensation to the owners."[28]

Although initially hesitant on the question of colonization, by
1821 almost all of the early white abolitionists endorsed some
scheme of black expatriation as a convenient way of reconciling abolition with the racial antipathies of the white population, including
themselves.

By 1830, however, buffeted by a resurgent slave system and insistently independent activity by militant blacks, the conservative abolitionist movement gave way to a new and militant movement.

The key defining characteristics of the militant abolitionists after
1830 were that all favored immediate emancipation without compensation, and they generally opposed emigration proposals. The
American Anti-Slavery Society demanded the "instant" abandonment of slavery, and added: "We maintain that no compensation
should be given to the planters emancipating their slaves." The militants argued that to compensate a slave owner for freeing his slaves
was tantamount to admitting the legitimacy of slavery.[29] On the
question of colonization the Society stated: "We regard as delusive,
cruel and dangerous, any scheme of expatriation which pretends
to aid, either directly or indirectly, in the emancipation of the slaves,
or to be a substitute for the immediate and total abolition of
slavery."[30] The militants proposed to achieve their ends through
constant and active agitation against slavery: "to convince all our
fellow-citizens, by arguments addressed to their understandings and
consciences, that Slaveholding is a heinous crime in the sight of
God. . . ." This echoed the activist note struck by Garrison in the
first issue of the *Liberator:* "Let Southern oppressors tremble
. . . let their Northern apologists tremble—let all the enemies of
the persecuted blacks tremble. . . . Urge me not to use moderation

in a cause like the present. I am in earnest—I will not equivocate—
I will not excuse—I will not retreat a single inch—*and I will be
heard.*"

Beyond this point, however, there was considerable discord
among the militants; not the least of which was a fundamental dis-
parity in philosophy between the reform-minded and radical abolitionists. Historian Aileen Kraditor defines the radicals as "those
abolitionists who, like Garrison, believed that American society,
North as well as South, was fundamentally immoral, with slavery
only the worst of its many sins, and who looked forward to a
thoroughgoing change in its institutional structure and ideology."
In other words, the radicals were universalists who perceived a wide
range of issues and struggles as related, and indeed interlocked. The
other wing of the militants were reformers who "considered Northern society fundamentally good and believed that abolition of slavery
would eliminate a deviation from its essential goodness and thereby
strengthen and preserve its basically moral arrangements."[31] There
was no hard and fast line separating these two camps, but Kraditor
argues that, especially after 1837, the factions increasingly disagreed
over basic questions of strategy. The Garrisonian radicals tended
to adopt a broad, all-embracing approach to social change, whereas
the anti-Garrisonian reformists proposed a more limited, single-issue approach. After 1839 the two groups also split over the question
of whether agitation and moral suasion, or political action and voting were the proper and sole methods of attaining abolition.

In terms of concrete issues there were several that divided the
two militant factions. One was the question of the role of women
in anti-slavery work. In fact, this was the overt issue that split the
American Anti-Slavery Society in 1840. It must be borne in mind
that at this time in history the only socially acceptable role for the
middle-classs white woman was to be a wife, mother and mistress
of a household. Poor white women were active in the hired work
force and black women, of course, were exploited as slaves. However, it was unheard of for a middle-class white woman to step
down from the pedestal. The dominant values of the period miti-

gated against these women becoming vocally involved in political agitation.

White women took part in the founding convention of the AASS in 1833. However, they were not allowed to sign the Declaration of Sentiments or to join the society.[32] That same year black and white women in Philadelphia formed the Philadelphia Female Anti-Slavery Society. Other female anti-slavery societies were formed in subsequent years and in 1837 the first National Female Anti-Slavery Society Convention was held with 81 delegates from 12 states. The women were especially helpful to the abolition societies through their fund-raising work. Like their male counterparts they faced harassment from violent mobs, but the women persevered in their efforts.

Despite these early activities the "woman question" did not arise as an issue in the abolition movement until 1837. In that year Sarah and Angelina Grimké, two Southern white women who were former slaveholders, started lecturing on abolition to mixed audiences of men and women. This created quite a sensation, with the result that antifeminist abolitionists began dredging up arguments from the Bible to support their contention that women should not be allowed to speak in public, or that such unladylike activity was contrary to custom and a threat to the existence of the family.[33] On the other hand, the Garrisonian radicals, later including Douglass, argued not only that women should be allowed to speak in public meetings but they should also be granted full voting and office-holding privileges in the anti-slavery societies. For some time the radicals held sway and more and more women became active in anti-slavery work. Many of the early feminists were also active in the abolition movement, especially after 1848, but historian Benjamin Quarles believes that they may have done this not so much out of a commitment to abolition but because it provided them an opportunity to promote the cause of woman's rights.[34] In any event, the debate came to a climax at the 1840 meeting of the AASS, when Abby Kelley, a staunch Garrisonian, was appointed to the business committee. Then three other women, including Lucretia Mott, were elected to the executive committee. This was too much for the antifeminists, and a number of delegates walked out of the convention claiming that these actions had virtually merged the abolition and woman's rights movements. This only confused matters, they thought, and that very night the dissenters met and formed the rival American and Foreign Anti-Slavery Society. Although the woman question precipitated the split, it was symptomatic of a deeper and growing rift between the factions.

Interestingly, among the officers of the new anti-slavery group was Henry B. Stanton, husband of the feminist Elizabeth Cady Stanton. It was Mrs. Stanton who converted Frederick Douglass to a pro-feminist position after she returned from the 1840 World Anti-Slavery Convention held in London.[35] Thereafter, Douglass was a strong and consistent defender of woman's rights, as were several other leading black abolitionists. Indeed, it was not uncommon for black groups to pass resolutions endorsing woman's rights. However, a question must be raised as to whether the black male leaders intended the inclusion of black women in their pro-feminist resolutions. There is some evidence of tension between the sexes over the role of black women in organizations,[36] and Quarles suggests that black leaders may have found it opportune to make common cause with militant white women in an effort to secure additional allies for the struggle against racial oppression.[37] Black women were not indifferent to these matters, and some were active proponents of women's rights. It was a black woman, Maria W. Stewart, who was the first native-born American woman recorded as speaking in public.[38] She spoke out against slavery and rebuked the Colonization Society. Black women who supported woman's rights did so because (1) they wanted the right to attend and speak at anti-slavery meetings, and (2) they desired their full share of political rights.

Aside from the woman question, an issue which further separated the radical abolitionists from the reformers was the matter of religion. By 1839 Garrison had become a severe critic of the churches and clergymen. Although a fervently religious man himself, he scathingly attacked churchmen whom he accused of upholding or conciliating slavery. As far as he was concerned the churches were "a great brotherhood of thieves" because they gave their blessings to man-stealing. In 1840 the Anti-Slavery Society Convention formally condemned the churches for their pro-slavery stand: "The church ought not to be regarded and treated as the Church of Christ, but as the foe of freedom, humanity, and pure religion, so long as it occupies its present position."[39] About the only religious group that was not thoroughly denounced were the Quakers, because of their long-standing record of anti-slavery activity.[40]

Needless to say, these sharp jabs at organized religion brought thunder down upon the heads of the radical abolitionists, not only from conservative church figures but also from many religious abolitionists. The religion issue also played a part in Garrison's later break with Douglass. Douglass had recognized something Garrison failed to see. The slavery issue had split the churches, particularly Baptists and Methodists, right down the middle. This opened the door for abolitionist agitation in some of the churches, and Douglass therefore felt that a blanket condemnation of organized religion was unwarranted.

A third major difference between Garrisonians and anti-Garrisonians concerned the means for achieving abolition. Should oral and written agitation be the sole means or was some type of political action also necessary? Garrison refused to vote or participate in any way in a government that included slaveholders. He also opposed traditional political parties because of his belief that a party in a country where slavery existed must of necessity be a pro-slavery party. Garrison later went even further and propounded the view that the U.S. Constitution was a pro-slavery document which could not be supported by any true abolitionist. Because of this view he argued that the federal union should be dissolved, and a new country established, excluding the South, with a new constitution. His motto was, "No union with slaveholders."

Garrison's critics advocated voting for abolitionist candidates and engaging in political activity as practical ways of ending slavery.

They contended that the Constitution was anti-slavery in spirit and therefore it was correct to work for the abolition of slavery within the federal union.

Ironically, Garrison's position dovetailed very nicely with that of the Southern slaveholders. The Southerners asserted that slavery could not be prohibited by the federal government under the Constitution since it was a matter of states' rights. Political abolitionists denied this and argued that slavery was a question of federal policy. Garrison's assertion of the pro-slavery nature of the Constitution, combined with his insistence that abolitionists should abstain from political activity, was a position that could only give comfort to the slaveholders.

This debate over political action also put Garrison on a collision course with many black abolitionists. Many free blacks in the North who supported radical abolitionism on other questions did not accept this non-voting position. Samuel Cornish, a well-known black newspaper editor, asserted at an anti-slavery convention that the disfranchisement of blacks in New York State was the chief cause of their oppressed condition. He asserted that if two candidates ran for that state's Assembly seats with one favoring and the other opposing black suffrage, and both indifferent to the question of slavery, blacks would support the candidate favoring suffrage.[41] In later years Garrison and Douglass would also have strong disagreements over this question with Douglass drifting more toward political abolition and becoming involved with the Liberty Party, the Free Soil Party, and the Republican Party.

These, then, were the major issues which came to separate the reformist from the radical abolitionists. It should now be clear that these labels are less than satisfactory, since they suggest static groupings and do not reflect the dynamic of changing relationships. Leaving the labels aside, these issues also affected the relationship between black and white abolitionists, as has been suggested, and this matter will be taken up in more detail in subsequent pages.

However, it is necessary now to examine the leadership of the militant abolitionists and to consider their relationship to American society in general.

White Leadership and Northern Racism

The leaders of the white militant abolitionists tended to be middle-class intellectuals and professionals. Many of them were college-trained and ran the gamut of professions, including law, medicine, religion and education. A handful of businessmen joined the cause and even a few former slaveholders such as James Birney and the Grimké sisters. Before the 1840 split, their basic approach to abolishing slavery was to employ the intellectual's tools of newspapers, pamphlets and oratory at public meetings. Possibly because of their social background and the fact that most of them had never lived in the South, slavery was for many of them an abstract intellectual issue that did not concern their daily lives. As will become evident, when militant abolitionists advocated immediate emancipation, it did not necessarily imply that they also advocated political and social equality of the races.

Despite their shortcomings and ambiguities, militant anti-slavery workers were in a sense the ideological vanguard of Northern industrial capitalism. They were not necessarily conscious of this role, but their anti-slavery agitation helped make the general public more aware of the sharpening contradiction between the North and the South. In many ways the slave-plantation system of the South and the industrial system of the North were in fundamental conflict. Moreover, both systems were expanding rapidly and the question was, which would come to dominate the political power structure of the United States? In the decades before the Civil War a precarious balance had been maintained between the two systems. The industrial North dominated what is now known as the Midwest, but at the same time the slaveholding South, through the seizure of Texas and the war against Mexico in 1846,[42] had acquired large blocs of land in the Southwest. Every slave state that came into the Union meant more power in Congress for the South, whereas every free state meant more power for the North. Consequently, the conflict between North and South took the form of a political fight over the *expansion* of the slave system.

As detailed in what follows, the North was not particularly interested in ending racial oppression; its only goal was to weaken the
political strength of the South. This attitude found a reflection in
abolitionist thinking. White abolitionists saw the need to undermine
the power of the slaveholder in order to destroy slavery, but they
were not concerned to step beyond emancipation and attack racism
in all of its manifestations. Aside from their radicalism on the slavery issue, most militant abolitionists were very much products of
the society in which they lived.

Abolitionists' prejudices were reinforced by the attitude of the
Northern white population. Free blacks before the Civil War suffered many legal, social and economic limitations in the Northern
states.[43] By 1820 they did not have the legal rights and privileges
of citizens, and in fact their very citizenship was in question. With
few exceptions the State Department refused to grant passports to
free blacks, issuing certificates instead. The department claimed the
issuance of passports would amount to recognizing blacks as
citizens.

Questions of citizenship also affected the procurement of land.
Some abolitionists felt that given the extent of race prejudice in the
North as well as the South, blacks should be resettled on separate
lands in the West. This solution was never adopted; rather blacks
were kept out of the new Western lands whenever possible. Until
the Dred Scott decision in 1857 ruled conclusively that free blacks
were not citizens, Congress explicitly excluded blacks from land and
homestead bills in the 1840's and 1850's so as to reserve those lands
for white settlers.[44]

Free blacks were further restricted in their residence. Whites
were hostile to blacks settling in their towns and put pressure on
their legislatures to prevent black immigration. One form of restriction was to require the posting of bonds against pauperhood ranging
from $500 to $1,000. Although these were seldom enforced, occasionally they would be used to harass black residents.

In most Northern states black male suffrage was either restricted
or denied. Even in the New England states where full suffrage was

granted, social pressure kept many black men from exercising the franchise.[45] Black abolitionist agitation for suffrage resulted in popular referendums, but these were defeated. In fact, the movement to extend suffrage to all men led to the disfranchisement of black voters in some areas. Many opponents of universal suffrage could be won over only by limiting it to universal *white* manhood suffrage. In New York State, where there was qualified suffrage for black men, Gerrit Smith, a leading abolitionist, arranged for land grants to free blacks so they could qualify as voters.

Free blacks in the North thus faced tremendous discrimination. School segregation existed, jobs were limited to the most menial work, and blacks enjoyed little legal redress of their grievances. Whites justified their exclusion of blacks on the grounds that black people were incapable of achieving the standards of white society and that integration of the two races would necessitate the lowering of those standards.

White abolitionists proved not to be immune to such racially prejudiced reasoning.

Tension Between Black and White Abolitionists

The prevalence of racism in the North contributed to racial tensions within the militant abolitionist movement. Some historians have argued that militant white abolitionists resolutely fought against white supremacy. While this may have been true of some white anti-slavery workers, nevertheless it will be shown that to be anti-slavery was not necessarily to be anti-racist. Relations between white and black abolitionists were far from harmonious, at least partly due to the inability of many white abolitionists to accept blacks as fully equal and independent human beings.

Unlike their predecessors, the militant abolitionists accepted blacks as members and officers in the anti-slavery societies but not without misgivings and dissension.[46] On one side were some whites who contended that to discriminate against blacks was to betray the whole abolitionist cause. On the other were arrayed whites who felt it inexpedient to admit blacks since this might offend whites who were otherwise disposed to join the anti-slavery movement. There was, however, another dimension to this debate which both sides glossed over. When the militant abolitionists came on the scene in the early 1830's they had little support except among free blacks in the North. The Quakers who had been the backbone of the old abolitionist movement were alienated by the militancy of the new campaign, and their support fell off. Hence, aside from any question of principle, there was the simple fact that in its early stages militant abolitionism could count on finding diligent workers and loyal supporters only among a few people, many of whom were black. Those white abolitionists who sought to deny membership to blacks were calculating that by excluding blacks they could gain wider white support for the cause. In effect, they took the *hope* of winning more support among racist whites as valid grounds for alienating existing black supporters. They thereby fell victim to the illogic of white-supremacist thinking, a temptation that has consistently snared white social reformers.

The question of racial equality absorbed a great deal of the energy of abolitionist speakers and writers. Both black and white abolitionists spent much time arguing that the slaves were indeed men, in an effort to counter the almost universally held belief that black slaves were subhuman and biologically inferior to whites. However, in their arguments some interesting differences in purpose and perception were revealed, although it cannot be said that these differences break down strictly along black-white lines. From earliest times, black abolitionists constantly strove to prove to the world that they were the equals, the peers, of any white men.[47] Basically, they argued that, given full freedom, blacks could equal the achievements of whites. While some white abolitionists supported this contention,[48] the converse of this equality argument was also frequently employed; namely, that any person could be degraded to the status of a slave. Indeed, abolitionist orators often exhorted their listeners to imagine themselves in the place of the slaves. Recalcitrant listeners were apprised of the biblical injunction: "Remember them that are in bonds, as bound with them." The purpose of these admonitions was to induce complacent whites to empathize with the slaves, and hopefully join the anti-slavery cause.[49]

The most extreme form of this "empathy" theme appeared in the form of the "white slaves" argument. For example, in a Boston speech in 1829 Garrison asked his hearers to use their imaginations:

> Suppose that—by some miracle—the slaves should suddenly become white. Would you shut your eyes on their suffering, and calmly talk of constitutional limitations? No, your voice would peal in the ears of the taskmasters like deep thunder; you would carry the constitution by force. . . patriotic assemblies would congregate at the corners of every street; the old cradle of liberty would rock to a deeper tone than ever echoed therein at British aggression; the pulpit would acquire new and unusual eloquence from our holy religion. The argument, that these white slaves are degraded, would not then obtain. You would say that it is enough that they are white, and in bondage, and they are immediately to be set free. [50]

In this passage Garrison was seeking to generate empathy for the plight of the slave, but in so doing he appealed to the racist feeling that the enslavement of a white person was somehow more deplorable than the enslavement of a black person. Garrison later caught this error and affirmed that he did not consider white slavery more sinful than black slavery.[51] Other white abolitionists were not so astute.[52]

The point of the white slaves argument was to dramatize the fact that black slaves were not inherently more degraded than whites because the oppression of slavery was equally degrading to all people. This line of reasoning may be called the notion of equality in oppression. Most black abolitionists, on the other hand, were less interested in gaining the empathy of whites, and more concerned with demonstrating the notion of equality in freedom—the idea that given full freedom all humans have basically similar capabilities and potentialities. Thus, while sympathetic whites were trying to imagine themselves in the place of suffering slaves, militant blacks were raising the no-doubt-disquieting idea that they were perfectly capable of taking the whites' places! These very different perceptions of the question of equality resulted in the curious contradiction of Frederick Douglass being criticized by white abolitionists because his lectures were too eloquent; he no longer sounded like an illiterate slave.

Even white abolitionists who vigorously proclaimed the inherent equality of the races exhibited a proclivity to accept racist stereotypes. These writers described blacks as lacking practical business sense, and being "weaker in the direction of the understanding." Negroes were said to possess a "fervid African element, so childlike, exuberant, and hopeful." Abolitionist Theodore Tilton applauded blacks for their highly "religious nature," and added that the race's pronounced intuitive faculties made it "the feminine race of the world." That all blacks had rhythm and could make good music was denied by none. Such descriptions bordered dangerously close on Southern stereotypes of the indolent, sensual, happy-go-lucky slave. The overt purpose of these abolitionist writers was to demonstrate that racial equality should not be taken to mean racial sameness, yet in the differences they described there was an implicit assumption that the alleged "feminine" virtues of the black race were in fact inferior to the supposed "masculine" qualities of Caucasians.[53] This romantic racism was indicative of the extent to which the ideology of white supremacy permeated the North, affecting even those whites whose avowed purpose was to oppose it.

The pervasiveness of this racist ideology undoubtedly accounted for abolitionists' reluctance to fight for full equality for blacks. Slavery apologists constantly harped on the so-called horrors of social and political equality, suggesting that this would lead to "black domination." For the most part white abolitionists, ambivalent themselves and fearful lest they offend the sensibilities of sympathetic whites, failed to meet this argument head-on and instead capitulated to it. The American Anti-Slavery Society in its constitution proposed to elevate blacks to a level of "equality with the whites," but it carefully restricted this statement to mean equal enjoyment of "civil and religious privileges," not social equality. Aside from a reluctance to offend sympathetic whites, some white abolitionists were afraid—not without reason—that social intercourse with blacks might precipitate mob action, and others, such as James Birney, contended that the premature introduction of the social equality issue might defeat the struggle for civil rights.[54]

Despite the ambivalences of the whites, blacks were active participants in anti-slavery groups. Few whites, however, deigned to mingle with their black co-workers as social peers. Such conduct was both unpopular and uncommon. Racists asserted that social intermingling led to interracial marriages and thus defiled the "pure" blood of the white race. White abolitionists accepted this argument and went to great lengths to deny that they were amalgamationists. "We do not encourage intermarriage between the whites and blacks," said the New Hampshire Anti-Slavery Society in a notice to the public. "We would discountenance it expressly and distinctly."[55] Lydia Maria Child, an advocate of racial equality, termed the race mixing issue "a false charge, got up by the enemies of the cause, and used as a bugbear to increase the prejudices of the community." Yet she could not resist adding that "by universal emancipation we want to *stop* amalgamation." Even Garrison found it expedient to admit that "at the present time mixed marriages would be in bad taste. . . ."[56]

Black abolitionists could not help but regard the intermarriage issue with a cynical eye. David Walker discussed the subject in his pamphlet, not because he desired to marry a white woman, but because he believed whites' insistent objections to intermarriage were a graphic illustration of the low esteem in which they held the black race.[57] Black author David Ruggles argued similarly in 1834.[58]

Many white abolitionists opposed granting political rights to blacks because they were swayed by the common belief that political equality would lead inexorably to social equality.[59] Other white activists were influenced by anthropological writings which erroneously asserted that blacks had never exhibited any capability for self-government.[60]

Black abolitionists did not tolerate these racist attitudes on the

part of their white co-workers. They charged the whites with har-
boring race bias and recounted many examples to support the accusation. A black newspaper editor wrote that one of the reasons some
whites joined the anti-slavery movement was their belief that it
stood for abstract principles to be applied to the South, without
requiring them to battle prejudice at home. Another editor warned:
"Until abolitionists eradicate prejudice from their own hearts, they
can never receive the unwavering confidence of the people of
color."[61]

One of the few white abolitionists who was never charged with
racism was John Brown. According to Quarles, "Brown's relationships with Negroes had been close, continuous, and on a peer
basis. . . . Apparently no Negro who ever knew Brown ever said
anything in criticism of his attitude or behavior toward colored people. Brown's attitude toward slavery and his grim and forceful response to it were shaped by many things, of which his own personal
experiences with Negroes was not the least."[62]

The Grimké sisters also stand out as unique among white abolitionists. They were the only Southern white women in the movement, having themselves been members of a slaveholding family.
They consistently opposed the idea that blacks were inferior to
whites, and in their own lives and organizational work demonstrated their rejection of race prejudice. The sisters believed that
social integration was the way to overcome race prejudice in whites.
Consequently they urged white and black women both to work and
socialize together. In their activities with the Anti-Slavery Convention of American Women they offered specific recommendations to
combat racism which included both private and public socializing
between the races, a daring and advanced position for their time.

They incorporated this recommendation into their own lives.
Both women sought friendships with black families. Sarah became
very close to a black Philadelphia woman, Sarah Douglass. Both
also protested the practice of segregated seating at Quaker meetings
by sitting with the black members. Angelina's wedding to Theodore
Weld was an interracial event, attended by many leading abolitionists.

Aside from calling on Southerners to free their slaves, the sisters also gave aid to former slaves of their own family. They sent them money and helped one man to become a self-sufficient truck farmer. After the Civil War they discovered that their brother, who had remained a slaveholder, had fathered two sons by one of his slaves. The sons, Francis James Grimké and Archibald Henry Grimké (later to become an outspoken black radical), had been freed by federal troops and had gone to Lincoln University to study. They were welcomed as family members by the sisters and Theodore Weld, the women raising funds from their abolitionists friends to help their nephews through school.[63]

A matter that particularly incensed black abolitionists was the generally patronizing attitude of white reformers and their hostility toward independent action by blacks. Blacks complained that white abolitionists set a double standard of achievement which strongly suggested black inferiority. Thus, whites who expected less of black pupils in the classroom or who accepted shoddy performances by black ministers and teachers, were themselves subjected to stringent criticism. "Our white friends," a black newspaper noted, "are deceived when they imagine they are free from prejudice against color, and yet are content with a lower standard of attainments for colored youth, and inferior exhibitions of talent on the part of colored men. This is, in our view, the worst feature of abolitionism. . . ."[64]

As early as 1839 the *Colored American* began to question the right of white abolitionists to speak for blacks. "As long as we let them think and act for us," the paper warned, "as long as we will bow to their opinions, and acknowledge that their word is counsel, and their will is law, so long they will outwardly treat us as men, while in their hearts they still hold us as slaves."

The black convention movement, which had begun in 1817 and was in full swing in the 1830's, also posed the question of black independence. Historian Leon Litwack remarks that "when the Garrisonian press claimed that separate Negro conventions perpetuated the idea of segregation, the *Colored American* and its supporters reaffirmed their defense of independent action by blacks."[65] Samuel Ward, a black reformer, asserted that the multiple wrongs inflicted on black people made independent black organizations absolutely necessary. This argument between black and white abolitionists continued unabated. Moreover, black abolitionists themselves were very much divided over the question of separate organizations.

Another major criticism leveled against white abolitionists by their black counterparts was the former's half-heartedness in carrying out the second of their stated goals, which was to work toward improving the status of free blacks. Nearly every abolitionist society had a special committee on the welfare of free blacks, but as a rule these committees simply did not function.[66] Black abolitionists were sharply critical of this inaction because they recognized that unless the economic situation of free blacks was improved, emancipation would be only a hollow victory. "When the *Colored American* reviewed the economic plight of the Negro in the wake of the Panic of 1837," Litwack reports, "it noted that not one local abolitionist had placed a Negro in any conspicuous position in his business establishment; in fact, it could not even find a Negro in the offices of the New York Anti-Slavery Society."[67] Black abolitionists entreated their white colleagues and urged them to correct this situation. However, whites who heeded this advice made only token efforts to help the black workingman, which mainly involved giving a few blacks menial jobs.

The American Anti-Slavery Society, for its part, designated four of its 65 agents to work with free blacks in the middle 1830's. These agents were employed to "forward the great work of elevating the pecuniary, social, intellectual, and moral condition of the free people of color" and to "investigate the actual condition of the colored people in the free states." These agents worked in New York, New Jersey, Pennsylvania, Ohio, Illinois, and parts of Canada. Although assigned the job of elevating the economic situation of free blacks, the anti-slavery agents apparently concerned themselves mainly with matters of education, temperance, moral reform, and taking social surveys.[68] Free blacks were urged to acquire trades or take up farming but there is little evidence of any concern with economic barriers to these occupations, such as racial discrimination by em-

ployers and trade unions, or the fact that free states like Ohio required blacks to post $500 bonds before they could settle there.

General indifference to the condition of free blacks stemmed not
only from race prejudice, but also from the white abolitionists' lack
of any kind of overall socioeconomic analysis of American society.
According to Aileen Kraditor, "There is little evidence in the abolitionists' writings of insight into the social sources of ideology or
the class nature of the slave system."[69] It simply did not occur to
most middle-class white abolitionists to think in terms of the workingman, white or black, and they never understood the degree to
which economic freedom was basic to other freedoms. For them
slavery was simply a question of individual morality, and the problem was to persuade the individual slave owner to free his slaves.
They had no comprehension of slavery as an institution, or its relationship to the American economy.

Thus, in the early 1840's both white and black abolitionists were
badly divided over a number of issues. Frederick Douglass at this
time was firmly allied with the Garrisonian factions in both camps,
but this was soon to change.

Douglass-Garrison Split

Douglass, a self-educated slave, ran away from his Maryland master in 1838 and settled in New Bedford, Massachusetts. He met
Garrison at an anti-slavery meeting in 1841. The two men impressed each other, and Douglass was recruited as an anti-slavery
lecturer. Within a short time he had become one of the most popular and sought-after speakers on the abolitionist circuit. Garrison
undoubtedly had a tremendous impact on Douglass' intellectual development, and Douglass' financial survival was largely dependent
on the good will of his white friends; nevertheless, the former slave
maintained a certain independence which eventually was to become
intolerable to Garrison.

Philip Foner in his biography of Douglass reports that "in 1849
Douglass was still a Garrisonian abolitionist. He still adhered to
the Garrisonian doctrines that moral suasion was the only effectual

instrument for the extermination of slavery; that the North should secede from a Union which protected slavery; that the United States Constitution was a pro-slavery document, and that consequently no sincere abolitionist could vote or hold public office."[70] However, the two men had already started moving apart.

Douglass told Garrison in 1847 that he planned to start his own newspaper. Garrison strongly opposed the plan. Garrison's biographer, John L. Thomas, states that the reason for Garrison's opposition was that he didn't desire any new competition for his own *Liberator.*[71] This may have been so, but there is more to the matter. Garrison argued that Douglass could be most effective in the anti-slavery cause as a lecturer. He continued: "It is quite impracticable to combine the editor with the lecturer, without either causing the paper to be more or less neglected, or the sphere of lecturing to be seriously circumscribed."[72] Douglass must have found this line of reasoning amusing since he was well aware that Garrison himself successfully combined the editor with the lecturer.

After some delay, Douglass went ahead and established his paper, *The North Star,* in December, 1847. In his first editorial Douglass wrote that it was the responsibility of black leaders to advocate the anti-slavery cause. "The man who has suffered the wrong is the man to demand redress," he said. "He who has endured the cruel pangs of Slavery is the man to advocate Liberty." The publication of the *North Star* was favorably received by blacks, and it helped bring Douglass into closer contact with his own people. In fact, James McCune Smith, a black New York doctor, wrote a friend that only since the start of his editorial career had Douglass been "seen to become a colored man! I have read his paper very carefully and find phase after phase develop itself as regularly as in one newly born among us."[73]

Garrison reacted to these events by complaining to his wife that Douglass had "never opened to me his lips on the subject, nor asked my advice in any particular whatever! Such conduct grieves me to the heart. His conduct about the paper has been impulsive, inconsiderate, and inconsistent. . . ."[74] Garrison was so discomposed by

Douglass' audacious independence that he could not even give an accurate report of what had actually transpired.

The final split between the two men did not come until the early 1850's. At issue were basic doctrines of the Garrisonian faith: (1) the interpretation of the Constitution and the role of political action; (2) the questions of pacifism and moral suasion; and (3) underlying it all, the issue of black independence.

Through reading and discussion Douglass had become convinced that the Constitution, in purpose and intent, was anti-slavery. Hence, it was the duty of the federal government to eradicate slavery, and Douglass felt that political action aimed at bringing this about was indispensable. Moreover, Douglass slowly arrived at the conclusion that there was no valid reason to break up the Union. "He saw clearly that disunion would isolate slaves and leave them at the mercy of their masters," Foner asserts. "For the North to secede, as the Garrisonians advocated, would relieve it of its share of responsibility for slavery and deny the slaves their most important allies."[75] Garrison's slogan was "No union with slaveholders." Douglass adopted "a more sensible motto, namely, 'No union with slaveholding.' " To Douglass' mind the real issue was the institution of slaveholding, not merely the region or individual slaveholder involved in the system.

In the decade leading up to the Civil War Douglass became ever more active in politics. He vacillated and switched parties frequently and obviously was not always sure which particular course to pursue, but he clearly had grasped the concept that slavery was based on political power and its eradication would require concerted political action.

Tied in with this was Douglass' changing view of pacifism and moral suasion. It is possible that his thinking on this subject was affected by John Brown whom he first met in 1847. In any event Douglass came to believe that moral suasion alone would never liberate the slaves. Increasingly, he started to justify the right of slaves to revolt. He found it disgustingly hypocritical that every Fourth of July the nation praised the revolutionary violence of the

American patriots, while at the same time it condemned the revolutionary violence of slaves who were seeking their own liberation from unjust tyranny. In 1843 Douglass had opposed Garnet's call for slave rebellions, but in 1849 it was Douglass who thundered: "I should welcome the intelligence tomorrow, should it come, that the slaves had risen in the South, and that the sable arms which had been engaged in beautifying and adorning the South were engaged in spreading death and devastation there."[76]

These and all other changes in Douglass' viewpoint were greeted by Garrison with vilifying attacks. Thus, in 1853 at the climax to his dispute with Douglass, Garrison was reduced to racist slanders, charging that "the Anti-Slavery cause, both religiously and politically, has transcended the ability of the sufferers from American Slavery and prejudice, *as a class,* to keep pace with it, or to understand the philosophy of its operations."[77] Such condescending remarks, Douglass noted, were indistinguishable from the racism of "the bitterest despisers of the Negro race."

Abolitionists and White Labor

Their self-righteous and moralizing individualistic approach to social problems also played a part in generating hostility between the abolitionists and white labor. Garrison's advice to white workers in 1840 was that they could help their cause most by self-reform, that is, by giving up drinking, loose living, and otherwise putting their domestic lives in order.[78] Needless to say, such a patronizing approach to the problems of labor tended to alienate white workers from the abolitionists.

There were further reasons why Northern white labor viewed the abolition movement with mixed feelings. Organized labor's basic interest was the improvement of conditions for Northern white workers, and it looked upon black labor, whether slave or free, as a threat to its interests.[79] Hence, support for abolition depended on whether organized labor assessed slave or free black labor as relatively more inimical to its interests. Abolitionists argued that slave and free labor were fundamentally antagonistic and that slavery would eventually degrade the free laborer to the status of a slave.

White workers replied by charging that abolitionists were not concerned with the problems of labor as a whole. Abolitionists had no program for Northern labor, it was asserted, and they had made no provisions for the livelihood of the slaves should they be freed. Moreover, some labor leaders contended that abolition should not concern the workers since in reality it was a political power struggle between Northern industrial and commercial capitalists and Southern agricultural capitalists.

But white workers were mainly alarmed by the thought of competition with black labor. Many feared that if slavery were abolished it would result in a flood of freed slaves into the North. They observed the depressed condition of Southern white workers and concluded that black workers, who were more desperate and therefore willing to work for lower wages, would necessarily depress the wages of Northern white workers. The abolitionists, possessing no economic analysis or program, had no way to allay these fears.

Political Parties, the Civil War and Its Aftermath

Many blacks, including Douglass, became active in the anti-slavery political parties after 1851. Black delegates were present at the Buffalo convention of the Liberty Party in 1843. Resolutions passed at this convention invited blacks into the party as fellow citizens, and urged all party supporters to work for the removal of racial discrimination in their own states.[80] The Liberty Party also nominated blacks for office. John Langston became the first black to be elected by popular vote to the office of clerk of a township. Douglass was the first black to be nominated for a prestigious office, Secretary of State of New York in the election of 1855. Unfortunately, the Liberty Party never received much support from the white electorate.

Militant abolitionist groups always included as an official part of their program a call for equal rights for free blacks as well as an end to slavery. The Free Soil Party and later its successor, the

Republican Party, were the first anti-slavery parties to separate the two issues.[81] Moreover, until 1861 these two parties limited their anti-slavery stand simply to opposition to the expansion of slavery,[82] further backtracking from the abolitionist position of the Liberty Party. The Free Soil Party gingerly avoided the equal rights issue in its national campaigns, although in local campaigns it did sometimes work against racial discrimination. With the removal of demands for equal rights from their platforms and through appealing to the self-interest of free white labor, the Free Soilers and later the Republicans were able to muster widespread support for the anti-slavery cause. This was based, however, on their concern for the detrimental effects of slavery on the white worker, North and South, rather than on any serious concern for the plight of the black slave. Although many political abolitionists rationalized that the white electorate would not support anti-slavery if coupled with a demand for equal rights, at the same time most did not see any contradiction between racial prejudice and anti-slavery as they were themselves uneasy about black populations in their own states and convinced of the intellectual inferiority of black people.[83] In addition, many supported anti-slavery in the 1850's to preserve the frontier for free white settlers and to prevent Southern interference with economic legislation beneficial to the North.[84] Expediency clearly was replacing militancy in the political abolitionist movement.

Douglass and other black abolitionists gave critical support first to the Free Soil Party and then the Republican Party, even though equal rights was compromised. They believed that politically this was all that was feasible, and that these parties could do most for black people.

Abraham Lincoln, who was to pilot the nation through the turbulent waters of secession and Civil War, was anything but an ardent abolitionist. Lincoln regarded slavery as an abstract evil, which he disliked. He pitied the slaves and their suffering, but he also believed that militant agitation for abolition was unsettling to national tranquility. As early as 1837, when the Illinois legislature passed a strongly worded resolution upholding the right of property in slaves, Lincoln issued a mild but revealing protest. Lincoln stated that "the institution of slavery is founded on both injustice and bad policy, but . . . the promulgation of abolition doctrines tends rather to increase than abate its evils." He went on to add that the U.S. Congress "has no power under the Constitution to interfere with the institution of slavery in the different States."[85]

Lincoln shared the common racial prejudices of his day, which led him to oppose social and political equality for blacks. But these were all "false issues," he asserted. The real issue was not these, nor even slavery, but the preservation of the Union. After being elected to the presidency, he wrote: "My paramount object in this struggle is to save the Union, and is not either to save or to destroy slavery."[86] Politically, Lincoln represented the forces that sought to restrict the spread of the slave-plantation system, to keep the free territories of the West open to settlement by small, independent farmers. These forces did not support emancipation, even after the war began, and even less did they favor black suffrage. Lincoln proclaimed emancipation only after it became clear that this step was necessary to successfully undermine the South's agricultural economy and simultaneously enhance the North's military strength by incorporating the manpower represented by the ex-slaves. Similarly, black male suffrage was granted only after this became politically necessary in order to maintain Republican dominance during Reconstruction.[87]

During and after the Civil War hundreds of abolitionists went South to teach and give economic assistance to the freedmen.[88] Many also agitated for passage of the Thirteenth Amendment, which would permanently outlaw slavery. However, on the matter of the Fourteenth and Fifteenth Amendments, which would make blacks citizens and voters, abolitionists were in disagreement. The underlying question of to what extent abolitionism advocated full racial equality was finally coming to a head.

Garrison argued in 1865 that the American Anti-Slavery Society's work was done with the accomplishment of full emancipation.

Many abolitionists disagreed with this, maintaining that the work of securing civil and political equality still had to be done. They kept the society in existence until 1870, agitating for passage of the Fourteenth and Fifteenth Amendments. Garrison resigned but continued to agitate for the rights of black people, although historians disagree as to whether he supported the franchise for freedmen.[89]

Black leaders such as Douglass and Garnet urged a strong program of black male suffrage, full social equality and land for the freedmen. Not all white abolitionists were behind such inclusive demands, although most supported black male suffrage. One key exception was the militant feminists of the woman's rights movement. They supported black male suffrage only if woman suffrage were granted before or along with it. They thus opposed the Fourteenth and Fifteenth Amendments because women were excluded. In 1867 the Equal Rights Association had been founded to work for universal suffrage, but in 1869 the white women dissolved the organization because they felt it was emphasizing black male suffrage at the expense of woman suffrage.

Among anti-slavery legislators Thaddeus Stevens and Charles Sumner were the most militant in their support of the black leaders' demands, but old age and eventually death took these two defenders of equality out of Congress before the end of Reconstruction.

By 1870 the Radical Republicans and militant abolitionists thought they had attained their goals of establishing civil and political equality with the passage of the Fourteenth and Fifteenth Amendments. Many now felt that their work was done. The anti-slavery societies disbanded, although they urged their members to work individually or in new organizations to end race prejudice in the North as well as in the South. Many abolitionists, including Douglass, believed that civil rights was outside the formal sphere of the anti-slavery societies.[90] Other abolitionists, however, had been working locally against school segregation and came to the conclusion that federal action was necessary if it were to be ended.[91] Aaron Powell and others organized the National Reform League to work on desegregation of schools and public accommodations and to agitate for enforcement of civil rights in the South. This organization never developed any strength and was defunct by 1872.[92]

In 1864 the National Colored Men's Convention had formed a National Equal Rights League demanding full emancipation, an end to discrimination, and black male suffrage.[93] The league set up a number of state branches, held national conventions and carried on political work. However, feelings that the National League duplicated the work of the Union Leagues caused its demise by 1869.

Union Leagues were formed in 1863 by Republicans to mobilize public support in the North for the war effort.[94] They moved South with the Union forces, being popular among whites until the end of the 1860's. Black Union Leagues were active until destroyed by intimidation and terrorism. By 1874 they, too, were gone.

Thus, abolitionists had disbanded their anti-slavery societies in a period when organized support for blacks' rights was weakening. There were no strong organizations to take over and urge support of integration and enforcement of civil rights. Moreover, the coalition of Radical Republicans was breaking apart.

Many former Radical Republicans had become disillusioned with the ineptness and corruption of the Grant administration and had joined the Liberal Republicans, a group that advocated amnesty for the white South with no stipulations guaranteeing the civil rights of the black population. Many of these men were former abolitionists, such as Horace Greeley, their Presidential nominee in 1872; yet they felt that their obligations toward black people had been discharged by the passage of the three amendments. Blacks were now free, they believed, to improve their own condition without institutional restraints. The Liberal Republicans courted the white South for support and turned their interest to developing and exploiting the resources of that region. Only Charles Sumner, who joined the Liberal Republicans because of personal and political differences with Grant, argued that civil rights must be a precondition for amnesty. He tried attaching his civil rights bill to an amnesty bill, but this failed. Congress granted amnesty with no provisions for ensuring black civil rights. Sumner also stood alone among the Liberal Republicans in denouncing the racist theories of Northern scholars who supported the South's contentions concerning the inferiority of black people.[95]

Many abolitionists such as Garrison, Wendell Phillips and Douglass supported Grant during the election of 1872, Douglass' active support being instrumental in winning black voters to Grant.

The Civil Rights Act of 1875 climaxed a decade of effort on the part of many abolitionists and Republicans.[96] Yet the bill that finally passed excluded Sumner's provisions outlawing school and cemetery segregation. In addition, the bill was passed by a lame duck session of Congress with 90 of the 162 Republicans not returning to Congress, and in an atmosphere of doubt about the constitutionality of the bill and a pronounced reluctance on the part of the Justice Department to enforce it. White populations both North and South were hostile to equal accommodations. Hence, the stage was set for the betrayal of 1877: abolitionists had dissolved their organizations, the two staunchest defenders of equal rights in Congress were dead, and the mood of the country opposed equality between the races.

CHAPTER III

Self-Interest and Southern Populism

The Southern Populist revolt of the 1890's is often interpreted by liberal white historians as an example of the extent to which racial hostility could be overcome, even in the South.[1] "It is altogether probable," wrote historian C. Vann Woodward, "that during the brief Populist upheaval of the 'nineties, Negroes and native whites achieved a greater comity of mind and harmony of political purpose than ever before or since in the South."[2] In a similar vein Norman Pollack asserts that the "dominant theme" of Populism was that it "sought to extend political justice to Negroes and to stand for policies which would benefit both races." Responding to charges that the Populists were duplicitous or opportunistic, Pollack states that, "in very few instances anywhere in the South does one find indications that expediency rather than principle underlay the Populist response to the Negro."[3]

More specifically, these historians argue, the economic self-interest of the Southern white farmers compelled them in practice to put aside their racial antagonism toward blacks. Evidence for this contention is found in statements made by Populist leaders. Perhaps the most widely known elaboration of the self-interest argument was published in 1892 by Georgia Populist leader Tom Watson. Writing in the periodical, the *Arena,* Watson noted that white and black tenant farmers were equally destitute, equally burdened with heavy taxes and high rents, and equally exploited by unscrupulous merchants. Hence they shared an interest in economic reform, but carefully nurtured racial antipathies prevented them from uniting politically to effect change. "You are kept apart," Watson advised black and white farmers, "that you may be separately fleeced of your earnings. You are made to hate each other because upon that hatred is rested the keystone of the arch of financial despotism which enslaves you both. You are deceived and blinded that you may not see how this race antagonism perpetuates a monetary system which beggars both."[4]

Such antagonism could not be easily overcome, and Watson developed his argument for cooperation as persuasively as possible: "Gratitude may fail; so may sympathy and friendship and generosity and patriotism; but in the long run, self-interest *always* controls. Let it once appear plainly that it is to the interest of a colored man to vote with the white man, and he will do it. Let it plainly appear that it is to the interest of the white man that the vote of the Negro should supplement his own, and the question of having that ballot freely cast and fairly counted, becomes vital to the *white man.*" Watson believed that the Peoples Party, the political arm of Populism, could achieve this racial unity and "settle the race question" by enacting a free ballot system in elections, adopting a platform "immensely beneficial to both races and injurious to neither," and, echoing his dislike for Northern interference during Reconstruction, "making it to the interest of the colored man to have the same patriotic zeal for the welfare of the South that the whites possess."[5]

Significantly, these statements represented strong arguments for black political participation *in support of* the white Populist rebels, but they did not imply political equality. There was no suggestion of electing blacks to public office nor of racial equality within the framework of the People's Party. True, blacks in some areas were elected to office in Populist campaigns and black men sometimes were chosen as People's Party officials, but, as will be shown, it was matters such as these, especially the former, that brought to light Populist misgivings about political equality.

Here we begin getting at a fundamental ambivalence in Southern Populism, which is key to understanding how the Populist move-

ment became a forerunner of the racist demagoguery that characterized Southern politics in subsequent years. White Southern
Populists attacked certain racist practices detrimental to the growth
of their political power, but they did not challenge the underlying
ideology of white supremacy—and in the long run this was to prove
their undoing. From the beginning Watson viewed the People's
Party as a white man's party that was compelled by necessity to
seek black support. For Watson this paternalistic pragmatism was
simply a matter of immediate self-interest. Blacks could not be ignored because they were enfranchised and formed a substantial portion of the Southern population. They were not going to disappear,
as some whites hoped, and unlike the relative handful of Indians
and Chinese, they could not be readily "disposed of" by the
dominant Anglo-Saxons.[6] Through intimidation and outright fraud
the Southern Democrats had succeeded in using the black "vote"
to maintain themselves in power. Hence, the black vote somehow
had to be turned against the entrenched Democratic Party.

To the white Populist mind this was a "practical" matter which
did not raise any questions of fundamental values and ideologies.
In fact, in the matter of racial ideology Southern Populists went
to great lengths to show that they were at one with Southern
Democrats: they wholeheartedly supported white supremacy. Even
in the famous *Arena* article cited above, which is often quoted by
liberal historians as evidence of Watson's pragmatic anti-racism, he
fell back upon the ideology of white supremacy in answering the
racist charge that Populism will lead to Negro domination. "There
is no earthly chance for Negro domination," he responded, "unless
we are ready to admit that the colored man is our superior in will
power, courage, and intellect." Watson stated further that those
"emasculated" whites who talked of black domination were nothing
more than a "degeneration from the race which has never yet feared
any other race. . . . I have no words which can portray my contempt for the white men, Anglo-Saxons, who can knock their knees
together, and through their chattering teeth and pale lips admit that
they are afraid the Negroes will 'dominate us.' " To allay any lingering doubts the Georgia leader pointedly wrote that Populists did

not advocate social equality. "Each citizen regulates his own visiting list—and always will."

These and even more blatantly white-supremacist sentiments typified the ideology of Southern Populism, and this fact is crucial to any understanding of why Populism failed to achieve power based on a black-white farmer's alliance.

Nature of the Southern Populist Revolt

The Populist movement in the South represented a revolt of the small, white farmers—mostly Democrats—"against the urban, business-oriented Democratic oligarchs who preferred industry to Arcadia and who were less solicitous for the small farmer than for the rich capitalist."[7] Moreover, there was a sectional element to the Populist revolt. Northeastern industrial capitalism had won a military victory over the Southern planters in the Civil War, and in succeeding decades it sought to extend its economic and political power to every part of the country, much to the despair of small farmers in both the South and the West. The Populist *Southern Mercury* editorialized bitterly in 1892 that the rulers of the Northeast had contrived that "every law that they have demanded has been enacted, during the past thirty years; and every law demanded put cash in their pockets and has taken cash out of the pockets of other sections of the country."[8] In sum, the farmers were angered by the monopolistic practices and exorbitant freight rates charged by Northern-controlled railroads, and by the economic hardships caused by the banks, trusts, landlords, and middlemen who dominated the Southern agricultural economy. Populism thus was the rebellion of a hard-pressed agricultural class against the encroachments of monopoly capital. Formerly, migration to the Western frontier had provided a safety valve for agrarian discontent, but now with the frontier closed, a rebellious agricultural population had little choice but to become involved in political action.

This was not an easy choice to make. It required years for the farmers' social circles and mutual aid groups of the 1870's and

1880's to mature into the political organizations of the 1890's. Furthermore, activists in the Populist movement found themselves the victims of constant harassment and persecution.

> They had to contend regularly with foreclosure of mortgages, discharge from jobs, eviction as tenants, exclusion from church, withholding of credit, boycott, social ostracism, and the endlessly reiterated charge of racial disloyalty and sectional disloyalty. . . . They contended also against cynical use of fraud comparable with any used against Reconstruction, methods that included stuffed ballot boxes, packed courts, stacked registration and election boards, and open bribery. They saw election after election stolen from them and heard their opponents boast of the theft. They were victims of mobs and lynchers.[9]

Black Populists were targets of special violence by racist mobs. Rev. H.S. Doyle, a young black preacher who made some 63 speeches in behalf of Tom Watson's candidacy for Congress in 1892, found himself threatened by a lynch mob and was forced to flee to Watson for protection. Watson issued a call for help to his Populist supporters and some 2,000 white farmers came to his aid. Doyle was fortunate, but some 15 other black Populists were murdered in Georgia during that election campaign. A similar pattern of intimidation and violence against black Populists was evident in other Southern states.

Clearly, the Populist farmers must have regarded their situation as grim indeed if they were moved to confront such hazards as these.

The White Farmer

One of the chief strongholds of southern Populism was among the upland whites—the so-called hillbillies—who lived in the mountainous backwoods regions of many Southern states.[10] It was among these and other extremely impoverished white farmers that Populism registered its strongest appeal. The reasons for this are not difficult to understand. After the Civil War these small farmers, both owners and tenants, were left in a chronic condition of abject poverty, having little ready capital for planting and harvesting crops, or acquiring new lands. Consequently, this class generated a constant demand for credit. Since the Southern banking system had been heavily damaged by the Civil War, this demand for credit was largely met by local supply merchants. These merchants did not lend money but instead advanced goods that the farmer needed, in return for a lien upon his growing crop, usually cotton.[11] High interest rates customarily were charged on these advances. Further, the crop that was mortgaged must be sold through the merchant who made the advance. The merchant class thereby increasingly gained financial control over the small farmers. In turn, the merchants were closely allied with the large agricultural and industrial capitalists—the Bourbons—who, with Northern aid, had risen to power in the South following Reconstruction. Hence, in the final analysis, the small farmer was subservient to the large corporations, railways and cotton manufacturing industries that were built by infusions of Northern capital. The railways and other corporations, according to Populist historian John D. Hicks, "were rarely scrutinized closely as to their methods and were almost never subjected to any genuine regulation."[12] Exploitive rates and prices, and other monopolistic practices, were the rule of the day. Thus, the farmers perceived their economic distress as due to the unregulated power of industrial capitalism. But regulation of industrial and financial institutions required government intervention, and increasingly the rural whites came to believe that control of state governments was the first step toward their economic salvation.

The Black Farmer-Sharecropper

In the aftermath of the War the black farmer was faced with even greater economic hardship than was the white farmer. Some blacks had sought to establish themselves as independent farmers. Indeed, in Georgia alone blacks purchased almost 7,000 farms in a period of three years.[13] However, the vast majority of black farmers were reduced to peonage under the sharecropping system. Sharecropping consisted of the landowner granting a plot of land to a tenant to work, in return for a portion of the crop—one-half or more—as rental. Having acquired some land the impoverished black tenant would then appeal to a local merchant for supplies. With luck, the tenant would get the needed supplies—in return, of course, for a lien on his crop, with interest rates running up to 30%. Thus, before the hapless tenant turned the first furrow he frequently was already doubly in debt.

Describing the difficulties of tenant farming in Alabama in 1889, Booker T. Washington wrote:

> Its evils have grown instead of decreasing, until it is safe to say that 5/6 of the colored farmers mortgage their crops every year. Not only their crops before, in many cases, they are actually planted, but their wives sign a release from the homestead law and in most every case mules, cows, wagons, plows and often all household furniture is covered by the lien. . . . After a merchant has "run" a farmer for 5 or 6 years and he does not "pay out" or decides to try mortgaging with another merchant the first merchant in such cases usually "cleans up" the farmer, that is takes everything, mules, cows, plows, chicken's fodder— everything except wife and children.[14]

Under such dire circumstances the black farmer shared the grievances of the white farmer, and the material basis for an alliance between the two groups was apparent.

The Rural Heritage of Race Relations

Although there was much to recommend an alliance between black and white farmers, several historical factors had contributed to a deep rift between the two groups. In the first place, many of the poor white farmers were hostile towards blacks, tending to regard them as economic enemies. The explosive advance of the cotton plantation system in the decades prior to the Civil War had seriously undermined the independent small farmers. Unable to compete with the large planters in cotton production they were inexorably pushed out of the fertile regions or forced to emigrate to the frontier.[15] Many of these ousted farmers became the "poor white

trash," "hillbillies," and "crackers" of the mountains and other in-
hospitable regions of the South. The class of poor rural whites was
thereby swelled by the growth of the slave plantation system. However, in the hysterical racist atmosphere cultivated by the big planters, the poor whites were prone to identify their distress not with
the slave *system* but with the slaves themselves. The unquestioning
acceptance of white supremacy demanded by the planters and their
allies combined with the formers' custom of employing poor whites
as harsh overseers between master and slave contributed immensely
to racial antagonisms.[16] The historic hostility between impoverished
rural white and black populations thus has roots that reach back
into the antebellum period.

Although the freedmen sought to ease these hostilities during the
brief Reconstruction interlude, their efforts proved to be in vain. The
enfranchised blacks, in possession of a measure of political power
in many Southern states, used this power to pass progressive legislation that benefited both poor blacks and poor whites. For instance,
the establishment of public school systems in parts of the South can
be traced directly to black Reconstruction.[17] Nevertheless, Southern
politicians and editors succeeded in stamping Reconstruction with
the brand of corruption and identified it in the public mind with
the Republican enemies in the North.

There was enough truth in the latter charge to drive a solid
wedge between black Republicans and white Democrats in the
South. Black Reconstruction was made possible because Northern
businessmen and politicians supported enfranchising the ex-slaves.
This, however, was an alliance of convenience in which the businessmen and politicians used black people as pawns in their attempt
to consolidate the economic and political control of the white North
over the white South. Black men were given the vote, not so much
out of sense of racial justice as to offset the political power of the
white South. After all, the North had won the war and Northern
leaders were anxious to ensure that their national political hegemony was firmly established. They believed this could be accomplished by allowing the freedmen to exercise the franchise within
the framework of the Republican Party.[18] After about ten years,

when the North was well on the road to achieving economic penetration of the South, black people were abandoned by their so-called friends.[19] In the infamous Compromise of 1877 the fate of black people was handed over to the most racist elements in the South, who had already launched a campaign of terrorism designed to disfranchise blacks or subject them to the political domination of the Bourbons who controlled the Democratic Party.

A further point should be observed in this connection. While black people enjoyed a degree of political power they still had no real economic power, despite the fears of poor whites. There had been talk during the war of partitioning confiscated plantation lands among the ex-slaves and Congress passed a limited land allotment act, but President Andrew Johnson ordered all Southern lands restored to their white owners.[20] Blacks might get the vote but they would not be given any substantial portions of land, even though the land belonged to sworn enemies of the Union. Few Republican leaders were ready to countenance such an obvious attack on property rights, especially when their business allies were looking to property-less blacks as a labor reservoir for industry. Consequently, black political power rested on the sufferance of the North; it had no independent economic base, and this made it much easier to undermine Reconstruction.

The Southern Democrats who played several roles in destroying Reconstruction and "redeeming" the South were credited with saving white supremacy from the threat of black domination. On this basis the Southern white population rallied around the Democrats and their racist idea of a "Solid South."

Relations between white and black farmers were further complicated by developments in the post-Reconstruction era. With the collapse of Reconstruction, black people were placed at the mercy of a new white master class whose political arm was the Democratic Party. This produced a curious situation in the Black Belt area of the South where Negroes far outnumbered whites. According to historian Hicks:

> This region was located in the relatively fertile low country that had been the heart of the old plantation system and had always had a pre-

ponderence of Negroes. When the slaves were freed many of them remained in the vicinity of their old homes, and of those who did migrate not a few came back. Landlordism in the Black Belt was at its worst; here the storekeeper-landowner held his Negro tenants in a bondage extremely like slavery. Political rights were of course denied the Negroes, and the landlords, supported by the townspeople, controlled nominations and elections to office. In the hill country, where the whites were more numerous than the ·blacks, the free farmers and the white tenants had the numbers necessary to rule locally if they chose. But in state politics the Black Belt politicians always won, for in all party conventions the black counties were represented not in proportion to the number of actual voters but in proportion to the population. Even when the population of the Black Belt was less than that of the hill counties, the ability of its politicians to manipulate conventions usually more than balanced the difference in numbers. Thus, since the one-party system made a nomination equivalent to an election, a small white minority located in the Black Belt and in the cities was in a position to control the political destinies of a whole state. Naturally the ruling caste used this power to preserve the privileges that it enjoyed.[21]

Black sharecroppers in the Black Belt, under the oppressive weight of Bourbon landlordism, found themselves disfranchised outright, or they were cajoled, bribed and intimidated into voting for the Democratic machine. Even when they refused to vote, they were "voted" by the machine. This scandalous situation evoked two contradictory responses from the white agrarian rebels. The more radical Populist leaders realized that a free ballot had to be instituted if the black vote were to be truly independent. But ingrained custom made it all too easy for many of the dissident white farmers to accept the white supremacist notion that blacks could never intelligently exercise the franchise, and therefore they concluded that blacks should be written off as incorrigible political enemies.

Thus, historically, two contradictory dynamics were at work among the white farmers of the late nineteenth century: one pushing them toward economic and political alliance with similarly exploited black farmers, and the second, based on white supremacy, moving them to economic and political hostility toward black farmers.

The Farmers' Alliances

Agrarian unrest among Southern farmers was brought to a head by the depression of 1873. As early as 1875 a group of frontier farmers in Texas had organized the first farmers' alliance. By 1885 the Texas Alliance claimed a total of 50,000 members spread among some 1,200 locals.[22] The Texas Alliance started its life as a combination social organization and purchasing cooperative, but it soon radically altered its character by drawing up a long list of demands whose implementation would require political action. Among other things the Texas farmers called for the prevention of speculative dealing in the agricultural produce market, more adequate taxation of the railways, new issues of paper money in the hope of thereby reducing credit costs, and an interstate commerce law. A committee of the Texas group was appointed to present these demands to the state legislature and to Congress.

Meanwhile, similar organizing activities were progressing independently in other states, and the Texas Alliance soon joined forces with groups such as the Farmers' Union of Louisiana and the Arkansas Agricultural Wheel. Southern farmers flocked into the consolidated group by the thousands, with the result that by 1890 the new Southern Alliance was estimated to have a membership of between one and three million.[23]

Very nearly the same train of events transpired in the North and West. The first unit of the Northern Alliance was formed in New York in 1877 demanding redress of grievances against the railroads and tax reform, among other things. The Westerners who came into the Northern Alliance sounded a note of economic radicalism. At their 1887 meeting the Western farmers suggested that government regulation of the railways might well be supplemented by actual government ownership of one or more of the transcontinental lines. These farmers also contended that the financial squeeze that gripped agrarian populations could be remedied by the free and unlimited coinage of silver. The federal government had stopped minting silver dollars in 1873, and instead paper money was issued by a number of private national banks acting in effect as subagents of the U.S. Treasury. The farmers believed that this arrangement gave the private banks control over the monetary system and that the banks exploited this control to keep the volume of money in circulation low, thereby keeping the cost of credit at a high level. Free coinage of silver, the farmers argued, would increase the volume of money in circulation and compel the reduction of interest rates. Free silver thus became a rallying cry of the embattled white farmers.

Black farmers were not admitted as members of the Southern Alliance. In fact, in the late 1880's when there was talk of the Texas Alliance combining forces with the Northern Alliance, one of the chief objections raised by the Southerners was the fact that blacks were eligible to membership in the Northern Alliance. The issue came up again at the 1888 meeting of the Southern and Northern Alliances. This meeting proposed to work out a merger between the two groups, but the Northerners objected to the exclusion of black farmers from the Southern Alliance. The Southerners suggested a compromise. They offered to strike the word "white" from their qualifications for membership, thereby leaving to each state organization the right to prescribe the eligibility of black farmers within its jurisdiction. The Southerners specifically wanted to keep blacks out of the national legislative body, the Supreme Council, but as a last concession to the North they offered to change their position on this point. However, by this time negotiations between the Northern and Southern groups had already broken down over this and several other issues. These disagreements ended immediate prospect of union between the two alliances.[24]

Nevertheless, in their own way, the leaders of the Southern white farmers recognized the need for black support. The whites organized a segregated but parallel group called the Colored Farmers' National Alliance and Cooperative Union. The first black alliance was established in Texas in 1886, and by 1891 the Colored Alliance claimed a million and a quarter members scattered among a dozen state organizations.[25]

The national leader and many of the organizers of the Colored Alliance were whites. "What we desire," one of the organizers explained in 1889, "is that the Farmers' Alliance men everywhere will take hold and organize or aid in organizing the colored farmer, and placing him in an attitude to cooperate intelligently and systematically."[26] A Southern white man, R.M. Humphrey, who had been a Baptist missionary among the black farmers, was the main force behind the organizing of the Colored Alliance, and he became its national head. All other officers were blacks.

Populist historian John D. Hicks repeatedly asserts that the Colored Alliance was "little more than an appendage" to the Southern Alliance. The attitude of white Alliance leaders and the virtual fusion of the two groups in 1890 would tend to support this interpretation; yet there were substantial areas of disagreement and discord between the two, and the black alliancemen tried, with little success, to chart an independent course.

At one point in 1891 the Colored Alliance proposed a strike of black cotton pickers. Circulars were mailed out demanding an increase in the wage rate to $1.00 per hundred pounds, and setting a date for the strike.[27] However, Col. L.L. Polk, president of the white Alliance, squelched the strike idea by advising the white farmers to leave their cotton in the fields rather than pay more than fifty cents per hundred to have it picked. Polk charged that the blacks were attempting "to better their condition at the expense of their white brethren. Reforms should not be in the interest of one portion of our farmers at the expense of another."[28] The white Alliance thus sought to prevent the black organization from acting independently, especially when such action seemed to threaten the immediate self-interest of the white farmers.

Underlying this dispute was a difference in class interest between the two groups. Many of the white farmers, especially the leaders of the agrarian revolt, were farm owners and their ideology tended to be that of a landowning class.[29] Between white and black farmers, who were overwhelmingly sharecroppers[30] differing only in degree from landless farm workers, there was a smoldering class conflict not altogether unlike the contemporary conflict between farm owners and farm workers. This class conflict theme was never articulated. Instead, Populist leaders constantly stressed the identity of interests between farmers and laborers.[31] Both groups had a common enemy in Eastern capital, they asserted. The Knights of Labor reciprocated this sympathy, but the American Federation of Labor dismissed the farmers as an employer class.[32] In later years following the decline of Populism and the growth of large-scale farm enterprises, the conflict between farmers and workers became more evident to all concerned.[33]

Politically, the Southern Alliance exhibited little positive concern for black people. Alliancemen had gained control of the 1891 Georgia legislature by electing 160 of its 219 members. While the Alliance platform proposed certain reforms, the Alliance-controlled legislature passed the largest number of anti-black bills ever enacted in a single year in Georgia history.[34] These included a law which laid the basis for the later establishment of the white primary, and a segregation statute which superseded an equal accommodations law won by black politicians during Reconstruction. The segregation bill required railroads to furnish separate coaches for white and black passengers. It also authorized streetcar conductors to segregate the races. The Georgia Colored Alliance, which was holding its state convention in Atlanta at the time, sent a delegation to the legislature to protest the segregation bill. A representative of the delegation argued that black people were not seeking social equality. "All the Negro wants is protection," he said.[35] Despite this protest from their black brothers, the white alliancemen passed the Jim Crow bill and it was signed into law on October 21, 1891.

Black farmers thus were caught in a position of economic and racial conflict with white farmers and their political representatives. However, unlike the Negro Conventions of the Abolitionist era, the black farmers lacked a truly independent organization through which they could develop and articulate their own program. Instead they were reduced to a subservient status in the agrarian reform movement. With the organization of state and national Populist parties in the early 1890's, this situation underwent certain changes in form but not in substance.

Populist Politics and the Black Voter

It must be borne in mind that during the 1880's the farmers in the Southern Alliance were almost to a man staunch supporters of the Democratic Party. Consequently, the initial political strategy which emerged in the Alliance was to try to capture the existing Democratic machinery. The reasoning behind this strategy, according to Hicks' *The Populist Revolt,* was that "loyalty to the one-party system as a guarantee of continued white supremacy would ensure that the Alliance, once it had won control, would have no formidable opposition party to contend with, and the Alliance program could be put through."[36] This strategy of fusion with the Democrats continued to affect Populist thinking even after the independent People's Party had been founded. For a number of reasons, however, the fusionist strategy was not very productive of concrete results, and gradually the Southern leaders began thinking of forming independent third parties.[37] Even so, the allegiance of the Southern white farmers to the Democratic Party struck so deep that only about half the members of the Southern Alliance supported the new Populist Party. "The rest," Hicks comments, "were unwilling to risk the reality of white supremacy in what might prove to be a vain struggle for a new order."[38] A thoroughgoing commitment to white supremacy thus presented a serious hindrance to Populist leaders in their attempts to organize a third party; and indeed, when the Populist movement fell apart after 1896, most of the white farmers simply drifted back into the Democratic Party, the champion of white supremacy.

As the Southern white farmers moved into the political arena, setting up statewide Populist parties and laying the foundation for a national third party, the necessity for black support, meaning black voters, became apparent if the rebels were to succeed in overthrowing the entrenched Democrats. Populist leaders and newspapers began openly calling on black voters for support. They contended that in some states the Republican Party could not represent black voters because it was too weak even to mount a campaign. At the same time they affirmed that they would not resort to the underhanded tricks commonly employed by Democrats in manipulating the black vote. A Georgia Populist paper summarized their proclamations succinctly:

> The Populists recognize that the Negro is a man and a citizen. They want him to see that his ballot is a sacred trust put into his hands to assist in shaping the destiny of the nation and not something to be bartered to designing demagogues who have the longest purse and the largest jug. The Populists will not resort to meetings in dark alleys or make secret promises which will not bear the light of day. On the question of social equality they stand where all other sensible men stand, irrespective of party or race, for to invade the sanctity of home and family by legal enactments would be the ruin of both races. But in the enjoyment of the rights granted to every citizen by the constitution the Populists advocate equal and exact justice to all men. . . .[39]

Populists were viciously attacked by racist Democrats who accused them of trying to undermine white supremacy. The racists asserted that the Democratic Party was "the white man's party" and that if the Populists succeeded in splitting the white vote this would result in black domination. In replying to these charges, Watson and other Populist leaders contended that the Democratic Party represented only the industrial capitalists and not the common white man. As early as 1880, when Watson made his political debut, Woodward tells us that he "called for a revolt from the rule of the industrial clique even if it meant splitting the white man's party."[40] In essence Populist spokesmen said a third party was necessary because the Democrats did not represent white farmers and laborers and the Republicans were repugnant because they were identified with the Southern defeat in the Civil War, and with Reconstruction. Reduced to its barest essentials, Populism was a class revolt within the Democratic Party. However, this class struggle did not really transcend racial lines; the supremacy of the white race was never at issue. On the contrary, Populism hoped to become the new white man's party—the party of the common white man, swept into power on the pivotal votes of his much-needed, but indisputably inferior, dark "brother."

Not all white Populists, however, were convinced that black support was needed to boost them into power. Not surprisingly, this disagreement was reflected in the Populists' stance on the question of the degree and kind of black participation in the movement itself. In states such as Georgia and Texas, blacks were active as officers of the local Populist parties. Watson spoke to racially mixed Populist audiences and shared the speaker's platform with black speakers. In Alabama, on the other hand, a Populist newspaper boasted that no black had ever held a seat in any local Populist convention, and in Virginia black Populists were segregated.

Understandably, black voters expressed ambivalent feelings about the Populist Party. For example, historian Clarence A. Bacote reports that in Georgia, "many Negroes were suspicious of the Populist Party, feeling that its members represented the uneducated class in the state and were responsible for the proscriptive legislation passed by the Alliance legislature of 1890-1891."[41] Most blacks were committed to the Republican Party but a black voter, writing to the *People's Party Paper* in Atlanta in 1892, appealed to blacks to break with the Republicans and join the Populists. The writer charged that the Democrats were hiring black ministers to stump for the Republicans in a drive to destroy the Populists. He then called for black voters to renounce the Republicans and "vote for wife and children and a chance for a home."[42]

Black leaders of the Colored Alliance rejected with one voice the thought of fusion with racist Democrats, advocated by Southern Alliancemen, but they did not share this unity on the question of a third party. At a joint convention of the alliances held in Cincinnati in 1891, all of the black delegates, except E.A. Richardson of Georgia, voted in favor of a third party. The following year at the St. Louis convention the entire Georgia black delegation withdrew when it discovered that Humphrey, the white leader of the Colored Alliance, was allowing whites to cast ballots of the Georgia Colored Alliance in support of a third party.[43]

Well aware of the misgivings of black people, many Populist leaders made a great display of seeking black support and promising to defend the rights of black voters. In 1893, when Georgia led the nation in lynchings, Tom Watson announced that it would be the object of the Populist Party to "make lynch law odious to the people." A year later, at a Populist state convention, Watson seconded the nomination of a black candidate "as a man worthy to be on the executive committee of this or any other party from the state at large." Again, in 1895 Watson denounced Ben Tillman of South Carolina for leading a movement to disfranchise black voters. Finally in 1896 the Georgia state platform of the People's Party carried a plank denouncing lynch law and terrorism and demanding justice for black people. Another plank called for abolition of the convict lease system that virtually made slave laborers of prisoners, imposing its heaviest burden on black people.[44] Examples such as these could be multiplied to cover several pages, but it must be understood that there were serious limitations to what Populists actually were willing to do on behalf of the black voter.

Yet with the Republican Party becoming ever more ineffectual and racist, many independent-minded black voters looked hopefully toward the Populist movement. Blacks had a fairly clear understanding of their needs, but the question was whether the Populists could come through with something more than empty rhetoric. As early as 1888 a convention of black leaders in Georgia spelled out a list of grievances that probably reflected the views of most black voters. They attacked the chain gang and convict lease systems, lynch law, and the spreading practice of segregation. They deplored the barring of blacks from jury duty and inadequate appropriations for black education. Finally, they denounced ballot-tampering, urging a free ballot and a fair count, and they called for black representation in the legislature.[45]

The black leaders did not have to wait long for a Populist response to their grievances. Populist platforms and campaigns routinely included a condemnation of the convict lease system, but this was apparently the limit of their interest in the subject. It would be left to the Progressives to reform the penitentiary system. Like the black leaders, Southern Populists decried lynching in general, but they failed to oppose *particular* lynchings and they offered no concrete proposals to combat this criminal activity. Indeed, the Populists' two-time nominee for governor of Texas was reluctant to endorse a strong anti-lynching measure proposed by the Democratic encumbent.[46] Opposition to segregation fared no better. Most Southern legislatures adopted Jim Crow laws in the late 1880's and early 1890's, and white reformers either endorsed or at least failed to oppose such measures.[47] As for the matter of jury duty, Populists exploited this issue to garner black votes, but blacks were not placed on juries even in Populist-controlled counties.[48] Watson elaborated the Populist position on schools by opposing racially mixed educational institutions. Instead he said that blacks should have their fair share of separate schools. But the agrarian rebels were unwilling to see black (or white) schools improved at the cost of federal intervention, as was proposed under the ill-fated Blair Federal Aid to Education Bill, which, had it been passed, would have provided millions of dollars for public education in the South.

An important test of Populist interest in black rights was seen in the Lodge Federal Elections Bill of 1890, designed to protect black voting rights through federal supervision of congressional elections. It passed the House but was eventually defeated in the Senate. Although the bill was defeated, it fanned the flames of white racism in the South and was a subject of lively controversy for years afterward. It was supported by the Colored Alliance and other black leaders, but white Populists, like white Democrats, were horrified at the thought of federal intervention in the affairs of the South. Tom Watson stated the Populist viewpoint on the federal elections bill in his 1892 *Arena* article. Watson had to play a close game since the Democrats were denouncing the bill as a Republican plot to impose black domination on the South. He tried to steer a course between alienating white voters on one hand and losing black support on the other. Watson therefore opposed federal interference because this "will lead to collision and bloodshed." He immediately added, however, that the People's Party "not only condemns federal interference with elections, but also distinctly commits itself to the method by which every citizen shall have his constitutional right to the free exercise of his electoral choice. We pledge ourselves to isolate the voter from all coercive influences and give him the free and fair exercise of his franchise under state laws." Watson thereby rejected federal intervention—which had in the past proved, and was in the future to prove, the only effective way of securing and protecting black suffrage—and instead offered more promises of Populist fair play.

The Southern reformers were ready to plead states' rights when matters affecting the status of blacks were concerned, but when it came to regulation of railroads or prohibition of dealing in agricultural futures the Southerners were only too willing to endorse federal intervention. They thus consistently chose to interpret the self-interest of blacks as alien to their own needs—a fatal mistake.

Populists talked of political rights for blacks, but their inflexible allegiance to white supremacy led them to undermine the only factor that could have brought them into power—the black voter. In the face of Democratic opposition white Populists had four basic options: (1) They could openly confront the Democratic machine and work to see that the black voter was protected from intimidation and allowed to cast a free ballot that would be fairly counted; (2) they could fuse with black and white Republicans to oust the Democrats, assuming blacks were free to vote the Republican ticket; (3) they could compete with the Democrats in fraudulently manipulating and abusing the black vote; or finally, (4) they could join with Democrats in disfranchising black voters in the hope that they would gain a relative advantage by narrowing the electorate to whites only. For a short time and to a limited extent Georgia Populists chose the first option, while in North Carolina fusion with the Republicans was tried with surprising success. In Mississippi and South Carolina Populists were not above using the same exploitative tricks and manipulation used by Democrats in controlling the black vote. But in the end disfranchisement was the course taken throughout the South. The reasons for this can be illuminated by examining Populist political activities in Alabama and Virginia, and North Carolina and Georgia. In the former two states Populists almost from the outset exhibited hostility to black voting, while in the latter two the black vote was sought by the reformers. However, in all four states black disfranchisement was the final result.

Alabama-Virgina

Black-white cooperation in Alabama was evidently never more than the hope of a very few of the white agrarian reformers. White organizers from the Southern Alliance had established parallel Colored Alliances throughout the state with an estimated membership of 50,000 by 1889.[49] However, the black organizations did not enjoy the full support of the white Alliance, and they were adamantly opposed by the Bourbon Democrats.

With the change in focus from economic to political activity in the 1890's blacks were prevented from participating in the Alabama Populist Party.[50] In the 1892 gubernatorial campaign Populists allied with a dissident faction of the Democratic Party and ran Reuben Kolb for governor against incumbent Thomas Jones. Kolb appealed for black support, but he lost by a narrow margin. Jones won because of majorities tallied in the Southern black belt counties, but analysis of the vote count revealed the use of highly questionable procedures, to say the least.[51] A Democratic paper forthrightly reported: "The truth is that Kolb carried the state, but was swindled out of his victory by the Jones faction, which had control of the election machinery and used it with unblushing trickery and corruption."[52] Nevertheless, the *Southern Mercury,* an important Populist paper published in Texas, probably reflected the views of Alabama Populists when it reached the amazing conclusion that Democratic juggling of the vote count was "proof" that Democrats relied on black support to perpetuate themselves in office![53] The *Mercury* further asserted that Kolb was the "white man's" candidate.

In the 1894 election the Jeffersonian Democratic-Populist fusion group eschewed all pretenses of seeking black support. Kolb ran unsuccessfully against the regular Democratic nominee, General William C. Oates. A black Republican leader who approached the Kolb forces was driven away from their convention hall in Birmingham, and one Kolb leader announced that he favored shooting "every damned Negro who offered to vote."[54] One plank of the fusion platform favored voluntary colonization of blacks in order to ensure white dominance in Alabama.[55]

Despite Populists' frankly white supremacist stand, Democrats screamed "Negro domination" in their effort to scare white voters away from the new party. Moreover, the Democrats soon began pushing for a constitutional convention for the purpose of disfranchising blacks and eliminating once and for all the possibility of any white dissidents gathering support from that quarter. The convention finally was held in Montgomery in 1901. One Democrat piously explained its purpose: "If we abridge or deny the Negro the right to vote, we take this action not in hostility to him as a race . . . but because his exercise of suffrage without restriction makes it unsafe to the life of this state and detrimental to all the interests of the people among whom he resides. . . . The white race must dominate because it is the superior race, and in that domination the Negro will find the safest pledge and guarantee of just and impartial administration. . . ."[56] As though that were not enough, another white leader implied that blacks were the cause of corruption in Alabama elections and that by disfranchising blacks "we will have stricken down forever fraud and corruption in elections. . . ."

There is no account of Populist leaders opposing this insidious move, although their white constituents in the hill counties voted against holding the constitutional convention.[57] Instead the Alabama Populist leaders seem to have adopted the attitude that the white politicians who cheated them out of elections were more to be trusted than their black victims.

In Virginia a variation on this theme was repeated. Prefacing an essay on the rights of black people, a Virginia Populist wrote,

"This is a white man's country and will always be controlled by the whites."[58] This statement fairly well summed up the attitudes of the Virginia reformers. The earlier Readjuster era* in Virginia history, interpreted by the Democratic press as a period of black domination, had turned the state's reform leaders away from any thought of a radical alliance with blacks.[59] In fact the Populist candidate for governor in 1893 had earlier proposed black disfranchisement, and the Populist Party actively sought to dissociate itself from the black vote lest the party be accused of promoting black dominance.[60]

Rampant fraud and intimidation practiced by the Democrats succeeded in keeping the Populists from power. Nevertheless, the Democrats proposed disfranchisement as a way to forestall potential opposition, and also to remove the temptation to cheat.[61] A white Republican found this argument most paradoxical. "The remedy suggested here is to punish the man who has been injured," he commented. Blacks were to be disfranchised "to prevent the Democratic election officials from stealing their votes."[62]

Unlike other areas in the South, Virginia Populism was led by the "better" class of whites, the patrician families of the Black Belt regions. Yet these Southern aristocrats, often regarded as friends of the black race, evidenced no greater interest in black political equality than did many of the poorer Populists. Indeed, the constitutional convention called to disfranchise black people was presided over by a former Populist. The evidence reveals it was the upper-class whites, rather than the poor whites, who sparked the move to bar blacks from the ballot box in Virginia.[63]

North Carolina-Georgia

Populism rode to power in North Carolina by fusing with the Republican Party, which then still had a large black contingent. How-

---

* The Readjuster era was a forerunner of the Populist period. The reformers' goal in that movement was to "readjust" the state debt so that taxes could be reduced, and black votes were actively sought.

ever, this was a matter of "practical" politics and did not represent a revolt against white supremacy. In fact it was the Republicans who opened
the way to fusion in 1894, while anti-black sentiment within the Populist
Party constituted a major threat to the alliance.[64]

During the brief fusion period several major reforms were
enacted, including a new election law that greatly expanded the size
of the electorate by extending the franchise. Moreover, hundreds
of blacks were elected or appointed to local and state offices.

The Democrats countered with their usual scare tactics, but the
Republicans managed to hold the alliance together even though in
1896 the national Populist Party had fused with the Democrats.
Continued black Republican support, although not without internal
bickerings, contributed significantly to fusionist electoral majorities.
But anti-black propaganda spread by the Democrats was already
corralling some Populists back into the folds of the old party.

In 1898 the Democrats made an all-out drive against Negro
domination, claiming this was the goal of the fusionists. The
Populists, becoming ever more uncertain, turned first to the
Democrats who flatly rejected their overtures.[65] They were reluctant
to fuse again with Republicans who were the chief targets of Democratic attacks. At the last minute, however, the two parties joined
forces against the Democrats. However, Populist and Republican
leaders capitulated to racism and countered by charging that the
Democrats had been the first to institute black office-holding, and
therefore they should not be blamed for originating this breach of
the Southern code. But Populist leaders went further and insisted
that the Republicans should remove all black candidates from their
ticket. "I have all along strenuously opposed any cooperation if negroes were to be on the ticket," a member of the Populist executive
committee announced.[66]

The tide had turned, however, and Democrats swept back into
power on the white supremacy issue. They immediately moved to
disfranchise blacks and thereby eliminate this base of support for
any future opposition. Meanwhile, the blatant racism of the 1898
campaign led directly to the Wilmington race riot in which scores

of blacks were beaten and killed by a frenzied mob which had been incited by the Democratic press to destroy the "big burly black brutes" who "dominated" the city.[67]

Tom Watson's Georgia Populists avidly sought black support and even invited blacks to participate in their state conventions.[68] Blacks flocked to hear Watson as he stumped for the Populist cause. At times it seemed that the two races might really unite in a common struggle for better lives for all.

Yet there were portents of the racist turn Watson was later to take. In fact, one recent commentator, who re-examined the evidence, has suggested that Watson did not suddenly undergo a mysterious metamorphosis late in life, but was quite consistently racist all along. Watson is pictured by this scholar as a man filled with nostalgic dreams of the glories of the old slave South. Charles Crowe writes that "as a member of the planter class by birth and one of the largest exploiters of oppressed labor in the state, Watson shared the obsessions of his peers in a hatred of Reconstruction and black aspirations and in a consistent devotion to white supremacy. Nothing in his career prior to 1890 would lead one to suspect him of racial heresy or a radical future."[69]

Watson's earlier anti-black voting record in the Georgia Legislature brought him under fire from black audiences when he ran for re-election to Congress in 1892. His attempts to explain his record were apparently met with skepticism, and his supporters were compelled to argue that Watson was somehow transformed into a new man when he first entered Congress in 1890.

Upon re-examination, even the well-known incident in which Watson shielded a black minister, Rev. H.S. Doyle, from a lynch mob speaks less well of Watson's courage and anti-racist intentions than some have suggested. Watson took pains to explain that he handled the whole matter with proper Southern etiquette. He ordered "his darky" to stay in the "nigger house" behind the big plantation house, he said. Moreover, he did not go against the local authorities but instead, Crowe reports, he "sought and secured the full cooperation of the Democratic mayor, the Populist county sheriff and other local officials who reprimanded the more violent Democrats." Watson thus took considerably less risk in defending his "darky" than has previously been supposed.

The dispute over Tom Watson's early role undoubtedly will continue. Less ambiguous is the record of the Georgia Farmer's Alliance, already discussed, the Georgia Populists' political record and Watson's later behavior. Populism reached its high point in Georgia, as elsewhere, with the elections of 1892 and 1894. The People's Party vigorously pursued the black vote, and it is probable that more blacks voted in the 1892 election than in any since Reconstruction.[70] Nevertheless, Bourbon fraud and manipulation kept the Populists, including Watson himself, from victory. The Populists tried again in 1894 but they were already beginning to have second thoughts about competing for the black vote. Even so, the election returns, again disappointing to the Populists, showed that every county carried by the Populists was the result of black support.[71] The Democrats were so distrubed by this that within a few months they passed a law establishing district registration committees, which they controlled and which they could use to remove from the rolls any blacks who seemed inclined to vote for the Populists. This ensured that the Populists had not the slightest chance in the 1896 elections.

Despite this clear record of black support, some Georgia Populists concluded that the black voter was a liability since Democrats continued fraudulently to amass an overwhelming black vote. Also, these Populists felt that their frantic pursuit of the black vote, combined with hypocritical Democratic warnings of black domination, had alienated many white supporters, and they increasingly came out for disfranchisement as a way of "solving" the whole problem.[72]

After the collapse of Populism in 1896 Watson retired from politics. When he again emerged in 1904 he had resolved any lingering ambivalences he had about the black vote. Watson concluded that disfranchisement was the only way to get the black vote out of the Democratic pocket. Mississippi had led the way in 1890 by changing its constitution. In Georgia the same thing had been accomplished through the simple device of the white primary. However, since the white primary was merely an internal rule of the Democratic Party it could be laid aside any time the Democratic machine needed to muster the black vote. When a split occurred in the Georgia Democratic Party in 1906, Watson was convinced that only if the black vote could be eliminated permanently would the remnants of Populism hold the balance of power between the two factions. "The white people dare not revolt so long as they can be intimidated by the fear of the Negro vote," he explained. With blacks disfranchised "every white man would act according to his own conscience and judgment in deciding how he should vote."[73] This anticipated white revolt never materialized, instead race hatred was built to an unprecedented pitch as blacks were made the universal scapegoat. The hysterical racist campaign of 1906 contributed to a climate that made possible the Atlanta race riot later that year. This was the most violent race riot in the history of the state. Dozens of black people were lynched, maimed and driven from their homes.

Watson had by now become the prototype of the racist Southern demagogue, loudly decrying Yankees, pretending to speak for the "common white man," and constantly slandering black people. No racist slur was too low for him. He talked of the "hideous, ominous, national menace" of Negro domination; and the man who once denounced lynching now openly advocated this criminal practice. "Lynch law is a good sign," he wrote. "It shows that a sense of justice yet lives among the people."

In trying to explain his desertion of the black voter Watson argued that this was the only way Populism could triumph in the South. But this was only a flimsy rationalization since the evidence in Georgia and North Carolina supported precisely the opposite contention. Watson never realized the extent to which the ideology of white supremacy, in the form of fancied threats of black domination, was the enemy of the Populist cause. Like most other Southern Populists he was a white supremacist from the beginning and never really changed. He was willing to exploit the black vote to advance the Populist cause, but in the final analysis he refused to see that black support was a key ingredient in any Populist victory. Watson would not recognize that the black voter was not simply an appendage to be abandoned when convenient, but was the indispensable cornerstone of any movement to reform political relations in the South. This was a general failure of the Southern Populist movement. White Populists, instead of giving top priority to the fight for a truly free and unintimidated black vote—including federal intervention if necessary—chose to opt for white supremacy and joined with the Democrats in disfranchising blacks, thereby assuring the defeat of Populism.

The Black Response to Populism's Collapse

At the height of its strength in 1896 the national Populist movement committed suicide. Populism was co-opted by the free silver forces, who wanted to narrow the reform movement to a single issue,[74] and by a shaken and divided national Democratic Party that was frantically casting about for a winning issue. Opportunist Democrats believed that by endorsing free silver they could steal Populism's thunder. And that is precisely what happened.

The Populist Party fused with the Democrats because of its own internal divisions and weaknesses. Western Populists and free silverites pushed silver as *the* issue in Populism, while Southerners and radical Populists held that silver was no panacea. Yet the radicals feared making a principled stand against the silverite fusionists lest they permanently split the Populist Party.[75] So in the name of party unity and with a vague hope of winning new adherents to Populism from the folds of the Democratic Party, the radicals opted for fusion. This spelled disaster. Historically, Populism was a revolt within the Democratic Party and it had long been the goal of that party to frighten or cajole the dissidents back into its ranks. Shouting "nigger domination" was an effective stick for beating and scaring Populists in the South, and free silver proved to be the carrot national Democrats had sought. Even though the Democrats lost the 1896 Presidential election they accomplished their major goal since the independent reform movement was undermined and dispirited Populists drifted back into the old party.

Some historians have interpreted the events of 1896 as a sellout to the Democrats, while others contend that Populists were attempting a radical last stand.[76] Regardless of the merits of this scholarly debate it is clear that from the standpoint of black Populists, fusion was nothing short of a catastrophe. The few blacks at the 1896 national Populist convention opposed fusion since they feared it would result in the triumph of the Democratic Party and accelerate the process of disfranchisement occurring in the South.[77] They wanted Populism to continue as an independent movement in the hope that it would yet make good on its promises to black voters. Their pleas were in vain, however, and the majority of white Populists happily proceeded to cut their own throats.

Well before Populism's demise, blacks in the South had good reason to fear that the agrarian reform movement would release a wave of racism more vicious than anything seen during Reconstruction. The passage of segregation laws by Southern legislatures in which white reformers were active, the reactive campaign for black disfranchisement by Democrats and reformers alike, and spreading racial violence—all were signs that no sensible person ignored. There could be little hope of progress in these threatening times. Survival itself was at stake. It was this ominously shifting tide of events that no doubt shaped Booker T. Washington's approach to the race question. In his famous 1895 address Washington proposed a tactical retreat in order to ensure racial survival in the South. He advised blacks to accept social segregation and to eschew politics while doing everything possible to improve their skills in manual labor, farming and business. He later counseled blacks to avoid radical movements, since experience had shown that the radicals were often racists and in any event they certainly had no power to protect blacks from the wrath of white bigots.

While Washington thought it wise to create among whites the impression of a non-threatening, acquiescent black population, he nonetheless was privately deeply involved in efforts to prevent disfranchisement and other forms of discrimination.[78] Moreover,

Washington amassed a considerable amount of personal political power and influence in the belief that he could use this to the best interests of the race, although in later years younger black leaders accused him of abusing this power.

Even militant black Populists found it the better part of wisdom to follow Washington's example after the break-up of the Populist movement. Thus, John B. Rayner, a militant leader of Texas Populism from 1894 until 1898, was forced to withdraw from politics temporarily following the resurgence of the Democratic Party. He bitterly noted in his diary: "The faith the South has in the Democratic party is much stronger than the faith the South has in God."[79] Interesting himself in self-help and black education projects, Rayner adopted a self-effacing attitude which led one reporter to describe him as having the "air and bearing of the old time darkey." For a proud and independent man such as Rayner this servile posture must have been exceptionally difficult to maintain, and he could cling to his sanity only by scribbling out his anguish in a personal diary.

For some black leaders, however, continued deterioration of living conditions for Southern blacks proved totally unacceptable. They proposed a mass migration similar to the great exodus to Kansas and the West which followed upon the defeat of Reconstruction. But this time Africa was the chosen land. Georgia's Henry McNeal Turner, Bishop of the African Methodist Episcopal Church, sounded the call for a move to Africa. In an apparent jab at Washington, Turner said that to stay in the South and accept the denial of social and political equality was to accept "perpetual servility." He added: "If the Negro is to be a man, full and complete, he must take part in everything that belongs to manhood. If he omits a single duty, responsibility or privilege, to that extent he is limited and incomplete."[80] Turner had traveled in Africa and he believed that only there would blacks be fully accepted. However, his and other emigration movements did not win very many adherents. Most Southern blacks couldn't afford to emigrate to the next county, not to mention Africa, and there seemed to be a widespread feeling that, come what may, black people's fate was bound up with Southern destiny.[81]

It was to be in the North that a militancy similar to Turner's would reawaken. But the young black intellectuals who entered the reform struggle during the Progressive Era were not interested in emigration. They braced themselves for a head-on confrontation with white supremacy.

CHAPTER IV:

Progressivism: Expediency and Accommodation

Many of the same economic factors that precipitated the Populist revolt in the farming regions of the South and West also gave rise to the Progressive impulse at the turn of the century. Indeed, the Progressive movement may be described as essentially a reaction of the old independent, urban middle classes to the consolidation of monopoly capital, and its subsidiary manifestations in government and labor. The Progressives sought to use the power of government to regulate the large monopolies, in the process staking out a secure niche for a new middle class of salaried employees within the ever-growing bureaucracies and industrial organizations that dominated American society.

In the years following the Civil War a great transformation occurred within the U.S. economy. Over a brief span of thirty years manufacturing replaced agriculture as the backbone of the national economy and, in fact, by 1894 the U.S. had become the leading manufacturing nation of the world, having usurped the position formerly occupied by Great Britain. Certainly the factory system had existed prior to the Civil War, but it was only in the closing decades of the nineteenth century that large-scale industrial production became a way of life in America.

The transition to an industrial era was accompanied by a remarkable expansion of the economy. Capital formation and productive output climbed rapidly. Between 1869 and 1899 capital invested in American industry increased almost six-fold, while the value of manufactured products nearly quadrupled.[1] Investment capital was absorbed by industries such as mining, petroleum production, iron and steel manufacturing, and other capital goods industries; but by far the largest share of investment was poured into the burgeoning and wide-ranging railways.[2] As a consequence of this industrial activity the Gross National Product more than tripled. However, the lion's share of the increase in total national wealth found its way into the hands of the great captains of industry. Huge personal fortunes ranging between $25- and 100 million each existed side by side with glaring poverty and hardship. Progressive writers never tired of exposing the shocking inequalities of wealth and income spawned by American industrial capitalism in the Gilded Age.

The creation of gigantic family fortunes was a result not merely of industrialization; it proceeded more directly from the process of economic concentration. The great trusts and monopolies in railroads, manufacturing and banking were organized during these years and brought inexorably under the control of the leading finance capitalists, the Mellons, Morgans, Rockefellers, Vanderbilts and others.[3] It was not free, competitive enterprise but rather cunning manipulation and unbridled monopoly that gave birth to America's "Sixty Families."

Rise of Imperialism

Internationally, the consolidation of monopoly capital corresponded with the advent of a period of American imperialist expansion that was to shape the course of world history. The appearance of American imperialism was prompted by several factors. In the first place the closing of the Western frontier seemed to mark the geographical limits of the domestic market. Internal imperialism directed against the Indian population had proved highly successful in "opening up" vast stretches of land for white settlers, thereby generating a constantly expanding market for growing American industries. With the ending of this westward expansion American businessmen began searching for new markets, especially in Asia, for their ever-increasing industrial output. The federal government was not insensitive to the needs of the industrialists. Prodded by the newly organized National Association of Manufacturers and other business groups, President William McKinley promised that his administration would give attention to the "worthy cause" of overseas economic expansion.

Second, soaring profits due to industrial expansion and monopoly practices generated large quantities of surplus capital. Some outlet, some area of investment had to be found for this surplus capital lest it contribute to already severe problems of economic instability. Writing in 1898, a prominent journalist and economist warned that the entire fabric of the American economic order might be "shaken by a social revolution" unless new opportunities were created for foreign investment of surplus capital.[4]

Finally, contributing to the rise of American imperialism was the need for military control; in particular, sea power was of great importance. If the United States was to protect its new foreign markets and ocean trade routes, and further expand its imperial dominion, it needed naval bases in strategic locations, especially in the Pacific and Caribbean oceans. Consequently, at an early date the U.S. government began acquiring islands that could serve both as plantation colonies and as refueling stations for the Navy.

The U.S. Navy established a station in the Samoan Islands in 1872, and this arrangement was confirmed by a treaty in 1878. Later, after a decade of rivalry, the islands were divided between the U.S., Great Britain and Germany. Meanwhile, the U.S. had gained control over a string of other small islands in the Pacific, including Wake, Midway, Palmyra and Howland.

In 1884 the U.S. leased Pearl Harbor in the Hawaiian Islands as a naval station. American businessmen had already put a considerable amount of investment capital into Hawaiian sugar plantations, but with the added lure of military protection surplus capital poured into the islands. Moreover, the American minority, distrustful of the "inefficient" native government, agitated vociferously for annexation of the islands to the U.S. Native Hawaiians feared that annexation would mean the importation of American racism to the islands. Determined to have their way, the American residents engineered a revolt against the royal government in 1893. The new government immediately negotiated a treaty of annexation. After some delay, Congress approved the treaty in 1898 during the McKinley administration.

The year 1898 also witnessed U.S. intervention in the Cuban war of independence against Spain. American newspaper publishers, seeking to increase their circulations, sensationalized the Cuban war and demanded intervention on "humanitarian" grounds. To their outcry were added the voices of American business interests concerned about the safety of their substantial investments in Cuba. American diplomacy in the months before the war made intervention all but inevitable, the sinking of the *Maine* only serving to spark an already smoldering conflict. With the conclusion of the Spanish-American War the U.S. acquired political and economic control not only over Cuba, but also Puerto Rico and the Philippine Islands.

Thus, by the turn of the century, the United States was well on the way to acquiring an empire composed primarily of darker peoples, people of African, Indian, Polynesian, Japanese and Chinese extraction.

A convenient rationalization for this policy of aggressive commercial and territorial expansion was conjured up in the myth of Anglo-Saxon racial superiority. This myth had been given a name in 1845 with the coining of the phrase "Manifest Destiny" on the eve of the American war against Mexico. The Mexican people were warned by American imperialists that they would face utter destruction, as the Indians had, unless they submitted to the will of the Anglo-Saxons.[5] The imperialists contended that in the great struggle for survival the Anglo-Saxon race had proved itself superior to all other races, and therefore it was destined to conquer the continent and eventually dominate the hemisphere. This was nothing but crude Social Darwinism—the notion that one race had been chosen through natural selection to rule over other races. Derived by analogous reasoning from Darwin's theories of biological evolution,

Social Darwinism became a rage among America's upper classes, including businessmen, politicians and scholars. Its great virtue was that it provided "scientific proof" that (1) those who were on top of the social and economic ladders deserved to be there, and (2) the domination of the white over darker races was ordained by nature.

As might have been expected, Social Darwinist thinking gave a distinctly racist tinge to emerging behavioral sciences as represented by the writings of such men as Herbert Spencer, William Graham Sumner, Madison Grant, William A. Dunning and William McDougall. Interestingly, even those scholars who opposed Social Darwinism and its implicit selfish individualism did not oppose Social Darwinist racism. On the contrary, writers such as Lester Ward, Charles H. Cooley, E.A. Ross and John R. Commons, while attacking Social Darwinism as it affected social relations within white society, nevertheless were as one with their scholarly opponents in propounding the inherent inferiority of the darker races.[6] The sole exception to this statement was the anthropologist Franz Boas who was a strong advocate of field study of non-Western peoples as opposed to relying on biased accounts by white travelers, and who insisted that the culture and institutions of a given people must be judged within the context of their particular social history rather than measured against an arbitrary "standard."[7] Boas, however, was not an agitator and his studies did little to lessen the racism of the period. Even the great Darwin himself seemed to support the contentions of the racists. Writing in *The Descent of Man*, Darwin stated that "there is apparently much truth in the belief that the wonderful progress of the United States, as well as the character of the people, are the results of natural selection. . . ."[8] Darwin glorified the Anglo-Saxon race, and saw it as the most crucial force shaping the course of history in the Western Hemisphere.

In the decades after 1885, historian Richard Hofstadter asserts, the racist myth of Anglo-Saxon superiority "was the dominant abstract rationale of American imperialism."[9] By fueling frenzied race antipathies, at one extreme, or rationalizing the "white man's burden," at the other, this convenient social myth served to justify a militaristic policy of economic and territorial expansion at the expense of nonwhite peoples. Furthermore, it provided the essential ideological link between imperialism abroad and racism at home. If Anglo-Saxon superiority were an established scientific "fact" then imperialism and racism were both justified since they were in accordance with "natural laws."

One of the ironies of this stage in American history is that even many anti-imperialists freely employed racist arguments to support their position. This was particularly true of Democrats who were anti-imperialist at the time. The Democrats did not wish to challenge the argument of Anglo-Saxon superiority, especially in the South, so party leaders simply inverted the race argument and used it to oppose expansionism. They contended that by annexing overseas territories, such as the Philippines, the U.S. was opening its doors—and eventually the rights of citizenship—to alien and inferior races. "There is one thing that neither time nor education can change," declared an anti-imperialist Southern senator in 1899. "You may change the leopard's spots, but you will never change the different qualities of the races which God has created in order that they may fulfill separate and distinct missions in the cultivation and civilization of the world."[10] He did not need to add that the dark races were destined to cultivate while the whites would be in charge of civilization. Imperial expansion, the Democrats smoothly concluded, far from being a benefit, actually posed the threat that Anglo-Saxon civilization might be inundated by inferior colored immigrants.

In California, the president of Leland Stanford Junior University even managed to convert Social Darwinism into an anti-militarist, anti-imperialist argument. David Starr Jordan proposed that war was a biological evil rather than a biological blessing, as the proponents of natural selection insisted, because it resulted in the maiming and death of the physically and mentally fit while leaving behind the unfit to marry and reproduce.

It should now be apparent that there were strangely contradictory sides to the Social Darwinist and imperialist positions. This situation produced some curious social types: conservatives who were Social Darwinists but opposed to imperialism, progressives who favored both Social Darwinism and imperialism, and reformers who challenged Social Darwinism but saw no reason to question imperialism or racism. The thread that unified these disparate positions was the ideology of white supremacy. No matter how the prevailing arguments for and against Social Darwinism and imperialism were manipulated, adherence to white supremacy stands out as a consistent theme which ran through most of them. The turn of the century was a time of excited debate and agitation, and although white supremacy shaded and slanted every debate, it was so intrinsic to white thinking that it was seldom itself the subject of debate. It was as though white supremacy had been absorbed into the very atmosphere—always present but infrequently noticed. Nevertheless, the full contours of the Progressive Era cannot be appreciated without taking the enveloping racism into account.

The Middle-Class Revolts

The rapid growth of monopoly capital resulted in the concentration of wealth and power in fewer and fewer hands. This, combined with the all-too-apparent collaboration between government and Big Business interests and consequent widespread corruption, provoked a "growing uneasiness amongst the middle class—small business and professional men—who looked with fear upon the program of the captains of industry." Progressive historian Vernon L. Parrington reports, "The little fish did not enjoy being swallowed by the big, and as they watched the movement of economic centralization encroaching on the field of competition they saw the doors of opportunity closing to them."[11] It was this great body of the petty bourgeoisie—the independent middle class—who provided the popular base of the Progressive movement. It was they who became excited by exposés in muckraking journals, who applauded speeches by reform-minded intellectuals and scholars, and who voted the Progressive politicians into office. Indeed what unity there was in the early years of the Progressive movement existed more in its social composition than in its programs and organizations. For in reality the Progressive movement was several movements—for social justice, for political reform in city and state governments, and for political and economic reform at the national level. Many different kinds of groups were active in these movements, and only after 1912 did progressivism achieve some measure of organizational unity in the form of a national Progressive Party.

The response of the middle class to monopoly capital was not a simple and straightforward matter. It involved two divergent and even contradictory tendencies. On the one hand, there was a pronounced sentimental yearning for a return to the romantic past of frontier individualism and independence; to re-establish a world of primitive capitalism where, with much work and a little luck, an individual could still make his fortune. This romantic nostalgia, symbolized the "psychic crisis" of an old middle class which perceived rampant industrialism as a threat to its independence, and possibly its very existence. Simultaneously, however, an opposing tendency was at work by which the petty bourgeoisie was transformed into a supporter of the liberal corporate social order that slowly rose to dominance in succeeding decades, finally triumphing with the New Deal. The central proposition of this tendency called for rationalizing the economic system by regulating competition and imposing uniform standards. Most of the reforms of the Progressive Era were aimed not so much at destroying monopoly capital but at making it more "reasonable" and efficient through government intervention and regulation.[12] Demanding strong national regulation of interstate corporations, the Progressive Party platform of 1912 explained: "The corporation is an essential part of modern business. The concentration of modern business, in some degree, is both inevitable and necessary for national and international business efficiency. But the existing concentration of vast wealth under a corporate system, unguarded and uncontrolled by the Nation, has placed in the hands of a few men enormous, secret, irresponsible power over the daily life of the citizen—a power insufferable in a free government and certain of abuse. . . ."[13] Torn between these opposing tendencies, the old middle class in effect sacrificed its independence, while integrating itself as a "white collar" elite within the new corporate social order which it helped bring into being.

These conflicting ideological strains were interlaced throughout the career of Theodore Roosevelt, the man who became the controversial political symbol of the Progressive Era. The son of a respectable New York family, Roosevelt was a young gentleman-scholar who entered politics out of a driving sense of mission. He despised the very rich, whom he accused of being concerned only with money-making, but at the same time he feared and hated the working classes and the poor. In Hofstadter's opinion, "What Roosevelt stood for, as a counterpoise to the fat materialism of the wealthy and the lurking menace of the masses, were the aggressive, masterful, fighting virtues of the soldier. 'No amount of commercial prosperity,' he once said, 'can supply the lack of heroic virtues,' and it was the heroic virtues that he wished to make central again in American life. His admiration went out most spontaneously to the hunter, the cowboy, the frontiersman, the soldier and the naval hero."[14]

Roosevelt's romantic infatuation with the "heroic" past made him a jingoist par excellence, ever ready to unleash a campaign of military conquest, particularly against peoples whom he regarded as racially inferior. He approved heartily of the genocidal domestic imperialism which decimated the Indian population. "I don't go so far as to think that the only good Indians are dead Indians," Roosevelt mused in 1886, "but I believe nine out of every ten are, and I shouldn't like to inquire too closely into the case of the tenth. The most vicious cowboy has more moral principle than the average Indian."[15] In his major historical work, *The Winning of the West*, Roosevelt rehearsed the white settlers' struggles against the Indians and concluded that white imperialism was not to be halted even at the cost of a racial war to the finish. He described "the spread of the English-speaking peoples over the world's waste space" as "the most striking feature of the world's history," and asserted that only "a warped, perverse, and silly morality" would condemn the white conquest of the American West.

Such racist fantasies produced in Roosevelt an energetic architect of American imperialism. In fact, from the standpoint of some U.S. businessmen who preferred economic penetration of foreign markets to military conquest, he was too energetic. The practical men of affairs were troubled by Roosevelt's headstrong disposition. It was Roosevelt who, as Assistant Secretary of the Navy during the Spanish-American War, ordered the attack on the Spanish fleet in the Philippines, without authorization from his superior. Later in the war, Roosevelt gave up his desk job and organized a volunteer calvary regiment, the famous Rough Riders, and went off to fight in Cuba—further fueling the fears of those who regarded him as flamboyantly impetuous.[16]

Although Roosevelt, the Rough Rider, may have been regarded by some of his critics as a throwback to an earlier age, in his economic thinking he was right in line with the shrewder representatives of big business. Although he ranted against the rich, his chief advisers and many of his supporters were representatives of industrial and finance capital, and he privately assured business friends that he would govern both in the interests of the corporations and the country as a whole.[17] Putting his finger on the Progressive dilemma, Roosevelt wrote in 1911 that "real progressives" were hampered by the romantic Progressives who wanted to return "to the economic conditions that obtained sixty years ago." The real reformers, he asserted, wanted to get on with the business of rationalizing the industrial system.[18]

Like the more thoughtful capitalists, Roosevelt recognized that regulation of corporations and certain concessions to organized labor in the form of social legislation were needed in order to forestall more radical demands and actions. In 1902 he launched an antitrust suit against a large railroad monopoly. When the railroad lobbyists began agitating against this action Roosevelt advised them that their campaign would only strengthen the radical movement which sought to have the railroads nationalized. Also in 1902 Roosevelt set a precedent by intervening in the anthracite coal strike and proposing arbitration of the dispute, much to the consternation of old-fashioned capitalists who would have preferred to put down the strike without government interference.[19] Like many progressive leaders, Roosevelt thought of himself as a member of an educated, responsible elite whose role was to dispense "justice from above" by mediating disputes between the wealthy classes and the workers in the interest of conserving social stability.[20]

Regulation, not destruction, was Roosevelt's solution to the problem of monopolies and trusts. Anticipating the Progressive Party platform, he told Congress in December, 1902: "Our aim is not to do away with corporations; on the contrary, these big aggregations are an inevitable development of modern industrialism, and the effort to destroy them would be futile unless accomplished in ways that would work the utmost mischief to the entire body politic. [Apparently a reference to the threat of socialism–R.L.A.] We draw the line against misconduct, not against wealth.[21]

Roosevelt acquired a reputation as a "trust-buster" but historians have noted that the Taft administration brought 90 antitrust suits in four years as against Roosevelt's record of 54 proceedings in seven years. Roosevelt was indeed responsive to the very interests he claimed to oppose. "The most intense and rapid growth of trusts in American business history took place during Roosevelt's administrations," Hofstadter concludes.

In 1910 Roosevelt assumed leadership of the Progressive movement with the unveiling of his program of "New Nationalism," which was a combination of his old doctrines and some of the more challenging progressive ideas.

> Specifically Roosevelt endorsed the initiative, referendum, and recall, popular election of Senators, and direct primaries. He shocked conservatives by assailing the federal judiciary for obstructing the popular will, and advocated that decisions of state courts nullifying social legislation should be subject to popular recall. He supported compensation laws, limitation of the hours of labor, a graduated income tax, inheritance taxes, physical evaluation of railroad properties to enforce "honest" capitalization, and government supervision of capitalization of all types of corporations in interstate commerce.[22]

Roosevelt evidently believed that reform was necessary in order to ensure the security of existing property and power relationships. Although he proclaimed that democracy must be economic and not merely political, Roosevelt feared the "extreme democracy" advocated by radical Socialists. He repeatedly reminded his wealthier supporters that to ignore the demands of the working classes and the poor was suicidal. "The friends of property must realize," he wrote in 1904, "that the surest way to provoke an explosion of wrong and injustice is to be shortsighted, narrow-minded, greedy and arrogant, and to fail to show in actual work that here in this republic it is peculiarly incumbent upon the man with whom things have prospered to be in a certain sense the keeper of his brother with whom life has gone hard."[23] As for the new labor unions, Roosevelt pronounced them beneficial but made it clear that as they became powerful they must accept regulation by the state in order to avoid "abuses."

Roosevelt summed up his views in 1910. "What I have advocated," he said, "is not wild radicalism. It is the highest and wisest kind of conservatism." This was certainly a perceptive description of his role. To use Hofstadter's phrase, Roosevelt represented the curious paradox of the political conservative cast in the role of progressive reformer. This paradox goes far in explaining the position of the Progressive movement on the question of racism.

Progressive Response to Racism

The opening of the twentieth century found the United States gripped in a frenzy of racism. Disfranchisement, segregation and violence were freely employed to suppress the domestic colonial population, that is, blacks and other nonwhite peoples in the U.S. In two decades—from 1890 to 1910—blacks were virtually stripped of the vote in the South as eight states rewrote their constitutions to exclude the black voter. Earlier, the U.S. Supreme Court decision of 1883, declaring the civil rights law of 1875 unconstitutional, paved the way for the statutory establishment of segregation, confirmed by the "separate but equal" decision of 1896. Where segregation had been informally practiced before, it was now given legal sanction by the nation's highest tribunal. Finally, the continuing entrenchment of racism was made obvious to all by the increase in lynchings and race riots. In the last 16 years of the nineteenth century there were more than 2,500 lynchings. The vast majority of the victims were blacks, with Mississippi, Alabama, Georgia, and Louisiana accumulating the highest totals in the nation. In the first years of the new century, before the outbreak of World War I, an additional 1,100 blacks were lynched.[24]

Racial violence was not confined to the South. Anti-black riots occurred in New York in 1900, in Springfield, Ohio, in 1904 and 1908, and in Greensburg, Indiana, in 1906. John Hope Franklin concludes that "rioting in the North was as vicious and almost as prevalent as in the South."[25]

On the West Coast Asian-Americans were victims of racist attacks, segregation and an exclusion movement headed by labor leaders and progressive politicians. The anti-Japanese movement was especially strong in California, and it was only after protests by the Japanese government that this movement was for a time restrained.

Indicative of the hysteria of the period was the production and showing of the racist film, *Birth of a Nation,* which brutally distorted Reconstruction history and pictured blacks as rapacious savages bent on prostrating white civilization. The film was roundly denounced by the black community, but its endorsement by such a highly respected reformer as Woodrow Wilson gained it wider acceptance and larger audiences than it might otherwise have enjoyed.[26]

A call for government action against lynching, disfranchisement and segregation was given top priority by black protest groups beginning in the closing years of the nineteenth century. Since the federal government was in the hands of reformers after the turn of the century, close attention must be paid in the following pages to their response to these demands in analyzing the impact of racism. Interestingly, the first official proposal for a federal anti-lynch law was put forward by President Benjamin Harrison in the early 1890's. However, historian Rayford Logan reports that "Harrison's proposal came as a result of the lynching of 11 Italians and the subsequent demands of the Italian government. This first anti-lynching law, therefore, would have protected only foreign nationals in the United States. . . . It remained for the last Negro in Congress during this period to introduce a bill to prevent the lynching of American citizens."[27] The bill was not passed.

In analyzing the Progressive response to racism, it will be useful to divide the Progressives into two categories. In the first category were the political Progressives; that is, reform-minded politicians, especially those holding positions in federal and state governments. In the second category will be located the social welfare Progressives; the early social workers and urban reformers who generally worked through philanthropic and social reform organizations. These two categories were not mutually exclusive nor were they antagonistic, although, as will be shown, somewhat different dynamics were at work within them. There was a considerable degree of overlap and cooperation between Progressives of both types. Indeed, the same person could at different times assume one role or the other, or both. What united the two types was a common paternalistic desire to help the less fortunate classes to better themselves within the limits set by the industrial capitalist system. The shrewder political Progressives, such as Roosevelt, realized that this noblesse oblige attitude was immeasurably useful in obscuring the mounting signs of class conflict in American society.

First in order is an examination of the political Progressives, especially those in the federal government who held the power to halt the institutionalization of racism. While earlier federal administrations had done little to warrant black support, the election of Roosevelt in 1900 brought some rays of hope to the black population. One month after he took office Roosevelt invited Booker Washington to dine with him at the White House, and Washington soon became a close adviser to the President. Even more encouraging, Roosevelt seemed willing to attack racism in the South. He appointed a black man to a federal post in South Carolina, and he temporarily closed a post office in Mississippi to signal official disapproval of the fact that local whites had forced the black postmistress to resign her position. Black people praised these actions and hailed Roosevelt as "our President—the first since Lincoln set us free."[28]

Roosevelt's period of enlightenment was short-lived. In his second term he made clear to blacks the limits of his friendship.[29] Not all black leaders were surprised by this turnabout since it was in keeping with the old Roosevelt they had known before. Some remembered all too well Roosevelt's scurrilous attack on the black troops who had served with him in Cuba. Although there was vocal black opposition to American imperialism,[30] several black outfits fought in the Spanish-American War. The black troops who went to Cuba fought well. In fact it was black soldiers who, in one battle, saved Roosevelt and his Rough Riders from annihilation. Roosevelt at first praised the black soldiers but later, as he climbed higher on the political ladder, he reversed his stand and accused the black troops in Cuba of being cowards and deserters.[31]

The record of Roosevelt's second term fell right in line with this precedent. It soon became apparent that the Republicans intended to do nothing about black disfranchisement. Moreover, Roosevelt had adopted a policy of appointing fewer blacks to federal positions, a policy that he claimed had the approval of Booker Washington.[32] Roosevelt further alienated blacks by failing to oppose "lily-white" Republicanism, offering a quasi-defense of lynching, and dishonorably discharging a battalion of black soldiers for allegedly participating in a riot in Brownsville, Texas.[33] Actions such as these brought him under heavy attack from Northern black radicals, led by William Monroe Trotter.

Matters continued to deteriorate under Roosevelt's chosen successor, William Howard Taft. Shortly after his election, Taft toured the South and assured his listeners that the Southern white man was black people's best friend, that the government had no intention of enforcing "social equality," and that he saw no inconsistency between the Fifteenth Amendment and disfranchisement.[34] Taft appointed even fewer blacks to federal positions than Roosevelt had, explaining that he would not appoint blacks over the objections of whites. He completely capitulated before the lily-white forces, and did not oppose the informal establishment of segregation in federal offices in Washington.[35]

Roosevelt returned to the national political scene in 1912 to run as the Progressive Party candidate. However, he succeeded only in disillusioning black voters even more. At the Chicago Progressive convention Roosevelt supported a move to exclude black delegates from the South, while at the same time black delegates from the North were admitted. Roosevelt justified this policy on the spurious grounds that the Northern blacks had "won the respect of their communities" and they were "the peers of the Northern white men."[36]

Moreover, Roosevelt successfully opposed adoption of a resolution demanding equality for black people and protection of black suffrage. The rejected resolution had been penned by W.E.B. Du Bois who at first endorsed the Progressive movement.

The political reasons for the racism of Roosevelt and other national Progressive leaders are not difficult to find. Roosevelt had become convinced that the only way the Progressive Party could prosper in the South, and indeed throughout much of the nation, was by excluding blacks and appealing to white supremacy, in the same way that his old party, the Republicans, had turned to "lily-whitism." At first Roosevelt had tried to avoid the race issue as divisive, but he soon was compelled to take a position in which he attempted to straddle the fence. He wrote a long letter which later was circulated as a pamphlet entitled, "The Negro Question: Attitude of the Progressive party toward the Colored Race." In this document Roosevelt avowed his concern for the welfare of Southern blacks, but at the same time he unequivocally embraced lily-white Progressivism in the South. He went on to state that the party would appeal for the support of the "better class" of black voters in the Northern states, and that delegates from this area would be seated at national conventions. By this little stratagem Roosevelt undoubtedly hoped to avoid alienating white voters in the South and black voters in the North. Southern blacks could safely be ignored since they had already been disfranchised.

However, the maneuver failed. The pamphlet and Roosevelt's subsequent behavior at the Chicago convention angered the North-

ern black delegation. He sought to pacify some of the black delegates by inviting them to dinner, a tactic that had worked well in
the past, but which now failed miserably.

Roosevelt's expedient refusal to confront racism plus Taft's obvious weakness left many black leaders with little choice but to support Woodrow Wilson in the upcoming election. Wilson was billed
as a reformer, a man who proposed to implement a "New Freedom." Despite platitudinous assurances of good intentions Wilson
proved to be a severe disappointment to his black supporters. Some
who had opposed him pointed an accusing finger that said, "I told
you so." They reminded Wilson's supporters that as president of
Princeton University he had discouraged black applicants on the
argument that their presence might disturb the social peace of the
great university.[37] Moreover, as Governor of New Jersey Wilson
had pointedly ignored the Newark Negro Council's request for assurances of his concern to alleviate black oppression.

While running for the presidency, Wilson was hailed by white
Southerners as one of their own. He did not disappoint them.
Blacks were shocked to learn that segregation was being officially
instituted in federal government offices, including the Treasury and
Post Office. An enraged William Trotter personally confronted the
President over this issue only to be curtly dismissed. Several white
Progressives active in the National Association for the Advancement
of Colored People also protested the new policy to no avail.[38] Wilson
maintained that segregation was in the best interest of black employees.

Even more ominously, the Civil Service Commission started requiring that applicants for positions furnish personal photographs
with their applications. The official reason for this new policy was
to prevent fraud in taking the civil service examination, but black
leaders feared with good reason that the procedure would be used
to identify and eliminate black applicants.

Wilson had promised Oswald Garrison Villard, white chairman
of the board of the NAACP, that he would recommend the creation
of a National Race Commission to study ways of improving race
relations, and that he would speak out against lynching. However,

he quickly dropped the former proposal to avoid antagonizing Southern Senators, and he managed to avoid making a public denunciation of white mob violence until the summer of 1918. Even so, his proclamation attacking mob action as a betrayal of democratic principles was prompted more by military necessity than adherence to principles of justice. Army Intelligence had reported serious unrest among black soldiers concerned about violence directed against their civilian brothers and sisters. These troops, who were needed in the fight "to make the world safe for democracy," must be pacified by a gesture of presidential concern and good will.[39]

At the Versailles Peace Conference Wilson maneuvered to reject a Japanese-sponsored resolution requiring recognition of the principle of race equality in the League of Nations Covenant.[40] Wilson reasoned that such a resolution would provoke an undesirable debate and sidetrack the conference from the issues which he considered paramount.

The national Progressive Party tried to win power again in 1924. At its convention that year the party, including such radical leaders as Robert La Follette, sought again to dodge the race issue as divisive. The Progressive platform said absolutely nothing about the matter. When accosted by the NAACP, the political Progressives blandly affirmed that "the Negro is an American citizen and is included in all that the Progressives seek for the American citizen."[41] However, they firmly refused to attack the lawlessness of the revived Ku Klux Klan, or oppose racial discrimination in labor unions, or defend black voting rights—except in a last-minute appeal opportunistically issued just days before the election.

On the regional level the racial record of the political Progressives was anything but impressive. In the South Progressivism was "for whites only,"[42] and this was reflected in the political reforms adopted. Progressives in all sections of the country had demanded the institution of the direct primary system of nominating party candidates, contending that this would return political decision-making power to the hands of the people. As reform administrations swept into power in Southern state capitals the direct primary system was adopted. The catch was that these were *white* primaries, which served as a simple and highly effective method of disfranchising black voters. Thus, the promise of Populism, that the common white should have a greater say in his government, was finally fulfilled by the Southern Progressives at the cost of totally excluding blacks from political participation.

On the West Coast Progressives were in general agreement with other white Californians that the state should be preserved for white settlement.[43] Anti-Asian agitation was a common occurrence, first against the Chinese who suffered harassment, intimidation and even murder at the hands of angry mobs. Anti-Chinese agitation finally led to the passage by Congress of a Chinese Exclusion Act in 1882 for ten years. This was renewed in 1892 and made permanent in 1902.

After the turn of the century, the Chinese were no longer seen as a threat and attention turned to the growing number of Japanese in the state. Anti-Japanese sentiment was based both on economic and social arguments. White labor resented the competition of Japanese labor, white farmers the skill and success of Japanese farmers, while all saw the Japanese as unassimilable and a threat to the preservation of the white race.

Because Asian immigrants were ineligible for citizenship, they maintained the citizenship of their native lands, and Japan, in contrast to China, had emerged as a world power. Thus, treatment of the Japanese in California would have repercussions on foreign relations with Japan.

It was for this reason that Roosevelt used his influence, specifically on Progressive governor Hiram Johnson, to curtail any blatant acts of discrimination against the Japanese in California. Roosevelt agreed with the Californians' racist ideas regarding Asian immigration, but he saw California's hysteria on the question as politically inopportune. While in office he sought to limit and curtail overt anti-Japanese legislation in California and, in return for California's compliance, he engineered a Gentleman's Agreement with Japan which limited Japanese immigration to family members of Japanese workers already in the U.S. In addition, he signed an executive order barring Japanese immigration from Hawaii, Mexico, and Canada. These measures did not stem the tide of racism toward the Japanese, however, as women were still coming into the country and thus the Japanese-American population would grow naturally. As important, the Japanese were proving to be highly successful farmers, many times using land that whites had been unable to farm. Economic jealousy and competition combined with general racist feelings toward the Japanese continued to flourish in the state.

Although anti-Japanese legislation was continually introduced into the California legislature, Hiram Johnson was able to prevent any from passing until 1913. But with Wilson's election in 1912 Johnson owed no more loyalty to Washington. Wilson himself had been advised by James Phelan, a California Progressive who was prominent in the anti-Japanese campaign, to come out against Asian immigration as part of his campaign platform, much as Roosevelt had been advised to endorse black political exclusion. Wilson agreed, issuing a statement drafted by Phelan calling for a national policy of exclusion.[44]

Wilson took no effective action to prevent the California legislature from passing an anti-alien land act in 1913. The Japanese government, in an effort to stop the proposed legislation, had offered to voluntarily halt the immigration of Japanese picture brides, but Wilson's Secretary of State, William Jennings Bryan, ignored this offer and gave California no incentive to refrain from passing the bill. Thus in 1913 the Heney-Webb bill passed with the active support of Progressives in the California legislature. The Californians conceded to Washington a provision which would allow aliens to hold land to the extent that treaties between the U.S. and their home countries permitted it. This was to protect European investments.[45]

Interestingly, the bill in itself proved ineffective. Although aimed specifically at the Japanese, and recognized as such by Japan, Japanese immigrants were able to find ways around the bill, most simply by putting the land in the names of their American-born children. As Johnson knew even before its passage that the bill would be ineffective,[46] one is forced to conclude that the political Progressives in California were opportunistically catering to the racist sentiments of the electorate.

Revealed by all of this is a pattern of rank opportunism on the part of both national and state Progressive leaders. The national political Progressives sought desperately to avoid the race issue and to leave the status quo untouched, as in the South. Only when confronted by external considerations, as occurred on the West Coast, did they move to temper regional race antipathies. Even here they were more concerned with the *appearance* of restraint than actual suppression of racial extremists. Progressive leaders at the state level, left to their own devices, enthusiastically endorsed the local brand of white supremacy, whether in the South or the West, and they frankly appealed to the racism of the white electorate in their drive to gain power.

Social Welfare Progressives

Among social welfare Progressives a different dynamic was at work, chiefly because they were not concerned with the strategy of winning elections. These early social workers and urban reformers were sincerely concerned with uplifting the poor and less fortunate members of society. Among this element of the Progressive movement were seen the beginnings of the welfare paternalism which was later to come to full fruition with the New Deal. This developing trend was particularly evident in New York where a host of reformers sought to alleviate the suffering of the masses of poor blacks and foreign whites who immigrated to the city. The reformers established settlement houses and did social work among the immigrants, and they busied themselves with studying and writing about the social and economic condition of the Northern black population.[47]

The welfare movement was promoted by the middle-class black women's clubs, organized in the 1890's to foster racial solidarity and self-help.[48] In 1897 a black woman, Mrs. Victoria Earle Matthews, founded the White Rose Industrial Association in New York, which opened a home for black working women who were coming up from the South and falling into the hands of unscrupulous employment agents. Mrs. Matthews was followed by white reformers such as Frances A. Kellor and Mary White Ovington. Mrs. Kellor founded an organization known as the National League for the Protection of Colored Women. Miss Ovington, a member of a socially prominent family, was a social worker who was also an executive of the Committee for Improving the Industrial Conditions of the Negro in New York City, a forerunner of the National Urban League, established by a black high school principal.

Many idealistic young white women—Mary Ovington, Jane Addams and others—from well-to-do families were active in the settlement movement. William O'Neill attributes this fact to the growth of feminism. By becoming involved in social action the young female reformers "dealt the Victorian stereotype of women a fatal blow." Moreover, in their work the settlement workers played a pivotal role in the women's movements by providing "evidence that the social concerns of free women would not disrupt the existing order."[49] The women reformers, and their male counterparts, had no desire to overturn the social system. They sincerely wished to bridge the gulf between proletariat and bourgeoisie by encouraging cooperation between the classes and blunting class conflict.[50]

Describing the overall work of the Northern reformers, Gilbert Osofsky states that they "were primarily concerned with finding jobs and decent homes for Negro migrants, opening playgrounds for Negro children, breaking down the color barrier in employment opportunities, improving health and sanitary conditions [in black districts] and protecting Negro domestics from the exploitation of employment agents."[51]

In short, the reformers were seeking to improve the social and economic situation of blacks in the North, something black abolitionists had demanded more than 60 years before. But conditions in 1900 were far different from what they had been in 1840. If free blacks had been integrated into the Northern economy earlier in the nineteenth century it might have been conceivable for blacks to share in the gains made possible by the unprecedented growth of the industrial system. By 1900, however, the revolution of industrial

capitalism had already bypassed the black population, and the actual effect of social reformism was simply to help blacks to accommodate and integrate themselves into the lowest levels of an already
rigidly stratified economic system, where they would be kept by the
racism of employers and labor unions. This was well illustrated
by the early history of the Urban League. Founded by black and
white reformers in 1911, the League aimed to improve the social
and industrial conditions among black people. However, the national office and local branches were dominated by conservative white
industrialists and philanthropists who often used the League as an
anti-union, pro-strikebreaking organization, whose chief social work
function was to pacify black workers, urging them to be happy with
their lot.[52] It was not until the 1930's that the League was able
to break out of this conservative mold.

It is also worth noting that the Northern municipal reformers,
in their campaign to cleanse city politics by destroying the system
of political bosses and machine politics, undermined an institution,
albeit corrupt, which had served as a traditional vehicle through
which ethnic groups achieved some degree of political power in
urban areas. The reformers' assault on patronage and political fa-
voritism sharply constricted this illicit channel of social mobility.
It is another sad irony that corruption in city politics was not effectively attacked until blacks began moving into the urban political
arena.

In the South the Progressive movement was lily-white but victories won by the social reformers did benefit blacks indirectly.
Thus, the convict leasing system was officially abolished, a start
was made in the regulation of child labor, legislation to control the
liquor traffic was adopted, and increased appropriations were made
for public education, health and agricultural services.[53] Unfortunately, any benefits that accrued to blacks from these reforms were more
than offset by the race-baiting tactics of the Southern political Progressives. Furthermore, the industrial education movement supported by white philanthropy may have hurt blacks as much as it helped
them. Industrial education was promoted by whites who viewed it
as an effective way of reaching a compromise between the white

South, the capitalist North, and black people.[54] Industrial education would create a stable and trained supply of black workers who would not be inclined to challenge white supremacy. The joker was that industrial education came into vogue at a time when blacks were being pushed out of skilled trades by racist unions, and technology was making many old industrial jobs obsolete. Hence, black workers would have to take the worst jobs with the poorest pay. In addition, the funds provided by white philanthropists to black schools sometimes afforded racist Southern legislatures an excuse for smaller appropriations for black education.[55]

On balance, philanthropy and social reformism, in failing to attack racism, left intact a chief obstacle to genuine progress. Of course, radical change was not really the goal of most of the Progressive reformers. Both political Progressives and social welfare Progressives wanted to bring about more "harmonious" relations within the existing order. They were conservative reformers.

Concretely, this meant to curb racist excesses only insofar as these obstructed the smooth incorporation of blacks, and others of the dispossessed, into the lower reaches of the urban proletariat. Hence, both groups of reformers approved of and supported Booker T. Washington because he did not openly challenge white supremacy, and his program of industrial education for blacks dovetailed nicely with their program of conservative reform. Only the black radicals attacked white supremacy head-on, but their assault was blunted by Washington and further weakened as they were absorbed by the social welfare Progressives.

The Radical Assault

It is commonly believed that the first militant black organizations arose at the turn of the century as a reaction to the conservative accommodationist policies of Booker Washington. This is only partly the case. It would be more accurate to say that the defeat of Reconstruction and consequent suppression of black political and civil rights, combined with growing racial violence, were the direct contributors to a resurgence of the kind of militant activity which was seen before among black abolitionists.

However, the new militants achieved only limited effectiveness because, unlike their predecessors in the Negro Convention Movement, they lacked a reliable and independent base of support. Furthermore, they experienced severe financial difficulties and were wracked by internal dissension. These troubles were multiplied in later years by the efforts of Washington, backed by his white supporters, to undermine and destroy the militant groups. The conflict between Washington and the militants dramatically polarized the black freedom movement into antagonistic conservative and radical camps, but it must be understood that the militants had been active long before Washington rose to prominence in 1895.

As early as 1887 T. Thomas Fortune, the militant editor of the *New York Age,* conceived of forming an organization to oppose the growing institutionalization of white supremacy. Fortune called for the organization of a National Afro-American League, and at the founding convention in 1890 he listed seven reasons which he felt justified the group's existence:

1. The almost universal suppression of our ballot in the South. . . .
2. The universal and lamentable reign of lynch law. . . .
3. The unequal distribution of school funds. . . .
4. The odious and demoralizing penitentiary system of the South, with its chain gangs, convict leases and indiscriminate mixing of males and females.
5. The almost universal tyranny of common carrier corporations in the South—railroad, steamboat and other—in which the common rights of men and women are outraged and denied by the minions of these corporations.
6. The discrimination practices of those who conduct places of public accommodation. . . .
7. The serious question of wages, caused in the main by the vicious industrial system of the South, by the general contempt employers feel for employees, and by the overcrowded nature of the labor market. . . .[56]

One hundred and forty-one delegates from 23 states gathered in Chicago to form a permanent national organization as outlined by

Fortune. This was intentionally an all-black meeting since some of the militants "were convinced that white men interested themselves in the affairs of Negroes only to dominate them."[57] This sentiment echoed the separatism debate that shook the convention movement half a century earlier.

The assembly adopted a program along the lines suggested by Fortune, and it declared that it would accomplish its goals "by the creation of a healthy public opinion through the medium of the press and the pulpit, public meetings and addresses, and by appealing to the courts of law for redress of all denial of legal rights." Hence, at this early date the militants proposed the basic strategy of agitation and litigation which was to characterize later protest organizations, including the Niagara Movement and the NAACP.

Perhaps because of its militant program the Afro-American League experienced considerable difficulty attracting mass support among the black population, and at its second national meeting held in Knoxville in 1891 only a handful of delegates showed up.[58] This lack of support posed financial problems for the League and made it impossible to launch a test case of the Jim Crow practices of the railroads. In August, 1893, Fortune announced that the League was defunct because of lack of funds, lack of mass support, and lack of support from other race leaders.

The continuing deterioration of black people's status in the South, however, provoked calls for a revival of the League, and in 1898 the organization was reconstituted as the National Afro-American Council. It adopted a list of objectives almost identical with the original platform of the League. The council achieved some prominence in the black community, but soon was weakened by an internal fight over Booker Washington's leadership.

Almost every meeting of the council became a battleground between supporters and opponents of Washington, who had achieved national stature as a black leader. Washington's ideology flew in the face of the militants' demand for full social and political equality, but by 1902, using the political machine his white friends had financed, Washington was able to take over the council and oust the militants, including Du Bois and Ida Wells-Barnett, from control.

Thrown into disarray by this development, the militants were unable to reunify their forces for several years, although many gravitated toward Trotter's newly founded Boston *Guardian*. When they again established a national organization, the Niagara Movement, in 1905, they adopted the same strategy of agitation and litigation initiated by the old League. By this time, however, Washington had firmly consolidated his control over black ministers, newspaper editors and leaders of civic organizations, and the radicals therefore found themselves virtually cut off from any mass base of support. For this and other reasons the radical leaders adopted an elitist approach to social change that, in the long run, only isolated them further from the masses and resulted in their being compromised by the white Progressives who conceived and organized the NAACP.

To understand this development we must look at two chief figures who provided continuity between the old Afro-American Council and the new Niagara Movement: William Monroe Trotter and W.E.B. Du Bois.[59]

In certain ways Trotter was an enigmatic character, given to moody shifts and changes that baffled friends and enemies alike. To say that he was his own man is an understatement. Born in 1872 the son of a petty government official who also dabbled in small business ventures, Trotter spent his childhood in an interracial neighborhood in Boston's Hyde Park.[60] Trotter's family was fairly prosperous but not complacent; his father had long been an agitator for racial equality.

Young Trotter was a good student and he entered Harvard College in the fall of 1891. He was a serious undergraduate who did well in his studies. In fact, Trotter was the first black student at Harvard to be elected to Phi Beta Kappa. He graduated magna cum laude in June, 1895, just a few months before Washington made his famous address in Atlanta.

Now in his early twenties, Trotter was a graduate of the nation's most prestigious university, heir to a small fortune and apparently well along the way to solid middle-class respectability. In 1899 he married into a socially prominent family that also boasted of a tradition of racial militancy.

Racial militancy, however, was far from being a pressing concern of Trotter at this time. Certainly he had met racial rebuffs in college and in his later search for employment, but these failed to dampen his ambition to become a successful businessman. After holding a series of clerking jobs, he established his own real estate and insurance agency. His clients were mostly white, but business was good and he soon became a man of property in his own right. As Stephen Fox notes in his biography of Trotter: "His life was falling into a pattern much like that of his father—working with white people, living in a white neighborhood, keeping a strong but somewhat aloof interest in the race's welfare, and dabbling in politics. He was already into politics on a rudimentary level, working for Republican congressional and municipal candidates and serving as an alternate delegate from his ward at several conventions."[61]

What was it that broke this pattern, that halted Trotter's drift toward complacency and respectability? Trotter was not an insensitive man. He was aware of the growing seriousness of conditions in the South, and the spread of these conditions to the North; he was aware of the anti-lynching campaign started by Ida Wells-Barnett; and he was also aware of the public acquiescence of Booker Washington, a submissive stance that contrasted sharply with the attitude of his own father. "The conviction grew upon me," he wrote years later, "that pursuit of business, money, civic or literary position was like building a house upon the sands, if race prejudice and persecution and public discrimination for mere color was to spread up from the South and result in a fixed caste of color."[62]

Trotter entered his new calling of racial agitation with characteristic fervor. He turned first to Boston's black elite classes and helped organize the Boston Literary and Historical Association. Then he joined a more overtly political group known as the Massachusetts Racial Protective Association; and, finally, along with an associate, George Forbes, he founded his later well-known weekly newspaper, the *Guardian*. All of this occurred within the span of a few months in 1901. In establishing his newspaper, Trotter, very self-consciously, thought of himself as acting in the radical abolitionist tradition of William Lloyd Garrison. In 1907, as a symbolic gesture, he even moved the office of his paper to the same building where Garrison had published the *Liberator*. For better or worse, the two men did exhibit certain similar traits. Both were fiercely independent agitators, and, significantly, both addressed their appeals to the literate middle classes in the hope that these classes would have sufficient influence to bring about progressive change.

In his *Guardian* editorials Trotter mounted a constant attack on the politics of Booker Washington. At times it appeared as though the volatile Trotter blamed Washington personally for the worsening oppression that afflicted the race. Giving no quarter to his opponent, Trotter asserted that the policy of compromise had failed and "the policy of resistance and aggression deserves a trial."[63] Where Washington spoke of duties, Trotter spoke of rights. Where Washington spoke of self-help, Trotter spoke of political agitation for equality. Where Washington extolled the virtues of industrial education, Trotter called upon blacks to prove themselves by succeeding at the highest forms of education. When Washington was silent, Trotter denounced disfranchisement, segregation and lynching.

Washington fought back with every means at his disposal—using his influence with the white press, underwriting rival black newspapers to compete with the *Guardian,* placing spies in the opposition movement, and using political appointments to buy off members of the opposition.

The historic confrontation between the two men, which catapulted Trotter into national prominence, occurred at a meeting of 2,000 people at a Boston church in July, 1903. Washington had accepted an invitation to address the Boston branch of the National Negro Business League. Trotter and his supporters had drafted a series of nine questions with which they intended to challenge Washington from the floor of the meeting. Each question was highly provocative, and although Trotter later denied that there was any plan to break up the meeting, that was in fact what happened. Fist fights broke out between pro- and anti-Washington men, and Trotter and an associate were arrested as they attempted to shout questions at Washington during the melee.

The so-called Boston Riot widened the gulf between Washington and the radicals. Among those affected by this incident was W.E.B. Du Bois, then a teacher at Atlanta University. Du Bois was himself a product of New England's black elite. Although his immediate family lived in "genteel poverty," he could count among his ancestors independent small farmers, businessmen and professionals. Like Trotter, Du Bois passed his childhood in an interracial setting. When he grew older he won a scholarship to attend Fisk University, which gave him his first contact with black people in the South. He delighted in this experience, but then, and when he later returned to the South to teach, he was appalled by the realities of white racism. After leaving Fisk Du Bois moved on to Harvard where he earned M.A. and Ph.D. degrees. He then undertook two additional years of study at the University of Berlin. In Europe he became acquainted with socialism and came to regard himself as a Socialist.

By the time Du Bois arrived in Atlanta in 1897 he had decided to attempt the first comprehensive study of black life. He believed that careful scientific research and dispassionate discourse could be effective in altering white attitudes and racist stereotypes.

Du Bois had been in the Tuskegee camp in the 1890's but gradually he came to take offense at Washington's dictatorial tactics against blacks and submissive philosophy vis-á-vis whites. Du Bois' book, *The Souls of Black Folk,* published in the spring of 1903 spelled out his criticism of the Tuskegee program. He called for "ceaseless agitation and insistent demands for equality." To Washington's philosophy of industrial education Du Bois counterposed a program of higher education with special emphasis on what he termed the "Talented Tenth," an elite group that he felt should inspire and lead the black masses.

The arrest and imprisionment of Trotter in 1903 outraged Du Bois and dislodged him from his scientific aloofness. He wrote a letter supporting Trotter but was reluctant to take any further steps. Du Bois would make a valuable ally and Trotter knew this. Over the next few months Trotter incessantly pressed the Atlanta scholar to consolidate their nascent political alliance. Finally in the summer of 1905, after an attempted reconciliation with Washington, Du Bois made the inevitable break. Du Bois, Trotter and other Washington critics planned a secret meeting for later that year. Du Bois issued invitations to a limited number of trusted individuals asking for "organized determination and aggressive action on the part of men who believe in Negro freedom and growth."[64]

Twenty-nine black professionals and intellectuals from all over the country gathered on the Canadian side of Niagara Falls and formed what they called the Niagara Movement. Following the tradition of Frederick Douglass and basing themselves on the tenet that "Persistent manly agitation is the way to liberty," Trotter and Du Bois drafted a statement of principles for the new movement calling for, among other things, black male suffrage, full civil rights, economic opportunity and education of black youths according to ability. The Niagara militants would brook no talk of the black man meekly accepting his assigned lowly place in the hierarchy of white America. "We refuse to allow the impression to remain," they thundered, "that the Negro-American assents to inferiority, is submissive under oppression and apologetic before insults. Through helplessness we may submit, but the voice of protest of ten million Americans must never cease to assail the ears of their fellows so long as America is unjust."[65]

Thus Trotter's lone editorial voice was now joined with others in organized protest. The radicals were in possession of a new national organization with a program and strategy very much similar to the old Afro-American League.[66] The Niagara group undertook a campaign of agitation that succeeded in raising the level of political consciousness of many black people, especially educated blacks. The group also actively campaigned against segregation laws, lobbied for civil rights legislation, and appealed successfully to the courts in a Jim Crow case.[67]

But these were the limits of the group's success. The young organization was beset by financial difficulties and engaged in a sharp struggle with the "Tuskegee Machine." Furthermore, internal dissension began to trouble the movement. Du Bois and Trotter, having only recently concluded their alliance, found themselves in disagreement over admitting women to the organization. Du Bois organized a women's auxiliary and appointed the wife of a friend to be National Secretary for Women. Trotter, a staunch anti-feminist, at first opposed this move but eventually agreed to admit women.[68] Despite this compromise internal strife continued to plague the group. The two men clashed again when Trotter became suspicious of another member, a long-time friend of Du Bois, who appeared to have personal political ambitions. This violated Trotter's recently acquired but purist sense of social commitment, and the resulting hostile sniping further demoralized the group.

These troubles were further complicated by the movement's strongly elitist tone. Du Bois had insisted that membership be open only to the "very best class" of "thoughtful" and "dignified" black men,[69] and in fact most of the members were drawn from among the college-educated and professional classes. This elitism made communication between the organization and the masses of black people difficult. As Elliott M. Rudwick observed: "The organization was composed of men who occupied a privileged position in Negro society, and they were quite conscious of that fact. No small number considered their education as primarily a symbol of social prestige, which divorced them forever from intercourse with the masses. Aside from the higher social status which a university education conferred, such training gave these people a relatively intellectual outlook. There is a degree of social distance within any group between the educated and less educated segments, and this observation was especially true within the Negro race whose Talented Tenth was actually a talented hundredth."[70] With such an orientation the movement necessarily had a narrow base of support, especially since not even a majority of the college graduates and professional men supported it.[71] Elitism thus fostered class snobbery, which weakened and isolated the Niagara Movement even more.

In 1908 Trotter split from the movement and went his own way, organizing the Negro-American Political League (which later became the National Equal Rights League) as his chosen instrument. Du Bois picked up the pieces and held the Niagara group together for a while longer; then in 1910 he urged its members to join the newly formed National Association for the Advancement of Colored People.

The Springfield race riot of 1908 had horrified white social welfare Progressives and prompted them to issue a call for a conference on the racial crisis. The conference was held in 1909 and proved to be a tumultuous affair. After a long and heated debate, the militants, led by Trotter, Du Bois and Ida Wells-Barnett, succeeded in persuading the conferees, many of whom were white, to adopt a watered-down version of the Niagara program.[72]

Within a short time, however, the white-led NAACP tried to patch over the schism between the radicals and Washington, a move that alienated Trotter.[73] Trotter did not join the NAACP. He distrusted its white leaders, thinking them prone to compromise, and he disliked their patronizing attitude toward militant·blacks. He probably did not suspect that this decision marked a major turning point in his career. Although there were other climactic moments in his life of agitation, basically from that time on Trotter and his group were overshadowed by Du Bois and the well-financed NAACP.

Du Bois, on the other hand, did join the NAACP, and thereby became its only black officer. Du Bois was not particularly fond of whites but to a degree he had no choice. The Niagara Movement had declined, and he was fearful that his radical activity might jeopardize the shaky financial security of Atlanta University; consequently, he was seeking a new position. However, the only other job offer he received during this period was quietly dropped, presumably because of his militant views. Thus, when he was asked to become Director of Publications and Research for the NAACP, he readily accepted. The new job would give him an opportunity to continue his research and writing, but it also posed a serious problem since he knew that the NAACP's white leadership expected him to tone down his criticism of Tuskegee.[74]

Thus by 1910 Trotter and Du Bois had helped in launching a militant protest movement of national proportions. But because these two radical leaders had no independent mass base of support in the black community their success was compromised. Trotter

eventually went his own egocentric, individualist way, gradually losing his effectiveness; while Du Bois was forced to rely on the doubt-
ful support of white liberals who were anxious to effect a rapprochement with Booker Washington and unify the black movement under
their guidance.

There are many reasons Trotter and Du Bois adopted an elitist
rather than a mass approach to radical activity. Some part was
played by their background and training. Both were the sons of
an aspiring black elite which sought to differentiate itself from the
mass—white as well as black. Du Bois recalled years later that although his family was not well-to-do they shared the class snobbery
of their white neighbors and tended to look down upon the poor
white immigrants who comprised the bulk of the working class in
his hometown. Trotter's father instilled a fierce pride in his children, setting high standards and virtually demanding that his son
excel his white classmates in every respect.

Both men may have been influenced by the elitism and class consciousness of Harvard. Trotter certainly was. He used his Harvard
degree as a club to beat his pro-Washington opponents. In later
years he reproached the black masses and urged them to "observe
the better class of people," especially white people, in order to learn
proper behavior and decorum. To him true Americanism consisted
in the democracy, to use his word, that he had enjoyed at "dear
old Harvard."[75]

Clearly Trotter was a man of his times and his class. He spoke
for the Northern black petty bourgeoisie—who previously felt themselves safe—when he sounded the alarm against the white lawlessness and violence spreading up from the South. He spoke for the
interests of this class in advocating racial integration (implicitly
along class lines) on the one hand, and black capitalism (petty bourgeois nationalism) on the other. Unlike Trotter, Du Bois had a
great deal of empathy with the masses, probably because of his early
schooling and teaching experiences in the South. However, he dis-
dained mass leadership saying that he "could not slap people on
the back and make friends of strangers" nor "easily break down
an inherited reserve."[76] Both men sought to prove, to blacks and

to the whites with whom they frequently associated, that educated, middle-class blacks were the peers of educated, middle-class whites. This desire probably contributed to their expressed interest in social equality and civil rights, and it certainly motivated their passionate commitment to higher education. Unfortunately, it opened a wide chasm between them and the masses of poor Southern blacks who were more concerned with bread-and-butter issues and physical survival than with proving themselves equal to whites.

While these comments may reveal some of the personal factors contributing to the elitist thinking of the two, especially Trotter, they are insufficient as a full explanation. For further insight it is necessary to discuss briefly the radicals' perception of the social base to which they addressed their appeals.

Du Bois, in his autobiographical writings, shed much light on this matter. He contended that the dictatorial power of Washington and the Tuskegee Machine "aroused increasing opposition among Negroes, especially among the younger classes of educated Negroes. . . ." He then went on to suggest some specific reasons for this opposition: "After a time almost no Negro institution could collect funds without the recommendation or acquiescence of Mr. Washington. Few [black] political appointments were made anywhere in the United States without his consent. Even the careers of rising young colored men were very often determined by his advice and certainly his opposition was fatal."[77]

Evidently Du Bois believed that a new class of black intellectuals and professionals was beginning to chafe under the old-line leadership of Washington. These were the graduates of pioneer black colleges set up in the South during Reconstruction, or they were part of the increasing numbers graduated from white schools in the North. As this class developed, a challenge to Washington seemingly became inevitable. Since Tuskegee enjoyed the active or passive support of almost all of the established black politicians, preachers and editors, and the tacit approval of a considerable portion of the Southern black population, it was natural for Du Bois and Trotter to turn to what was actually an alienated intelligentsia when they launched their attack. There is some evidence to support Du

Bois' analysis, although the dynamic he outlined was probably more complex and moved at a slower pace than he expected.[78]

Du Bois gave a second reason for his focus on the Talented Tenth. He believed that the college-educated black intelligentsia should assume leadership of the black masses since otherwise the masses would have to accept the questionable leadership of sympathetic whites.[79] At this time he apparently did not consider—or he discounted—the possibility of militant leadership arising directly from the masses, as was to be seen in some of the later struggles of black workers.

The radicals thus addressed themselves to those classes they thought *should lead* the masses, instead of speaking primarily and directly to the black masses. This elite strategy had two consequences. In the first place it meant that the radicals could be undercut by a Marcus Garvey who went directly to the masses with his "Back to Africa" campaign. Second, in speaking to the intellectual elite the radicals did gain an audience for their ideas, but these ideas were defused and watered down as they were filtered through the special class interests of this group. The new black intellectual and professional classes may have favored militancy but like the white Progressives they abhorred genuine radicalism; it threatened to upset the very social order into which they were demanding admission.

In a sense Trotter and Du Bois cannot be blamed for their elitism. After all, the massive Northern migration had not yet reached the flood proportions, which were to bring widespread impatience with the old oppressions and a readiness for militancy and protest. Yet Trotter's bitter hostility toward the Garveyite movement showed he did not understand that this movement was an expression on a mass level of many of the nationalist sentiments that also motivated the radicals. Du Bois at least understood this, but he engaged in a personal feud with Garvey that destroyed any hopes of an alliance.

In the final analysis, the elitism of the middle-class radical leaders drove them either into isolation or into the arms of white Progressives who were concerned less with eradicating white supremacy, being instead more interested in building a smoothly running reform organization that could take all segments of the black movement under its wing. Certainly the NAACP did much for the protest cause, campaigning against lynching, segregation and disfranchisement; but its early domination by white Progressives produced continuing tensions between Du Bois and the leadership. Du Bois wanted the Association to mount a sharper attack on white racism and the economic causes of black oppression. Moreover, he espoused black self-determination, a concept that simply went beyond the understanding of the white NAACP officers. As Broderick points out in his study of Du Bois:

> The Association was in many respects a typical progressive cause: an attempt by men of good will to recover basic American democratic traditions through publicity, legislation, and court action. Its laissez-faire bent required the removal of barriers that held the individual back from his own full development through his own powers. It knew no grouping between the individual and the nation. It knew no color line. Villard told one correspondent that the Association desired "to help one race quite as much as the other." If Du Bois were to join the Association's chorus, he had to sing this tune. Yet fundamentally Du Bois sang in a different key: he was a Negro, fighting for Negroes, committed to Negro self-help. . . and distrustful of white men. . . . While the Association cautiously assailed legal barriers, Du Bois's shots ranged freely over the church, industrialists, labor unions, philanthropic foundations, and even hit his white liberal colleagues. When he went one step further and suggested the possibility of separate, independent Negro development perhaps through an Association more tightly geared to "our objects, our aims, and our ideals," he left white liberalism far behind. In Du Bois's view, the path upward was blocked by hurdles uncleared by progressivism.[80]

While on the personal level many white social welfare Progressives sincerely opposed racism, nevertheless the social role they played was that of a buffer group in a time of societal crisis: collectively they acted to blunt conflicts rather than force their resolution. Thus they tended to undermine or confuse the radicals' attacks on white supremacy and economic oppression, sidetracking these into less "extreme" and more socially acceptable channels.

Despite its weaknesses, however, the NAACP was to be for many decades the chief bastion against unbridled white supremacy. A share of the credit for this by no means insignificant accomplishment must be given to the early black radicals who first sounded the alarm and formulated a basic program of agitation and litigation against racism.

In conclusion, it must be observed that both political Progressives and social welfare Progressives were acting in accordance with the principle of conservative reform that characterized the Progressive Era. The national political Progressives aimed to rationalize the monopoly industrial system from above by imposing regulatory laws and agencies designed to integrate the economic and political systems into a harmoniously functioning unit. To this group racial conflict was a divisive issue, a distraction best left ignored (i.e., quietly accepted), or reluctantly discussed only with an eye to manipulating black voters or due to external pressures. Opportunism was the order of the day. At the state and local level political Progressives crassly sought to use the race issue to their own political advantage, which in practice meant advocating the most virulent forms of racism.

Social welfare Progressives in effect attempted to rationalize the social system from below through activities and organizations that would help black and white immigrant groups "adjust" and accommodate themselves to the industrial system. Like the political reformers they were firmly allied with Big Business which they depended upon to support their welfare and philanthropic efforts. The social welfare Progressives sincerely opposed the more violent racial abuses—which hindered their work at racial accommodation—but they were at one with political Progressives in seeking to rationalize the social system within the framework of monopoly industrial capitalism and white supremacy.

A small group of black radicals tried to challenge racism. However, their relative isolation from the mass of the black population, and their resulting elitism, blinded them to the changing role of black workers in the U.S. economy. Black workers were being incorporated as a reserve pool of industrial labor. The black radicals attacked racism on moral grounds, but they failed to appreciate the fundamental changes in the political economy that sparked Progressivism and that, moreover, were altering race relations in the U.S. The policies of Washington, on the other hand, were right in line with the new racial accommodation sought by the Progressives.

Consequently, the radical assault failed because it was too narrowly conceived and too narrowly based. The radicals struck a blow at the cruder forms of racism, but at that point they didn't perceive the more sophisticated forms of racism that were developing. Moreover, since they were unable to build a stable organizational base their programs were slowly taken over by the social welfare Progressives who used them for their own purposes. The radical assault was an important foray, but without grasping the essential causes of Progressivism it could not but be deflected and re-channeled into a "militant" but carefully controlled move for racial readjustment.

CHAPTER V:

Woman Suffrage: Feminism and White Supremacy

The dislocations and changes taking place in nineteenth century U.S. society changed the nature of the home, resulting in many white women taking an active part in social reform. Though they were met with opposition and discrimination because such activity was deviant from their prescribed roles, they joined the abolition, progressive, labor and socialist movements as well as the moral reform for temperance. By the middle of the century they were organizing with other women to protest the legal and social discriminations they suffered as a sex: exclusion from higher education and the professions, and the loss of woman's rights in marriage, particularly her control over her own property and earnings. They demanded equal guardianship of their children and easy divorce from an oppressive husband. This protest movement culminated in a massive mobilization of white women around the issue of suffrage.

The demands for woman's rights reflected changes in women's lives which had been brought about by capitalist industrialization. From colonial times American white women had legally, politically and socially been under the control of their husbands. But before industrialization they had been responsible for the production of many important household items, without which a family could not survive. Their work was essential; they knew this and their husbands knew this. In such a situation the man might have ultimate legal authority but he was equally dependent on his wife's labor as she was on his, making her an integral and recognized

121

participant in the pre-industrial economy. However the factory system, which began to develop around 1800, changed this. Spinning, weaving, and food preparation all became socialized, with machinery and a social labor force replacing the individual woman producing those goods in her own home. The care of the young and the maintenance of the family (cooking, washing clothes, etc.), however, continued to be the province of the women in the home. Done in isolation and for no pay, this work stood in direct opposition to that portion of woman's work which had been taken out of the home, socialized and for which a wage was paid. Further, women who had until then been essential to the economic productivity of the family, now found themselves totally dependent on the man's earnings, which were now often incorporated into salaried jobs as a result of the undermining of the middle class's economic independence by monopoly capitalism. Economic dependence and isolation became the condition of many white women.

Women whose husbands could not earn enough to support the family became paid workers in the labor force at wages on the average of one fourth that of men doing the same work.[1] Training programs, promotions and higher paying occupations were closed to women, thus preventing advancement for most female workers. Unions mainly ignored them, using the same rationale that the capitalists used for paying lower wages: that women were temporary workers who would return to being housewives as soon as they were able. Married women were in a predicament because of their duties in the home, particularly child care, for if mothers worked to support their families, their children went unattended or went into the factories themselves. Working conditions in the factories were unhealthy and oppressive and the pay for women and children so low that returning to the home appeared to most people in the society to be a progressive step for married women. In this way, too, the factory appeared opposed to the home.

Yet not all women could marry or wanted to marry. For them and for poor women, returning to the home was not an option. By 1870, 14.7% of the female population over 16 were wage earners; by 1900 it was 20.6%.[2] Early in the 1800's women workers had begun organizing to improve their working conditions. When the suffrage movement was organized, many became active supporters because they hoped the vote would enable them to pass progressive legislation.

Character of the Female Reform Movement

The majority of female social reformers were middle-class women. Their status allowed them the opportunity to engage in this activity, both because of time and sense of priority. If they were married, their husbands' economic status was such that many could afford domestic servants, thus freeing middle-class women of much of the work of maintaining a home. Unmarried middle-class women were forced to combat economic and social discrimination to support themselves.

The unifying issue between these two groups of women was the common belief that higher education provided the way to overcome social exclusion and discrimination. Consequently, the first demands of middle-class women were for educational reforms. They argued that higher education, by making them more knowledgeable, would make them better wives and mothers and would provide single women with teaching credentials. By the middle of the nineteenth century, women's colleges had been set up and female graduates were emerging who would not be content within the narrow confines of the home but were determined to leave their mark upon the society. Their demands broadened to include ending all forms of discrimination against women.

Of the many women drawn into the agitation for woman's rights were three who became the major leaders of the early movement. Elizabeth Cady Stanton was the daughter of a judge. She had become aware of the legal disabilities of women through reading her father's lawbooks and talking with his students. Her own upbringing had prepared her to be an educated wife and mother but she found running a household and the company of children and servants stultifying, especially when her family moved to a small town in New York state. It was her desire to break out of the confines of the middle-class home that motivated Stanton to organize the first woman's rights meeting in 1848.

Susan B. Anthony met Elizabeth Cady Stanton in 1851 and formed a lasting alliance with her, Stanton providing the intellectual substance and Anthony the organizational talent for this team of social reformers. They became the prime movers behind a militant and wide-ranging movement for woman's rights, at the center of which was the demand for suffrage. Susan Anthony was the daughter of an early textile mill owner who went bankrupt and was forced to return to farming. She had been educated and had worked as a teacher to help support her family. Keenly aware of the inequities in pay for women workers, she believed that suffrage was the key to remedying discrimination in employment. Already a social reformer in the areas of temperance and abolition, Susan Anthony was well acquainted with prejudice toward women.

Lucy Stone was the daughter of a poor farm family in western Massachusetts who worked for nine years as a school teacher to save enough money to attend Oberlin College. She graduated from Oberlin in 1847, one of the first women to graduate from the regular (male) program. Having prepared herself to be a public speaker, Lucy Stone became one of the most effective and eloquent lecturers for the anti-slavery and woman's rights causes. In 1855 she married Henry Blackwell—after he agreed to protest publicly the laws which gave husbands legal control over their wives. In addition to this protest Lucy Stone maintained her own name. Yet marriage, and especially motherhood, had a restraining influence on the fiery agitator. Although she, her husband and their only child, Alice Stone Blackwell, were all active in the woman's rights movement throughout their lives, they aligned themselves with the more "respectable" and conservative elements of the movement.

All three led women who sought to integrate themselves into the social processes of the society by organizing as a sex as well as individually, pushing at the boundaries of their lives by moving into new areas of organizational and occupational work.

Millions of middle-class white women joined the woman's club movement, which organized literary and social improvement groups along with social welfare activities for those who were interested. The feminists, who advocated woman's equality as an end in itself, and other female reformers, who saw woman's rights as a means to effect other reforms, represented the more socially conscious elements of middle-class women. They challenged the prevailing social ideas about woman which emphasized her maternal and domestic role to the exclusion of all else, a reaction to the fact that the family structure was weakening, for many women were in fact moving outside the home and becoming workers. But with a few notable exceptions feminists and female reformers did not question the traditional view that men's and women's natures were different and that woman's maternal functions made her especially suited for nurturing the young and caring for the home.[3] They insisted, however, that marriage and domesticity not abridge the legal rights of women. They sought to establish woman's equality with man and to enlarge woman's sphere, to make a profession an alternative to marriage, and to supplement her role as wife and mother with education and social reforms. The seeming dichotomies of the factory (production) and the home, contributed to the female reformers' class bias. When the middle-class reformers spoke of expanding woman's sphere they did not include the factories. Rather they emphasized non-manual activities such as organizational work and the professions.

Female reformers did support the attempts of working women to organize and improve their working conditions, by providing relief during strikes, investigating and publicizing bad working conditions and agitating for protective legislation. But the involvement of middle-class and even upper-class women in strike relief work and on the picket line obscured the class nature of labor struggles. Further, the Women's Trade Union League, for example, withdrew support from the Lawrence strike led by the Industrial Workers of the World in 1912 on the orders of the American Federation of Labor.[4] The strike, taking place in Lawrence, Massachusetts, consisted of textile workers who had united twenty-five nationalities, skilled and unskilled workers, men as well as women and children, to protest against the reduction of wages. Yet it was the IWW which organized workers without discrimination while the AFL and the craft unions were most discriminatory toward women. It was the respective unions' politics rather than their commitment to women workers that influenced the female reformers. The middle-class women were committed to reforming the political economy, not overthrowing it. They aligned themselves with craft unionism because they believed that labor and capital could coexist. By their actions the female reformers confirmed that political and class differences did indeed exist among women.

The woman's rights movement lasted for almost a century, and the attitudes of the participants reflected changes in thinking among the middle classes. The early movement drew much of its politics from the abolition movement and was highly moral in tone. The natural right of woman to equality and man's and woman's common humanity was stressed, just as the common humanity of whites and blacks was an argument of the abolitionists. The woman's movement emerged at the time when the abolition movement was entering into electoral politics, and from the beginning suffrage was one of their demands. As social reform among the middle classes turned more and more toward electoral politics at the end of the century, woman suffrage became ever more popular among female reformers.

Yet the woman's rights movement never lost its moralizing tone. Some of the arguments for women remaining in the home after it had lost its productive functions emphasized woman's moral nature. Suffragists did not necessarily repudiate these arguments, but rather tried to turn them around as reasons why women should get the vote. Historian Aileen Kraditor notes:

> Especially in the later years suffragists saw women in two lights. Within her home she was the sex whose chief duty in life was bearing and caring for children, functions which naturally endowed her with capacities for love and service and with peaceful propensities. . . . Outside her home she was the half of the population that, whether inherently or by training, was more moral, more temperate, more law-abiding. . . . In both roles, then, woman would be a tremendous asset to government if enfranchised.[5]

This idealistic world outlook colored the female reformers view of all social problems. This, combined with seeing the factory and the home in opposition, led them to view woman's condition in an abstract, almost monolithic way. They had little understanding of woman's role in production. Insofar as they were concerned with economics, it was to demand admission to the professions.

As the nineteenth century progressed, women's gains in educational reform, their efforts in the North in support of the Civil War, and their increasing entry into the labor force undermined the traditional rationale that woman's inferiority prevented her from doing what man could do. Instead arguments against woman suffrage began to center on the different roles that women and men played, roles that were said to be separate but equal. Woman's "higher morality" and the function of the home as a peaceful haven would be destroyed if woman entered man's sphere, argued many men and even some women.

Much of the opposition to woman's rights, and especially woman suffrage, was based on arguments that appealed to passions and prejudices.⁶ But behind this were the fears of what women would do with the vote. Many capitalists, particularly those in the liquor industry, feared that the female vote would back legislative reforms aimed at curtailing the power of the monopolies as well as instituting prohibition. Further, they feared the increased voting power of the working class. One female opponent of suffrage warned: "If the great mass of ignorant women's votes are added to the great mass of ignorant men's votes, there will be constant demands for work, money, bread, leisure, in short, 'all kinds of laws to favor all kinds of persons.' "⁷

Middle-class suffragists were appalled at the thought of class struggle and accepted the basic structure of their society: they simply wanted to participate more fully in its affairs. They sought, therefore, to show that the woman's vote would benefit the existing social structure and that the reforms women would enact would not alter the basic social relations.

In an era when the Anglo-Saxon population feared the voting strength of immigrants and nonwhite peoples, they tried to show that woman suffrage would increase—or at least not limit—the

Anglo-Saxon majority. In the West, where the earliest woman suffrage victories were won, there was a relationship with native-born white men's attempts to maintain political supremacy. On the West Coast, for example, woman suffrage was associated with the anti-Asian exclusion movement. Nationally it was connected to the Progressive movement and shared with that movement the belief in white supremacy.[8]

With the exception of their demands for equal rights, feminists and other female reformers shared the same views as the men of their class. Because the early woman's rights ferment existed alongside the developing abolition movement, the early feminists were affected by the agitation for abolition and racial equality; some became committed to ending slavery before they became advocates of woman's rights. Further, the presence and support of black abolitionists motivated the early woman's rights leaders to make the ending of racial discrimination a part of their conventions' demands. But as organized support for black rights dissolved after 1870, woman suffragists were less and less challenged to extend their arguments for equal rights to include black people. Suffrage leaders for the most part agreed with the prevalent racism which blamed blacks for the failure of Reconstruction and their disfranchisement, and sought to win woman suffrage through demonstrating their allegiance to white supremacy. Feminism came to mean predominantly (although not solely) the fight of white women to be included in the rights and privileges of a racist society.[9]

Woman's Rights and Abolition

From 1848 until the outbreak of the Civil War numerous woman's rights conventions were called to discuss the status of women, resulting in speeches and petition campaigns seeking legal reforms from state legislatures. Anti-slavery women were in the leadership of these activities because their work in behalf of abolition had necessitated challenging traditional views about women. Over a decade before the first woman's rights convention in 1848, debates had flared up regarding the proper role of anti-slavery women when the Grimké sisters—former slaveholders now dedicated to abolition— began lecturing to audiences of both sexes. Women had been work- ing in the abolition movement, but separately, where they mainly raised funds and circulated petitions for male societies. But when the Grimké sisters began to speak to female anti-slavery societies, the novelty of actually hearing former slaveholders, and Angelina's reputation for eloquence, drew men to the lectures.

The spectacle of two women—and soon others—traveling from town to town to speak to mixed audiences provoked condemnations, especially from the churches, that such actions were contrary to God's will and threatened the existence of the family. Among aboli- tionists themselves, debates increased regarding the right of women to full voting and office-holding privileges in the anti-slavery societies, precipitating splits in the societies, including a very bitter one in the Boston Female Anti-Slavery Society.[10]

Among some abolitionists who supported women's right to be in- volved fully in anti-slavery work were those such as Theodore Weld, Angelina's future husband, who urged the women to go on about their anti-slavery work but to be silent on the general ques- tion of woman's rights, so as not to link the two causes in the public mind. But the Grimké sisters believed that the success of abolition necessitated an answer to the charges made against them. "This invasion of our rights was just such an attack upon us, as that made upon Abolitionists generally when they were told a few years ago that they had no right to discuss the subject of slavery," wrote Angelina to Weld and Jon Whittier in August, 1837. "Did you take no notice of this assertion? Why no! With one heart and one voice you said, We will settle this right before we go one step fur- ther. The time to assert a right is the time when that right is denied."[11]

The Grimké sisters also recognized that the arguments against woman were in the abstract similar to those justifying slavery. They countered biblical quotes with alternative interpretations of the Bible and challenged the idea that social custom was a legitimate justification for woman's inferior position. They wrote and spoke out for women's equality with men. In *Letters on the Equality of the Sexes and the Condition of Woman,* a collection of articles reprinted as a pamphlet in 1838, Sarah Grimké presented the first serious discussion of woman's rights by an American woman. The pamphlet was widely circulated, contributing to a growing consciousness about woman's condition. "I ask no favors for my sex," wrote Sarah. "I surrender not our claim to equality. All I ask of our brethren is that they will take their feet from our necks, permit us to stand upright on the ground which God designed us to occupy."[12]

The Grimké sisters were not the first women to speak publicly in the United States. The woman who had pioneered as a lecturer was Frances Wright, a freethinker who spoke widely in 1828 and 1829 on a variety of subjects, including woman's rights. The first American-born woman to lecture publicly was Maria W. Stewart, a free black in New England who was an outspoken abolitionist and an advocate of educational opportunities for women. Speaking in the early 1830's, Maria Stewart met with much opposition for breaking social custom.

What differentiated the Grimké sisters from these earlier women was that the Grimkés were a part of a social reform movement which by 1837 had organized groupings of women who could offer support. The female anti-slavery societies, for example, sponsored most of the lectures where the Grimkés spoke, and soon other female abolitionists were on the speakers' circuit. Women discussed the question of woman's rights in their societies and heard debates on woman's equality in the anti-slavery conventions. Further, some were able to meet women at these conventions who, like themselves, believed that the rights of women extended past their role in anti-slavery work.

It was just such a meeting at the World Anti-Slavery Convention in 1840 in London that set in process the thinking for the first woman's rights convention held in Seneca Falls, New York, eight years later. The female delegates from the United States had been refused delegate status and banished to the balcony with visitors.

Among them was Lucretia Mott, a respected leader of the Hicksite Quakers as well as a leading abolitionist and founder of the first female anti-slavery society. In the days that followed she had many conversations with Elizabeth Cady Stanton, who was later to become an intellectual leader of the woman's rights movement. A newlywed who had come to the convention with her abolitionist husband on their honeymoon, Elizabeth Cady Stanton was new to social reform. However, she was already a staunch advocate of woman's rights, since her upbringing as the daughter of a judge had given her ample opportunity to learn about the legal disabilities confronting women. The convention offered her the opportunity of meeting women who thought as she did. Especially important were her talks with Lucretia Mott.

The events at the convention underscored to both women the need to organize a society to press for woman's rights. Eight years later circumstances brought them together again in upper New York state, and, with the aid of three other women, they issued the first call for a public meeting to discuss woman's civil, religious and social condition. On July 19 and 20, 1848, 300 women and men arrived in Seneca Falls for the convention.

In preparing for this meeting Elizabeth Cady Stanton resolved to call for the right of suffrage for women, a demand so "outrageous" that Henry Stanton declared he would have nothing to do with the convention and left town. Lucretia Mott was uncertain about the resolution, thinking that perhaps the women should move more cautiously. But Frederick Douglass, who lived nearby, was asked his opinion and supported Elizabeth Cady Stanton on the necessity of suffrage to woman's cause. Reassured that she would have his support at the convention, the future president of the Woman Suffrage Association authored the first resolution calling for suffrage: "Resolved, that it is the sacred duty of the women of this country to secure to themselves their sacred right to the elective franchise."[13]

The Seneca Falls Convention of 1848 passed 11 resolutions; all but the suffrage demand—which passed by a slim majority—received unanimous support. The other demands called for the right

of woman to personal and religious freedom, to be equal in marriage and to exercise the same rights as men in testifying in courts,
owning property, acquiring an education and obtaining jobs. In addition they specifically claimed woman's right to equal guardianship
of her children, to control of her own wages and to equal pay for
equal work. At the end of the convention 68 women and 32 men
signed their names to a Declaration of Principles. Among the signers was Charlotte Woodward, the only person present at the convention who lived to see woman suffrage become a federal amendment.

The Seneca Falls Convention was the first of many such conventions held before the Civil War in New York, Ohio, Indiana, Pennsylvania and Massachusetts. The women who attended these conventions generally believed that men did not want the power they
held over women and could be persuaded to change unjust laws
if only women could overcome their timidity and demand action.
The Declaration of Sentiments of the Seneca Falls Convention had
accused men of being guilty of injustice toward women but many
women objected to this, saying that men too were victims of the
unjust laws which gave them power over women.[14] Yet support for
woman's rights was hard to find. Proponents of woman's inferiority
were quick to condemn the conventions and the new ideas, and it
was mainly among the more radical abolitionists that the women
found men who would support their demands.

Many of the early leaders of the woman's rights movement were
themselves abolitionists, and often had trouble keeping the two
issues apart. Lucy Stone, for example, provoked the anger of conservative abolitionists because she lectured on both anti-slavery and
woman's rights. Finally a compromise was worked out whereby she
lectured on abolition on weekends, as an agent for the Anti-Slavery
Society, and on woman's rights as an individual during the week.[15]

Even abolition was a more popular cause than woman's rights,
and the more conservative abolitionists feared that combining the
two issues would detract from the anti-slavery issue. The women,
on the other hand, found it helpful to ally their cause with abolition
because that cause was more popular and because most liberal-

minded men were already abolitionists. Thus the leaders of the woman's rights movement encouraged ties between their own struggle and abolition on the bases of both sympathy and expediency. For similar reasons many black abolitionists championed the women's claims. They both agreed with the women's demands and they hoped to win the white women to the fight against racial discrimination.

Role of Black Abolitionists

Among black abolitionists—female and male—there was disagreement about woman's proper role, some believing that woman's inferiority was God's will. Many, however, supported the woman's rights activities, recognizing that the white women were basing their demands for full citizenship and equal rights on the same moral premises as black abolitionists used in demanding equal rights. For black women the ending of both racial and sexual discrimination was essential for full equality. Harriet Tubman, for example, commented that in the South she had suffered discrimination as a slave, but in the North she met discrimination both as a Negro and as a woman.[16]

Black men were aware of the invaluable contributions of female abolitionists and many felt it their duty to support those who had worked hard in the anti-slavery cause. Among such supporters was Frederick Douglass who had identified himself as an advocate of woman's rights a year before the 1848 convention when he stated in the first issue of the *North Star,* "Right is of no sex." He had been won to the cause of woman's rights when he met Elizabeth Cady Stanton after she returned from the 1840 World Anti-Slavery Convention. Douglass was the only man at the 1848 Seneca Falls Convention to support the suffrage resolution. Seconding Mrs. Stanton's motion, he argued that political equality was vital to woman's cause. Two weeks later in Rochester, Douglass again defended the suffrage demand. This time the convention not only endorsed the motion but resolved to begin petitioning the state legislature until the elective franchise was granted to New York women. Douglass carried notices of woman's rights meetings in his paper and attended them whenever he could, reporting the proceedings favorably.

Douglass's loyalty to woman's rights was also shown in his activities with black abolitionists. Negro conventions of which Douglass was a part went on record as opposing discrimination on account of sex. In 1848 two such conventions invited women to participate in the proceedings, the one in Philadelphia inviting white women as well as black. This invitation brought Lucretia Mott to the sessions.[17] Douglass kept his commitment to woman's rights when working with white abolitionists as well. In 1860 the Radical Abolitionists, with Douglass on the executive committee, planned a convention to discuss the feasibility of establishing an anti-slavery political party. They invited women to participate in the proceedings, thereby becoming the first group in the U.S. to attempt to organize a political party without sexual or racial discrimination.[18]

Because of this black support, the early woman's rights meetings were integrated and the leaders affirmed their tie to the black abolitionists by including protests against racial discrimination in their statements.[19] But not all white women were eager to ally themselves with black abolitionists until they saw it in their interest to do so. In 1851 at a woman's rights convention in Ohio, for example, white women had begged the president, Frances Dana Gage, not to allow Sojourner Truth to speak because they did not want their cause associated with "abolition and niggers." As the meeting progressed, however, the white women were overwhelmed with heckling by antagonistic men. Timid about public speaking and unable to counter the arguments that women were unfit for equal rights, the white women were at a loss. It was Sojourner Truth who saved the day with one of the most electrifying speeches in the history of the woman's rights movement.

Attacking the charge that women were weak, Sojourner Truth raised her bare arm: "Look at my arm! I have ploughed and planted and gathered into barns, and no man could head me—and ain't I a woman?" The room became silent under her commanding voice and eyes of fire. Then turning to the clergy and the charge that women couldn't have the same rights as men because Christ wasn't a woman, she thundered to the audience "Where did your Christ come from? From God and a woman! Man had nothing to do with him." Commented Frances Gage on the effect of her speech, "I have never in my life seen anything like the magical influence that subdued the mobbish spirit of the day, and turned the sneers and jeers of an excited crowd into notes of respect and admiration."[20]

Sojourner Truth embodied a quality missing or suppressed in many of the middle-class white women who attended these conventions. She had been forced to labor like a man under slavery and her resulting physical strength was living testimony to the absurdity of opponents' claims that women were inherently too frail for the responsibilities of equal rights. The charge of frailty arose from the imposed bourgeois standard that "refined" women not do certain types of physical work, and dress in clothing which in fact hindered natural movement and healthy breathing. Living under these conditions many white women were indeed frail and others shared their society's conception of them regardless of their actual physical capabilities.

Sojourner Truth's effectiveness in countering men's attacks at abolitionist and woman's rights conventions, caused some men to jibe that she was really a man, so steeped were they in the mythology of woman's nature as passive. At one convention the black woman met that challenge head on, ripping open her blouse for all to see her breasts so as to silence once and for all the slander that she was not a woman.[21]

Among the black abolitionists were those who in principle supported woman's rights but did not have the time to involve themselves actively in the reform efforts. Outstanding among these was the resistance fighter Harriet Tubman. Like Sojourner Truth she was religious, but unlike Sojourner who was a pacifist, Harriet Tubman believed that the struggle to end slavery would have to be bloody. Whereas Sojourner Truth could and would stand up to any man and verbally defeat him, Harriet Tubman, only five feet tall, was unafraid to confront men with physical force when necessary, as she had already proved in preventing captured slaves from being returned South. Harriet Tubman was in essence an activist in the front lines of the anti-slavery struggle. A runaway slave herself she became the most renowned conductor in the underground railroad. She was an excellent speaker and an active participant in abolitionist meetings. Douglass considered her a "genius"; John Brown called her "General Tubman." Only illness prevented Harriet Tubman from being with John Brown at Harper's Ferry. She had helped Brown plan the raid and had intended to be there with him. This fortuitous change in her plans left her free to become an active soldier in the Union army during the Civil War. She headed the Intelligence Service in the Department of the South serving as a spy and became the first woman in the U.S. to direct a military campaign, leading black and white troops to victory.

John Brown considered Harriet Tubman "the most of a man naturally that I ever met with." In fact she was the "most of a woman." Her activities demonstrated the contribution that women could make to "worldly affairs." In practice she "enlarged woman's sphere" and after the Civil War actively endorsed the woman's rights movement.[22]

Harriet Tubman's militant opposition to slavery was not unique among slave women. What evidence there is indicates that black women were integral participants in slave resistance, helping to plan and execute slave uprisings, committing individual acts of sabotage against the master and his property through poisoning and burning, nurturing the consciousness of resistance in the slave communities and escaping whenever possible. Some went North when they escaped; others joined the maroon communities in the heart of the slave territory, from which they directed assaults against slave owners.[23]

Condition of Slave Women

White advocates of woman's equality had a tendency to equate the status of white women with that of the slave. In a resolution passed

at the Salem, Ohio, convention in 1850 the women stated: "Resolved, that in those laws which confer on man the power to control the property and person of woman, and to remove from her at will the children of her affection, we recognize only the modified code of the slave plantation; and that thus we are brought more nearly into sympathy with the suffering slave, who is despoiled of all his rights."[24] "A married woman has no legal existence; she has no more absolute rights than a slave on a Southern plantation," wrote Elizabeth Cady Stanton. "A married woman," she continued, ". . . takes the name of her master, holds nothing, owns nothing, can bring no action in her own name; and the principles on which she and the slave is educated are the same. The slave is taught what is best for him to know—which is nothing; the woman is taught what is best for her to know—which is little more than nothing, man being the umpire in both cases . . . . Civilly, socially and religiously, she is what man chooses her to be . . . and such is the slave."[25]

In fact, enslaved black women faced a totally different situation from that of the white women reformers. Slavery could be maintained only through brutal force. Women even when pregnant were subjected to beatings. Punishment for women caught in the act of rebellion was sometimes harsher than for men. In addition women were subjected to a form of terrorism reserved for the female: rape. This was a way of reducing the black woman to the level of her biological being, to break her will to resist. It was an attempt to negate the claim to humanity that was nurtured in the slave community, for the other slaves were powerless to protect a woman from assault. Slave women attempted to resist here as elsewhere the attack on their humanity.

The black woman's reproductive role as well as her productive activities were expropriated by the slave master. She was forced to bear children in order to increase the slave master's "property" and was allowed to have a family life only when this served the master's interests. Given the reality of slavery, the black woman's experience of womanhood was unquestionably different from white women's. Reduced to the level of beast of burden in the fields and to breeder of new slaves, the black woman maintained her humanity through

the consciousness of resistance. Her domestic role in the slave quarters was crucial to the slave community's ability to resist total dehumanization because it was the only labor not directly and immediately claimed by the white master. Thus domesticity played a very different role in the slave woman's life than it did in the middle-class white woman's. For the slave woman domesticity was the base which facilitated resistance against social conditions. It was not an end in itself.[26]

The tendency to equate their condition abstractly with slavery obscured some white women's collaboration in black women's enslavement and hid the very real differences between the discrimination felt by middle-class white women and the exploitation suffered by the female slave. This was a reality she not only shared with black men, but was often made more brutal because of her femaleness. The white women who began protesting their condition as women were struggling against a different reality. For instance, one of the primary complaints of the early advocates of woman's rights was woman's loss of control of her property upon marriage. Not only did the slave woman have no property but she herself was considered as such, to be bought and sold and worked for the profit of the slave-owning class which shared its wealth with white women, some of whom directly contributed to the brutality of slavery. Additionally, white women protested their lack of control over their children and their subordinate status in marriage, but the father of their children was their husband and they were asking only for a change in family relations. Slavery destroyed normal family life as such and marriage was often forbidden. As important, middle-class white women were not subjected to the brutality of slave labor, the attempt to dehumanize totally, and the terrorism that was an essential feature of this system.

This is not to say that the white women's demands were not just and their condition oppressive. The fact that many black abolitionists affirmed woman's cause indicates that they recognized the serious plight of all women. But black abolitionists were clear on priorities; they knew that the condition of slavery and the denial

of racial equality meant that the very survival of their people was at stake. This simply was not true for white women.

Reconstruction: The Fourteenth and Fifteenth Amendments

Woman's rights activity stopped for the duration of the Civil War while reformers threw their energies into pressing for Emancipation and building support for the war effort. Anti-slavery women organized the National Woman's Loyal League in May, 1863, which collected 400,000 signatures in support of the Thirteenth Amendment to abolish slavery. The League, which included Stanton, Anthony and Stone in the leadership, also passed a resolution calling for equal rights for blacks and women, although not without disagreement among them as to whether it was the appropriate time to do so.

The debate about whether to refrain from making demands for woman's equality until the questions of slavery and equal rights for blacks had been settled became a major issue among advocates of woman's rights during Reconstruction, eventually splitting the movement into two factions. The feminists who had worked hard during the war expected to be rewarded for their work by being included in legislation extending the franchise. But when the Fourteenth Amendment* was proposed to Congress in the summer of 1866 it explicitly limited its concern to male citizens. Militant woman suffragists were horrified. The proposed Fourteenth Amendment not only had no mention of woman suffrage but put the word "male" into the Constitution for the first time. Up to this point the Constitution had been silent as to sex and women had been excluded from suffrage by the individual states.

---

* The Fourteenth Amendment has five sections. It guarantees due process of law to all persons born or naturalized in the United States; prohibits persons who have engaged in insurrection from holding public office

unless such a person is approved by two-thirds of both Houses of Congress; provides that the United States government cannot be held responsible for debts incurred during aid to rebellion or from loss or emancipation of slaves; and gives Congress power to enforce all provisions of the Amendment. The section which aroused agitation among feminists was the second one which stipulates: "Representatives shall be apportioned among the several States according to their respective numbers, counting the whole number of persons in each State, excluding Indians not taxed. But when the right to vote at any election for the choice of electors for President and Vice President of the United States, Representatives in Congress, the Executive and Judicial officers of a State, or the members of the Legislature thereof, is denied to any of the male inhabitants of such State, being twenty-one years of age, and citizens of the United States, or in any way abridged, except for participation in rebellion or other crime, the basis or representation therein shall be reduced in the proportion which the number of such male citizens shall bear to the whole number of male citizens twenty-one years of age in such State." (Ratified July 28, 1868)

The Fourteenth Amendment had been proposed by the Republicans to ensure their party's domination when the Southern states were accepted back into the Union. Suffrage was not explicitly guaranteed to black men; rather one section of the Amendment guaranteed to the Republicans that blacks would not be counted in Southern representation unless black men were allowed to vote. If not allowed to vote, the South would lose almost half of its Congressional seats. The motivation behind this section of the Amendment was the fact that with emancipation, the former slaves would be computed as full persons in apportionment, instead of 3/5 of a person as had been done under slavery. This change in computation would give the South 13 additional representatives in Congress. If all the representatives coming from the Southern states were Democrats, that party would have the majority in Congress. The Republicans believed that if black men voted, they would cast their votes for the Republican Party—their liberator. If they didn't vote, the Republican Party would not be hurt, due to the provisions of the Amendment.[27]

Because of the agitation for woman suffrage the word "male" was inserted to make clear that this amendment covered only the question of male voters. Women were to be counted in apportionment as was customary, even though the states barred them from voting. The Republicans were not interested in supporting such a controversial issue as woman suffrage; most thought woman's claim to the ballot ridiculous. Many congressmen did not support black suffrage either. The Fourteenth Amendment was a compromise measure to ensure Republican supremacy and the black vote a vehicle to consolidate the national hegemony of Northern business through its representatives in Congress. This and not racial equality was the motive behind the Amendment. In this scenario, woman suffrage had no place.

The Fourteenth Amendment put feminists in a dilemma. The word "male" would be added to the Constitution and seriously jeopardize the women's claims to full citizenship. Yet the Amendment held the possibility—although no guarantee—of stopping the intense repression and virtual re-enslavement of blacks in the South, by giving the freedmen political power at the polls. For this reason the black abolitionists and their allies urged the white women to support it.

Susan Anthony, who had been in the Midwest organizing an equal rights league among black refugees and actively agitating for black and woman suffrage, returned East to lead the opposition to the Amendment on the grounds that it excluded woman suffrage. Joined by Elizabeth Cady Stanton she organized a petition campaign to Congress requesting that legislation be passed which would prohibit states from disfranchising any of their citizens on account of sex or color. This was the first time that Congress had been petitioned for woman suffrage; previous petitions had been directed to the individual state legislatures.

Many abolitionists believed that the efforts to secure woman suffrage legislation seriously jeopardized the Fourteenth Amendment. They refused, therefore, to sign the petitions. The Republicans were bound to present to Congress the petitions from their constituents which soon totaled over 10,000 signatures. But they effectively negated the point of the petitions by introducing them as supporting universal suffrage, which to most people was synonymous with universal manhood suffrage.

While the Republicans protested and obscured the petitions which called for black and woman suffrage, the Democrats, who opposed black male suffrage, volunteered to champion the women's cause. Feeling deserted by their former allies, the woman suffrage advocates accepted this offer of help, although it compromised the intent of their petitions. Woman suffrage became a vehicle to attempt to sabotage all proposed legislation to enfranchise black men. Even the white feminists' arguments in support of black women were used this way.[28]

The white women were not unaware that the Democrats used their petitions and feminist arguments to hurt the chances of black male suffrage but they defended their position by saying that since the Anti-Slavery Society did not require its members to support woman suffrage, why should they require their allies to support black male suffrage? The white women were bitter; they believed that their rights were being sacrificed and they smarted under the admonitions of their former allies that this was "the Negro's hour." They feared that if their cause were not pushed militantly, woman would be left disfranchised when Reconstruction was over. They knew that many men, both black and white, believed that woman should be the inferior of man and thus distrusted the abolitionists who reassured them that as soon as the black man's cause was won, woman suffrage would be championed. They reacted with moral outrage at the political maneuvers of the Republicans.

Essentially, many white advocates of woman suffrage did not believe that Congress would give the vote to black men before white women. They refused to believe that their cause was hopeless, and, forced into a situation of seeing their cause split from black suffrage, were determined to agitate for woman suffrage with all the means at their disposal, including working with racists and even employing racist arguments themselves.

In May, 1866, the first Woman's Rights Convention was held since the Civil War. The convention unanimously endorsed a proposal by Susan Anthony that "by the act of emancipation and the Civil Rights Bill, the negro and woman now had the same civil and political status, alike needing only the ballot, therefore the time had come for an organization which should demand universal suffrage. . . ."[29] The American Equal Rights Association was formed with Lucretia Mott as president and Elizabeth Cady Stanton and Frederick Douglass two of the vice presidents. Those who joined the Equal Rights Association supported suffrage for women, but were not necessarily united on the priority of pushing the issue at that time and many tried to convince the feminists to hold back on their demands because of the political situation.

The Kansas election of 1867 dealt a severe blow to the unstable unity of the Equal Rights Association. Two separate referenda were offered the voters in that state. One would have eliminated racial discrimination, the other sexual discrimination in eligibility for voting. The effect of two separate referenda was that both were campaigned for separately and at the expense of one another. The Kansas election was the first time that the question of woman suffrage was put to a vote, but the Republicans who had proposed both referenda, soon dropped active support of woman suffrage. The abolitionists who held black male suffrage as a priority also dropped their support. Abolitionist papers all remained silent until the last month when their endorsement was meaningless. Some Republicans actively campaigned against woman suffrage, including the black orator, Charles Langston. Both measures lost.

The feminists who had gone to Kansas to campaign for the woman suffrage referendum, regarded this lack of support as yet another betrayal. They campaigned despite it. While campaigning in Kansas, Stanton and Anthony were offered the help of a vicious racist, George Francis Train. Once again they accepted the help of an opponent of racial equality, so determined were they to try to win this victory for woman suffrage.

Stanton and Anthony emerged from the Kansas campaign as owners of a newspaper, *Revolution,* which was a gift from Train who both named the paper and gave it its motto: "Men, their rights and nothing more; women, their rights and nothing less!"[30] With

Anthony as publisher and Stanton one of the editors, *Revolution* became a comprehensive woman's rights paper covering a wide range of issues including discrimination in employment and pay, the plight of the poor woman, inequities in the marriage and divorce laws, and the prejudice against woman in religion. But the paper also opposed the Fourteenth and Fifteenth Amendments.

The determination of the feminists not to forsake their own cause in the face of woman's exclusion from the Fourteenth Amendment had set in motion the dynamics of opposition to the Fifteenth Amendment* which had been proposed in Congress to guarantee black male suffrage. Many of the woman suffrage advocates found the Fifteenth Amendment an insult and a reminder of women's powerlessness since women, black and white, were again to be left out of legislation extending the franchise. But the outlawing of racial discrimination in suffrage, stipulated by the Fifteenth Amendment, did not in itself hurt the woman's cause because it did not specify male suffrage. By this time, however, the militant feminists had so convinced themselves of the primary importance of woman suffrage that they fought the Fifteenth Amendment because since racial discrimination was prohibited, more men would be voting, specifically those whom many of the white feminists considered their inferiors. Furthermore, they knew it would be very difficult to mobilize support for a sixteenth amendment to extend the franchise once again, an alternative proposed by Douglass and other woman suffrage advocates who supported the Fifteenth Amendment.

Frederick Douglass tried on numerous occasions to convince the white feminists of the urgency of the ballot for blacks. As early as 1866 he warned that the Equal Rights Association was in danger of becoming solely a woman's rights organization and argued that whereas woman suffrage was desirable, black suffrage was a necessity. Later he added to this argument that woman suffrage depended

---

* The Fifteenth Amendment: "The right of citizens of the United States to vote shall not be denied or abridged by the United States, or by any State, on account of race, color, or previous condition of servitude." (Ratified March 30, 1870)

on the preliminary success of black male suffrage. He criticized Stanton and Anthony for their position that black men should not get the franchise before women, their association with the enemies of black people and their use of derogatory remarks against blacks in the *Revolution*. "I must say that I do not see how any one can pretent that there is the same urgency in giving the ballot to woman as to the Negro," he argued. "With us, the matter is a question of life and death, at least, in fifteen States of the Union. When women, because they are women, are hunted down through the cities of New York and New Orleans; when they are dragged from their houses and hung upon lamp-posts; when their children are torn from their arms, and their brains dashed out upon the pavement; when they are objects of insult and outrage at every turn; when they are in danger of having their homes burnt down over their heads; when their children are not allowed to enter schools; then they will have an urgency to obtain the ballot equal to our own." Was this not all true for the black woman, someone asked. "Yes, yes, yes," he replied, "it is true for the black woman, but not because she is a woman but because she is black."[31]

Charles Remond, a black abolitionist long sympathetic to the woman's cause, tried to convince the feminists that black men would indeed support suffrage for women once black male suffrage was won. He admitted that in principle the women were right to demand universal suffrage but necessity required that partial black suffrage be supported. Black abolitionist Robert Purvis agreed with the militant feminists, however, arguing that he would rather his son were never enfranchised unless his daughter could be also, since she bore the double burden of being both black and female. But his son felt differently. Young Purvis was one of a group of black men who denounced the women's plans to agitate for a woman suffrage amendment as jeopardizing the black man's cause. George Downing, another member of the group, declared that it was God's will that man dominate woman.[32]

It was anti-woman remarks such as Downing's that agitated the militant feminists' opposition to black men receiving the vote before women. The women's distrust of the male voter was well grounded in their experience as victims of many discriminatory laws, but the prevailing assumptions of white racial superiority caused the white women to assume that black men would be even worse towards women than white men had been. Elizabeth Cady Stanton answered Downing thus: "When Mr. Downing puts the question to me; are you willing to have the colored man enfranchised before the women I say no; I would not trust him with my rights; degraded, oppressed himself, he would be more despotic with the governing power than ever our Saxon rulers are. . . . If women are still to be represented by men, then I say let only the highest type of manhood stand at the helm of State."[33]

The arguments the feminists used to call for woman suffrage ranged from the traditional claim of the equality of all human beings to reasons why white women would be better voters than black men. The basic assumptions underlying their arguments were that with emancipation black men and all women were equally oppressed but that white women were qualitatively better potential voters than black men. Feminists were quick to point out, for example, that white women were more educated as a group than were black men. In addition, the feminists believed that women represented a new class of voters; whereas black male suffrage only added more men to the electorate. This assumption that woman was somehow different from man was a result of the sexual divisions in the society growing out of the separation of the home from production. Whereas the opponents of woman suffrage argued that woman's different nature made her unfit for the vote, the feminists argued that precisely this difference made the extension of suffrage to woman a necessity. But the emphasis on woman's essential difference contradicted the claims that men and women were first of all human beings who deserved the same rights.

The assumption that woman's nature was different from man's explains the white feminists approach to black women. Whereas black men were seen to be degraded and potentially more despotic because they suffered oppression, black women were thought to be more oppressed and more intelligent and capable of the vote than black men. White feminists championed the black woman in their arguments for woman suffrage, pointing out that black women had been equal in oppression with their men in slavery and if only black men received the vote, black women would now have new masters. Since they assumed that black men would be more oppressive than white men, they argued that it was not in black women's interest for black male suffrage to be granted before woman suffrage. Indeed Elizabeth Cady Stanton went so far as to say that it would be better for a black woman to be the slave of an educated white man than of a "degraded, ignorant black one."[34] Further, because of woman's different nature, if a choice had to be made, it was in black women's interest that white women receive the vote first, the feminists contended. White women, representing all womanhood, would end injustice, so this argument went, because of their alleged superior moral nature.

Conspicuously absent from the white feminists' arguments for woman suffrage was any discussion of racial oppression. Douglass and others constantly tried to impress upon the white women the very real differences between the condition of all blacks and of white women. Susan Anthony ignored the situation of millions of Southern black men and women, for example, when she answered Douglass by personalizing the problem: "When he tells us that the cause of black men is so perilous, I tell him that even outraged as they are by the hateful prejudice against color, he himself would not today exchange his sex and color with Elizabeth Cady Stanton."[35] However, it was not Frederick Douglass' personal situation or even the relative merits of being a black man or a white woman in the Northern middle classes that were at issue. But the militant white feminists were unable to see that the question of black male suffrage was more than a question of abstract legal rights; that it was a question involving the freedom and indeed survival of the entire race.

Those white men and women who understood the crucial

situation for blacks, especially in the South, advocated supporting the Fourteenth and Fifteenth Amendments. They agreed with Frances Harper, one of the few black women to attend Equal Rights Association meetings, who argued that race was more important than sex, if priorities had to be set.[36] Even Sojourner Truth, who spoke out clearly for equal rights for black women and men, did not actively oppose the amendments.[37] It was not, after all, the black man who prevented Sojourner Truth and other black women from receiving equal pay for equal work, or who taxed them without allowing them any political representation. Nor was it the black man who discriminated against black women because of their color.

Given these positions it was inevitable that the uneasy alliance in the Equal Rights Association would end. The final break came at the 1869 anniversary meeting when Douglass moved that the association endorse the Fifteenth Amendment. It is unclear what the final outcome of the debate was, but many of the more militant feminists fought against the resolution, even though it referred to the amendment as the "culmination of one-half of our demands" and called for the redoubling of "our energy to secure the further amendment guaranteeing the same sacred rights without limitation to sex."[38]

Stanton and Anthony had had enough of the Equal Rights Association, which they believed had betrayed their interest. They and their followers withdrew to form a woman suffrage association made up only of those who supported the priority of woman's cause. The National Woman Suffrage Association set as its goal a sixteenth amendment granting woman the franchise. Although they had disagreed with the white woman militants about the Fourteenth and Fifteenth Amendments, Douglass, Sojourner Truth and Harriet Tubman continued to support woman suffrage and to speak at conventions with Stanton and Anthony.

A second woman suffrage organization was formed six months later of those woman suffrage advocates who had supported the Fourteenth and Fifteenth Amendments—the American Woman Suffrage Association with Lucy Stone, Henry Blackwell and Julia Ward Howe in the leadership. Although many members had supported the amendments some had also appealed to racist sentiments in their advocacy of woman suffrage.[39]

The National American Woman Suffrage Association

For the following twenty years the woman suffrage movement was divided into two rival organizations—the National, led by Stanton and Anthony, and the American, led by Lucy Stone and others. The issue of supporting the Amendments proved to be only one of many tactical differences between the leaders of the two organizations.[40] The National was, at least at first, hostile to male leadership, although men were allowed to join the organization. They maintained that the preponderance of men in the American Equal Rights Association's leadership had been instrumental in the betrayal of woman suffrage and they looked upon those women who supported the Fifteenth Amendment as having been "duped" by men.

Most important, however, was the question of including other reforms in the suffrage campaigns. The leadership of the American Woman Suffrage Association opposed involving their organization in any other issue, and criticized the National Association for doing so.[41]

The *Revolution* answered the criticism of its policy of backing other causes. Laura Bullard stated that they were not dreamers and knew that the ballot would do no more for woman than for man. Suffrage would only affect political problems but "woman's chief discontent is not with her political, but with her social, and particularly her marital bondage." Indeed, the writer went on, marriage was a significantly more important reform than "any such superficial and fragmentary question as woman suffrage."[42]

Clearly this writer's defense of the National's multi-issue stance contradicted some of the militants' earlier arguments for woman suffrage taking precedence over black male suffrage. Stanton herself appeared to have altered her views slightly for she was quoted as saying, "The negro was *first* emancipated, and then suffrage was given him; and I am not sure that this is not the natural order for woman. She must demand first her deliverance from slavery, claim her right to herself, soul and body, and then ask for suffrage."[43]

The *Revolution* had always taken a comprehensive approach to the question of woman's rights. Yet the barrage of arguments the militants had created regarding the importance of woman suffrage in relation to black male suffrage and the support they had built up contributed to the momentum that soon made woman suffrage the dominant goal of the National as well as the American Woman Suffrage Association. By 1890, in fact, there was so little difference between the two organizations that the leaders put personal animosities aside and merged into the National American Woman Suffrage Association (NAWSA) with Elizabeth Cady Stanton as president. Two years later Stanton resigned the presidency and Anthony took her place.

By the time of the merger Stanton and Anthony, who had stood together against the Fourteenth and Fifteenth Amendments, did not fully agree on the primacy of suffrage vis-á-vis other woman's rights issues. Anthony was still convinced that the suffrage victory was all-important and the key to winning all of woman's other demands. Further, she believed that save suffrage, women had won all their fundamental rights. On the other hand, as woman suffrage became the central, and for many women the sole, goal of the woman's movement, Stanton began to think that other issues, especially religion, were more important. Yet Stanton in her earlier arguments against the Fourteenth and Fifteenth Amendments had contributed to the overwhelming interest among women in suffrage.

Susan Anthony held the presidency for eight years. When she stepped down from the presidency of the Suffrage Association in 1900 a new generation of leaders took over the suffrage movement. Although many came into the suffrage movement through the Women's Christian Temperance Union which, under the leadership of Frances Willard, had developed a broad campaign that included many issues other than temperance, the new leaders were dedicated to keeping the Suffrage Association free of any other controversial reforms.

The new president of the Suffrage Association was Carrie Chapman Catt, a brilliant organizer and strategist who had become chairman of the NAWSA's Organization Committee in 1895. Her husband's ill health forced her to resign the presidency in 1902, but thirteen years later she resumed the office and led the suffrage forces to victory. Active in the international woman suffrage movement, she was a proponent of organizing the suffrage forces to press for a constitutional amendment, rather than attempting to win state by state.

In the years between Carrie Chapman Catt's presidency, Anna Howard Shaw was the leader of the suffrage forces. A doctor and a minister, she was a brilliant orator and very popular as a speaker. But she was a poor organizer and the suffrage movement declined during her leadership when the focus was on state campaigns.

Southern white women, who joined the movement at the turn of the century, were instrumental in shifting the focus away from a federal amendment because of their adherence to states rights. They also contributed to the more explicitly white supremacist stance of the movement. Not all of the new leaders agreed with the extreme racial views of the Southern white women. A few even opposed racial discrimination and as individuals joined the NAACP. But all were willing to tolerate racism within the suffrage movement because they wanted to build as much white support as they could for their cause. They segregated their parades and informally discouraged black women's organizations from joining the Suffrage Association because they knew that many white women opposed this. Moreover, none of the white suffrage leaders spoke for the rights of black women at suffragist conventions or refused to support tactics which explicitly talked of reducing black political power.[44]

Suffrage leaders simultaneously attempted to convince blacks that they should support woman suffrage. For example, they published a pamphlet by W.E.B Du Bois on woman suffrage. Du Bois, Mary Church Terrell, and other black leaders addressed their conventions. But they ignored the pleas of the black leaders that they "stand up not only for the oppressed sex but also for the oppressed race."[45]

White suffragists generally shared the prevalent white supremacist attitudes toward immigrants as well as blacks. They argued that it was an insult for native-born Anglo-Saxon women to be the political inferiors of "foreigners." Their need to build electoral support for various state referenda, however, forced them to campaign in immigrant communities. When they discovered that the immigrant vote was favorable to woman suffrage, their attitudes toward the immigrants softened somewhat. Yet anti-foreign sentiment continued and coexisted with a more sympathetic view toward the immigrants' right to vote.

Suffragists formulated their arguments to counter the arguments of the opposition. One major argument used against woman suffrage was that it would increase the non-Anglo-Saxon vote. White Southerners were even more explicit: woman suffrage not only held the possibility of enfranchising black women, but a federal amendment could revitalize the question of black male suffrage and curtail the systematic disfranchisement of black men being carried out in the South at that time. This latter argument was partly responsible for suffragists concentrating on state campaigns for a number of years after the turn of the century. When it became clear that the white South would never grant women suffrage without a federal amendment, white suffragists argued that black women could be disenfranchised in the same manner that black men were being denied the vote.

In regard to the question of woman suffrage increasing the non-Anglo-Saxon vote, suffragists developed arguments showing that woman suffrage would increase or at least not limit the white native-born majority. In 1893, for example, the newly merged National American Woman Suffrage Association passed a resolution that, "without expressing any opinion on the proper qualifications for voting," noted that there were more white native-born women who could read and write than all black voters and all foreign voters combined, so that "the enfranchisement of such women would settle the vexed question of rule by illiteracy, whether of home-grown or foreign-born production."[46]

Although the National Association never took a formal position on qualified suffrage, many of its members did. In 1894 Elizabeth Cady Stanton created a storm of controversy by advocating that illiterates and people who could not speak English be barred from the polls. Among those who opposed her was her daughter, Harriot Stanton Blatch who had become an active suffragist. Stanton's position on an educational qualification contradicted her traditional arguments for woman suffrage which had always been based on the inalienable rights of the individual to participate in the government which ruled her or him. In subsequent years more and more white suffragists came to agree with her stance. But Stanton, for all her outrage that the "daughters of Jefferson" should be the political inferiors of black and immigrant men, did not agree with those who advocated excluding nonwhite peoples from the United States. She would, however, prevent them from voting until they—male or female—were assimilated.[47]

Susan Anthony remained opposed to an educational or property qualification throughout her life. Organizationally, however, she had separated herself from the fight against racism after she left the Equal Rights Association. She asked Frederick Douglass not to attend a suffrage convention in Atlanta, rationalizing that she did not want him to have to suffer insults. She also contributed to the exclusion of black women by refusing a request to help organize a black branch of the suffrage association as this effort might antagonize Southern white support.[48]

In 1899 the NAWSA national convention was held in Michigan, a state in which black women were welcomed in suffrage clubs. A black suffragist, Lottie Wilson Jackson, offered a resolution that suitable accommodations ought to be provided black women on railroads. Not surprisingly the Southern white women strenuously objected to the motion. Those Northern women who supported the motion, pointed out that the resolution neither attacked the separate coach laws nor questioned segregation; all it asked was that black women be provided with decent accommodations. In closing the debate Susan Anthony used her influence to defeat the motion. "We women are a helpless, disfranchised class," she said. "While we are in this condition, it is not for us to go passing resolutions against railroad corporations or anybody else."[49]

In 1903 Susan Anthony joined Carrie Chapman Catt, Anna Howard Shaw and other leaders in signing a statement to a New Orleans newspaper which had criticized the NAWSA's stand on race as being pro-equality. The letter articulated the view that the race question was irrelevant to the purposes of the Suffrage Association and that the doctrine of state's rights was recognized regarding the relation of local clubs to the national organization. Further, the NAWSA convention passed a resolution that year which sanctioned restricted associations and left state associations free to employ white-supremacist tactics.[50]

On a personal level Susan Anthony maintained a commitment to racial equality. For example, although she refused to help black women join the Suffrage Association she did speak to black women's clubs informally. Frederick Douglass credited both Anthony and Stanton as being among the very few who supported him in his marriage to his second wife who was white. Ida Wells Barnett, the anti-lynching crusader and suffragist, speaks in her autobiography both of Anthony's personal actions on behalf of racial equality and her refusal to make those same stands politically within the suffrage movement.[51] She told Susan Anthony that although this might have made gains for woman suffrage, it also confirmed white women's racism.

The contradiction between Susan Anthony's professed personal beliefs and her political stance in relation to racism was a characteristic common to many white social reformers, though her rationale was different. She accepted the popular belief that woman was more moral than man; thus she rationalized her compromises on the grounds that white women would end racism when they got the vote because of their higher morality. In effect this was a feminist version of paternalism. This reasoning compromised Anthony's commitment to woman's equality as well as her commitment to racial equality because it accepted as legitimate the assertion that men's and women's natures were essentially different.

Commitment to expediency within the suffrage movement was not limited to racial matters. The questioning of such issues as woman's domestic duties, marriage and free love were beyond the pale for all but a very few suffragists. Nor did suffragists tolerate their own members challenging other sexist institutions. In 1896 the NAWSA convention officially disassociated itself from a feminist critique of the Bible that had been written by Elizabeth Cady Stanton and others. Susan Anthony had opposed the resolution, vehemently arguing that one of the tenets of the association had always been the right of individual opinion. (It was on this tenet that Anthony had rationalized not taking a stand on racism within the Suffrage Association.) The resolution passed despite Anthony's opposition; both of the future presidents of the NAWSA were among those who gave it their support. This was a blow to Susan Anthony's convictions and she considered resigning the presidency of the association.[52] If suffragists could disassociate themselves from a founder of their movement and past president of their association because her views were controversial on other subjects, there was little basis to assume that they would prove morally superior to white men when they did receive the vote.

The woman's rights movement had become conservative as suffrage developed in popularity. The movement did not require its members to agree on anything other than suffrage and, indeed, suffragists did not necessarily agree even on why women should be given the vote. Since the goal of the movement was to win legislation, it was essential to build male support. Therefore, suffragists used any and all arguments that they thought would help win votes for woman suffrage. The result was that they made claims about the value of the woman's vote which had no basis in reality. Further, they attempted to keep their movement "respectable" and to demonstrate to the white male voters that women's views on other social issues were the same as the men's.

The sympathy the early white feminists had felt towards black women as women had almost totally disappeared by this time. Suffragists were not concerned with black women when they argued for suffrage. Indeed, many were willing to argue that perhaps not all women should receive the vote since the opposition to woman suffrage feared the increase in the nonwhite vote. Thus there was little relation between the activities of the white suffragists and black women at the turn of the century. Black women also organized as women and when possible joined both the white women's club movement and suffrage associations. But their major organizational activities were oriented to alleviating the effects of racism in their communities and, in some cases, to protesting racial oppression.

Social Activism Among Black Women at the Turn of the Century

The reality of racial oppression and the exclusionary practices of white suffragists prevented woman suffrage from being a primary focus for organizing among black women. Disfranchisement of black men and the continued repression in the South, along with anti-black riots in other parts of the country where suffrage was obtainable, were ample proof that legal rights in and of themselves were no guarantee to actual equality. Black suffragists had looked upon woman suffrage as enabling black women to help elect progressive, and particularly black, officials in the Northern cities where black men were developing some voting strength. Their primary concern was to attempt to alleviate the effects of racial oppression by both improving themselves and developing services for the black community. A few, such as Ida B. Wells, the anti-lynching crusader, protested injustices and organized sentiment against racial oppression.

Throughout the whole of the nineteenth century free black women, North and South, organized themselves into local groups to undertake or support educational and social welfare activities in the black community. The real growth and organization of black women's groups on a national basis occurred at the end of the century in the Northern cities, where a number of educated black women with some leisure time provided the leadership for drawing local black groups together. Whereas the needs of the local black community in part stimulated the growth of local groups and determined their major activities, the impetus for national organization was a common commitment to challenge the racist stereotypes that black women were immoral and to protest the large number of lynchings which were occurring throughout the country, especially in the South.

The early black anti-lynching campaign had been spearheaded by a militant black journalist, Ida B. Wells, whose main support in the United States came from black women's clubs. Born and reared in Mississippi, Ida B. Wells had been a successful editor of a black Memphis, Tennessee, newspaper when in 1892 three of her friends were lynched. Always an outspoken critic of segregation, she wrote scathing attacks against lynching and urged her people to leave the city in her paper. Threatened with lynching herself, she bought a gun, determined to die fighting rather than submit. Fortunately, she was out of the city when a mob, angered by one of her editorials, sacked and burned her newspaper office. Undaunted, Ida Wells presented evidence in the columns of the *New York Age* and other papers, and in speeches throughout the U.S. and England, that the charge of rape of white women was only a false cover-up used by apologists of lynchings.

The lynching of Ida Wells' friends in Memphis had not involved a charge of rape; rather her friends were successful businessmen in competition with a white-owned store, and had been singled out of a group of black prisoners by a white mob during a racial confrontation. "This is what opened my eyes to what lynching really was," stated Ida Wells in her autobiography, "an excuse to get rid of Negroes who were acquiring wealth and property and thus keep the race terrorized and 'keep the nigger down.' "[53]

Ida Wells set out to prove that the lynchings, which were occurring on nearly a daily basis, were not caused by black men's attempts to rape white women. She began to investigate every case of lynching she read about, discovering that in 2/3 of the cases black men were not even charged with assaulting white women. In some of the cases the lynch victims had been women and children. Ida Wells published a compilation of her studies of lynching in 1895 entitled *A Red Record*. Frederick Douglass wrote the preface to the book.

The first organizing attempts among black women in New York City and Brooklyn are attributed to women who came together to sponsor a meeting to raise money to help Ida Wells start a new paper soon after she had been driven from Memphis. The meeting launched Ida Wells on her speaking campaign that was to take her to England as well as across the United States. It also launched the club movement among black women, not only in New York but in New England as well. Ida Wells, at the invitation of Josephine St. Pierre Ruffin, traveled to Boston and other New England cities spreading her message against lynch law and encouraging black women to organize. When Ida Wells went to Chicago for the World's Columbian Exposition in 1893, she organized the first club there. It was with the help of the black club women and Frederick Douglass that she was able to publish and distribute a pamphlet at the Fair stating the facts about the oppression of blacks.

The club movement, which involved most black women activists, flourished in New England under the leadership of Josephine St. Pierre Ruffin. She was the wife of a prominent black judge in Boston, a suffragist and one of the first black women to belong to the New England Women's Clubs which were part of the white women's club movement. Josephine Ruffin organized the Woman's New Era Club of Boston which published one of the most important black magazines of its day, *The Women's Era*, under her editorship.

Black clubs drew their leadership from black women whose families had economic security and social standing in the black community, but the membership incorporated working women, tenant farmwives and other poor black women. In this the clubs differed from the white club movement.[54] Black clubs also engaged in many activities that were similar to the white clubs: education, self-improvement and community services. But with the black clubs these were combined with an emphasis on race pride and development. They maintained homes for the elderly, orphanages, kindergartens, day nurseries as well as activities specifically aimed at the needs of black women: employment counseling, job training, and housing.[55]

In 1895 the Woman's New Era Club of Boston issued a call for representatives of black women's groups to meet to organize a national body. There had been previous calls for a national organization, most particularly from Mary Church Terrell, who was a member of the Colored Women's League of Washington, D.C., patterned after the white General Federation of Women's Clubs. The event which precipitated this call to organize nationally was the charge, in a widely publicized letter to an English suffragist, that black women were immoral. The women felt that a national organization could do much towards proving the falsehood of these charges.

In her address to the representatives of 20 clubs which met in Boston in July, 1895, Josephine Ruffin declared that their purpose was to challenge the charge of immorality by a "dignified showing of what we are and hope to become" as an "army of organized women standing for purity and mental worth." She noted that the opposition of white women to black clubs' participation in the General Federation of Women's Clubs was in part based on the charge of black women's immorality.[56]

The meeting resolved to form a national organization with *The Women's Era* as its official organ. That year the National Federation of Afro-American Women was founded with Mary Margaret Washington as president. Mrs. Washington shared the conservative orientation of her husband, Booker T. Washington, in regard to accommodation, but the new organization issued statements in support of Ida Wells' work against lynching. The National Association of Colored Women was formed the following year by a merger of this organization with the Colored Women's League of Washington with Mary Church Terrel as the first president. By 1899 the association claimed more than 300 clubs. At their convention that year 146 delegates represented 46 clubs from 16 states throughout the U.S. In 1914 the association represented over a thousand clubs and 50,000 black women.

Like the white settlement workers, the social welfare work among black women attempted to patch up failures in the system. The majority of active black women, like their white counterparts in the white club movement, worked predominantly in areas that were considered acceptable for women at the end of the century. A minority followed Ida Wells' path of organizing protests against racial oppression. A few clubs organized civil rights and protest activities around segregation laws. Other clubs endorsed the work of racial militants.

Many black women as individuals and in their clubs endorsed woman suffrage because it could help their race but they were discouraged organizationally from joining the suffrage movement. As individuals, Northern black women became members of white suffrage clubs. Ida Wells Barnett (she had married in 1895) organized a black suffrage club in 1913 because she recognized that many black women did not support woman suffrage because of their distrust of the white suffragists.

Victory and Defeat

In 1920 women finally received the vote after 72 years of almost constant agitation. The federal amendment, which read "The right of citizens of the United States to vote shall not be denied or abridged on account of sex," had first been introduced into the Senate in 1878 and into the House in 1883. By the time the federal amendment became law, fourteen states had already granted women full suffrage and many others partial suffrage, such as municipal or school elections.

Only one woman was alive in 1920 who had attended the historic Seneca Falls Convention in 1848. All of the early leaders of the suffrage cause were dead; the movement had changed in character from a multi-issue woman's rights platform to a single issue campaign. The organizational efforts that went into winning this one reform were enormous. Hundreds of thousands of women were organized. Millions of dollars were raised, mainly in small sums. According to Carrie Chapman Catt, the NAWSA president who led the suffragists to victory, the women:

> were forced to conduct 56 campaigns of referenda to male voters; 480 campaigns to urge Legislatures to submit suffrage amendments to voters; 47 campaigns to induce State constitutional campaigns to write woman suffrage into State constitutions; 277 campaigns to persuade State party conventions to include woman suffrage planks; 30 campaigns to urge presidential party conventions to adopt woman suffrage planks in party platforms and 19 campaigns with 19 successive Congresses.[57]

Toward the end of the suffrage campaign, women picketed the White House, were arrested and went on hunger strikes in the jails. These demonstrations had been organized by the National Woman's Party which felt that the National Association's tactics were too passive.

The long and arduous campaign that proved necessary for women to win political equality in part explains the movement's tendency to narrow its scope. Educational and occupational gains combined with certain legal reforms regarding marriage and woman's right to control her own property and earnings, also made suffrage appear to be the major obstacle confronting woman's equality. But in narrowing their focus to a single demand, suffragists failed to organize any mechanism for mobilizing women's voting strength.

They presented woman suffrage as an answer to women's and to the society's problems but, in fact, the female vote had very little effect on U.S. politics.

With the winning of suffrage, the woman's rights movement went into a rapid decline. Older suffragists had worn themselves out concentrating on suffrage and had failed to lay a basis for younger women to take up the battle for ensuring women's rights. Forces which had united in the battle for suffrage now broke apart on such questions as the Equal Rights Amendment proposed by the Woman's Party and protective legislation supported by trade union women and social welfare progressives. The class question which the suffragists had attempted to ignore, now was exposed in terms of how women sought to utilize their new voting power.

Working-class women, social welfare Progressives and Socialists had supported woman suffrage but for reasons somewhat different from the feminists. They wanted woman suffrage in order to support what they believed to be progressive legislation. For many, protective legislation covering women and children was a primary goal. The middle-class feminists, on the other hand, opposed any legislation that differentiated men and women and wanted an equal rights amendment passed that would prohibit any differential treatment. They claimed not so much to oppose protective legislation as to oppose laws which excluded men, fearing that this would set up new forms of discrimination against women. Once again the question of legal equal rights came into conflict with legislation aimed at alleviating immediate exploitation and oppression.

The more militant Woman's Party understood that suffrage had not solved all of woman's problems; that she still suffered discrimination. But the Woman's Party was unable to mobilize support for an equal rights amendment and with the exception of a few individuals who continued to press for the amendment, woman's rights ferment disappeared for nearly fifty years. When it re-emerged in the 1960's the Equal Rights Amendment was a goal of this new generation of feminist reformers.

Black women attempted to register and vote in the South as well as in the rest of the country. Occasionally individuals were successful but generally black women in the South suffered the same fate as their men and were excluded from the polls.

White suffragists had assumed that black women would be kept from voting in the South, the same as black men, and even when they did not agree with this illegal disfranchisement, they did not see this as a concern of their organizations. The leaders of the Woman's Party, for example, declared that since black women were discriminated against in the same way as black men, it was not a question of woman's rights and, therefore, their organization had no obligation to defend the rights of black women.[58]

Throughout the 1890's and the first half of the twentieth century black women prodded and pleaded with white women to come out squarely against lynching and anti-black riots. A few token resolutions were passed by white women's organizations at the turn of the century. After the first World War an interracial organization was formed under the leadership of black women to support an NAACP effort to obtain a federal law against lynching. In 1930, forty years after black women had begun their organizing efforts against lynching, Southern white women organized the Association of Southern Women for the Prevention of Lynching. This organization's major contribution was the gathering of over 40,000 signatures of white women from all over the South repudiating the racist myth that lynching was done in defense of white womanhood. Yet five years later the organization still felt it premature to promote federal legislation against lynching and refused to endorse an anti-lynching bill proposed in Congress.[59]

Black women had attempted to enlist white women in the struggle against racism by appealing to them as women. But the connections between black and white women as women were not as strong as the white women's allegiance to white society. Women as a sex suffered many forms of discrimination, but the black woman, as Frederick Douglass and Frances Harper had tried to explain to the white feminists so many years before, suffered first and foremost as a member of an oppressed race.

CHAPTER VI:

Organized Labor: From Underdog to Overseer

No other reform movement has had such lasting impact on non-white Americans as the labor movement. The long-standing and decidedly hostile attitude of organized white labor toward nonwhite workers is a central theme of the nation's social history. Nowhere else can there be found a more revealing measure of the average citizen's commitment to the ideals of equality and fraternity; for in the crucible of conflict between labor and capital the very soul of white America is exposed to view.

Basing itself upon the masses of ordinary working people the labor movement has obtained the active participation of more individuals than any other reform campaign. Millions were drawn into the great labor struggles that marked the last century of U.S. history. The story of the effort to organize the working class comprises the longest history of any of the social change movements under consideration in this study. Its origins can be traced to the colonial period when free laborers began agitating for the full franchise and registering their dissatisfaction with inequalities in the tax structure and regulations that held wages down. Finally, the labor movement is the only mass-based reform movement that succeeded in establishing itself organizationally as a permanent part of the American power structure. The abolitionists drifted into obscurity after the Civil War; the Populists failed and disintegrated in 1896; the Progressives were literally absorbed by the new industrial order against which they had been reacting; and militant suffragists merged indis-

165

tinguishably into the white electorate upon getting the vote. Only the labor movement has been able to maintain its independent base of support—a substantial portion of American workers—and its separate organizational identity while at the same time achieving some measure of real power within the system. Indeed, today national labor leaders are a part of that triumvirate of big business, big government and big labor that predominates in formulating national policy. If success is defined as carving out a comfortable niche within the establishment, then the leadership of organized labor has been successful like nothing else.

It is, of course, no secret that blacks and other minority workers, who comprise the vast bulk of the nonwhite populations, have been largely denied by the economic and political gains achieved by organized labor. The history of the American labor movement is one long and shameful story of exclusion, discrimination, outright treachery and open violence directed against black, Mexican, Chinese and other nonwhite workers. This is a tremendously involved story that cannot even be sketched in a brief chapter such as this. Instead, attention must be focused on the broader outline. In analyzing labor history it is particularly important to note the role of labor federations and other nationwide labor groups, since, at least officially, these usually discountenanced racial discrimination. Yet their practices, especially in the American Federation of Labor, only contributed to the institutionalization of racism. True, there have been exceptional unions and labor federations, but these have not been without their own problems. Moreover, they were usually short-lived, or over time they have yielded to the conservatizing influence of the more firmly established labor bureaucracies. Thus, in the years after the Civil War the National Labor Union and the Knights of Labor hesitantly attempted to unite the whole working class without regard to race, sex or nationality; but these two groups disintegrated by 1890. The heyday of the IWW spread over only a few years following the turn of the century. A rebirth of the hope of labor solidarity accompanied the great organizing drives of the Congress of Industrial Organizations (CIO) in the 1930's and 1940's, but CIO leaders purged the more radical unions and leaders from their ranks and eventually allied themselves with the conservative AFL.

The taint of racism in the labor movement cannot be attributed solely to the misleadership of labor bureaucrats or the conniving of capitalist bosses. Certainly opportunistic leaders have tried to capitalize on racial antagonisms to solidify white trade unions and secure their own leadership positions; and the owners and managers of industry were never reluctant to pit race against race, and nationality against nationality in order to depress wages and hinder organizing activities. Yet the conclusion cannot be escaped that many rank-and-file union members have been and are just as racist as the more bigoted labor leaders and employers. One scholar has castigated labor historians who "wasted much energy debating the AFL's attitudes toward black workers, when the truly bitter, and functional, racial animosities were not at the national but at the shop level. Unions have too often directed their recriminations at anti-union Negroes, rather than conceding their own inability to control the racial hatreds of white members."[2] Summing up the contemporary situation, Julius Jacobson wrote: "The mounting evidence is that not 'some' members take a wrong-headed view but that the bulk of the union movement, on one level or another, follows discriminatory policies, and has successfully resisted the minimal internal union pressures and heavier external effort to bring full equality into the labor movement."[3]

Ante-bellum Origins of White Hostility to Black Labor

In the South the slave system victimized not only blacks but also non-slaveholding whites. This latter class was made up of small farmers, craftsmen and laborers. In the chapter on Southern Populism attention was called to the fact that the small farmers resented blacks because the slave-plantation system pushed many of the former onto the most barren and least productive lands. A similar social-psychological dynamic was at work within the Southern labor force where slave labor was thrown into competition with free labor in the towns and at industrial sites. Many slaves were trained as skilled craftsmen so that they could perform maintenance and repair tasks on their owners' plantations, which operated as self-sufficient economic units. Slaves trained in blacksmithing, masonry, carpentry and other mechanical trades were highly valued by their masters because (1) They could render numerous services on the plantation, which relieved the necessity of hiring outside skilled labor; (2) skilled slaves had considerably higher market value; and (3) skilled slaves could be hired out in the surrounding towns when they were not needed on the plantation, thus affording a profitable additional source of income to the masters.[4] Slaves were also hired out as industrial workers. By 1860 some 200,000 slaves were employed as industrial workers in Southern mills, mines, foundries and railroads.[5] Although there was considerable variation from one industry to another, and from one area to another, industrial slaves performed a wide range of tasks, sometimes including that of foreman or supervisor. Whether hired out as craftsmen or industrial workers, slaves were thrown into direct competition with white workers. Since there was little difference in quality of work, the determining factor in getting jobs became the wage rate. The slave artisan or industrial worker could be hired out by his master for lower wages because the individual slave, unlike the free laborer, need not be concerned with earning enough to provide himself with decent housing, clothing and food. These essentials were provided by the master or employer as part of his normal operating expenses. Needless to say, a gang of slave workers, housed in dilapidated barracks and supplied with only the coarsest of food and clothing, could be maintained at a much lower cost than an equal number of free workers.

Thus industrialism could exist beside a plantation slave system, but only in subordination to the slave economy. Surplus slave labor not needed on the plantations was available for hire, but the needs of the plantation system for ever more land and labor inhibited industrial investment and development. Moreover, the racial ideology of the dominant slave system—that blacks were no more than draft animals—promoted the corresponding notion that blacks were therefore incapable of performing industrial work using machinery. Even though this was patently untrue, the ideology mirrored the plantation system's great demand for agricultural, as opposed to industrial, slave labor. (Later this kind of thinking was to provide a rationale for the exclusion of blacks from industrial work after the Civil War.) Thus the organization and ideology of the slave South mitigated against the triumph of industrialism in that area. For industrialism to become dominant required the availability of a large and fluid or "free" labor force that could be hired, fired and easily shifted from job to job as the market dictated, and for which the employer had no economic responsibility beyond payment of wages for work performed. This was the basic contradiction in organization and labor usage between the North and the South.

In reality, then, the Southern "white artisan was not competing with the black slave artisan any more than the independent store-keeper of the present is competing with the manager of the chain store in his territory. The white mechanic was competing with the slave owner whose cheap slave labor, financial resources, and political power gave him every advantage."[6] Clearly, the slave system seriously encumbered the free laborer in his struggle for a livelihood. But at the same time the racial ideology of the slave system acted to deflect attention away from the system itself by identifying economic distress with competition from "degraded" black workers. The situation was further complicated by the fact that in the accelerating struggle between labor and capital the slave occupied an ambiguous position. To his owner he was at once capital and labor; he was valuable property in himself and his work contributed directly to the enrichment of his owner. Whereas the chief concern of the free laborer was to gain a greater share of his employer's wealth in the form of higher wages, to the slave such a struggle was utterly meaningless, since his status as chattel property decreed that his earnings were likewise the property of the master. Consequently, the existence of slavery within the capitalist system created a deep cleavage between slave laborers and free laborers; and since this economically induced division corresponded almost perfectly

with racial lines, it was a simple matter to picture it as a race conflict. Added to all of this was the employers' practice, beginning
in the 1840's as Southern white workers were trying to organize,
to bring slaves in as strikebreakers; in some instances, slave labor
gradually supplanted free labor.[7]

The white workers made some attempts to curb the use of slave
labor, but for the most part "the white workers accepted their lot,
blaming and hating the Negro for their plight."[8] Like the small
farmers of the day, the Southern white workers did not understand
that they were competing not against black workers per se but
against the wealthy white man's slave *system*. Instead they vented
their hostility against the visible symbol of the slave system, the
black worker, whether slave or free. The relative handful of free
black artisans who lived in the South were in the most difficult
position of all. They, too, had to meet the competition of slave labor
and in addition they felt the brunt of white workers' hostility, being
restricted by the whites both in their right to work in certain occupations and in their freedom of movement.[9]

If life was hard for the free black worker in the South, his fate
in the North was no better. Racial antagonisms fostered by slavery
bore down heavily on the black worker. He was even prohibited
from living in several Northern states and many local communities.
The driving force behind such prohibitions was the resentment of
white workers who strenuously objected to the use of black labor.
They contended that the presence of black workers resulted in
lowering of wages and standards of work. Backing up their objections with open violence and murder, white workers succeeded in
restricting Northern black labor mainly to domestic and personal
service occupations.

Although some white workers supported the anti-slavery cause,
many others were antagonistic toward the abolitionist movement.
Due in part to the repeated attacks made by middle-class abolitionists on the embryonic labor movement, there was another anx-
iety that was more important in feeding this sentiment. Many
white workers in the North feared "that abolition would bring
thousands of black laborers into the nation's industrial centers to

compete for jobs that unskilled white laborers wanted, and that the wages of the whole working class would be driven down."[10] White laborers who already resented the presence of a small number of black workers in the North were thus even more hostile toward the idea of emancipation.

Yet the Southern slave system was already weighing heavily on the Northern white worker as it oppressed his counterpart in the South. While slavery placed upper limits on both wages and job opportunities in the South, labor historian Joseph G. Rayback reports that "in the North employers were telling their labor force that they had to work as long and as cheaply as the slaves of the South in order to compete with the Southern manufacturer."[11] Some white workers recognized the doubly oppressive nature of the slave system, and they supported abolition on the grounds that slavery degraded all labor, white as well as black. However, it was not until the aggressive expansion of the slave system in the two decades preceding the Civil War that significant numbers of white workers in the North became anti-slavery. However, the majority were not pro-emancipation; they were merely alarmed by the *expansion* of the slave system into lands that they wanted reserved for their own settlement. Their first aim was to emancipate themselves from "wage slavery" by becoming small property owners in the Western territories, an outlook expressed by the Free Soilers. As with the Southern small farmers the lure of the frontier was a convenient safety valve for releasing discontent.

The First General Strike

Southern secession and the attack on Fort Sumter left the North with little choice but to go to war. Even so, the North entered the conflict with no intention of freeing the slaves. Northern political leaders wanted to contain and limit the slave system, not destroy it. Lincoln's motto was "The union, with or without slavery."

Emancipation became necessary as a consequence of what W.E.B. Du Bois termed a massive general strike by slaves during the early stages of the war. According to Du Bois, the South had counted on black slave labor to raise food and cash crops for civilians and the Confederate army. In a crisis it was even expected that slaves could be used for military purposes. "Slave revolt was an ever-present risk," Du Bois noted, "but there was no reason [for the Southerners] to think that a short war with the North would greatly increase this danger."[12]

Southern rebels made careful calculations of the usefulness of slaves in the war effort. In 1861 an Alabama newspaper editorialized: "The total white population of the eleven states now comprising the Confederacy is 5,000,000, and, therefore, to fill up the ranks of the proposed army, 600,000, about ten per cent of the entire white population, will be required. In any other country than our own such a draft could not be met, but the Southern states can furnish that number of men, and still not leave the material interest of the country in a suffering condition. . . . The institution of slavery in the South alone enables her to place in the field a force larger in proportion to her white population than the North. . . ."[13] Clearly, then, the South determined that the slave system gave it a significant advantage in the coming conflict.

But advantage turned to liability as the black slaves surprised both the South and the North by using the civil conflict as the occasion for a gigantic general strike. Thousands upon thousands of slaves escaped from the plantations and headed for the Northern lines. "This was not merely the desire to stop work," Du Bois believed. "It was a strike against the conditions of work. It was a general strike that involved in the end perhaps half a million people [out of a total slave population of four million]. They wanted to stop the economy of the plantation system, and to do that they left the plantations."[14]

The white politicians and military commanders of the North at first did not appreciate the significance of this development. Instead, officers of the Northern armies ordered their men to round up the escaped slaves so they could be returned to their masters. It was more than a year before the Northern leaders realized that the general strike afforded the North a tremendous opportunity. If the

North would sanction the strike, if the North would encourage slaves to leave, it could break the economic backbone of the South. An emancipation proclamation would encourage even more slaves to run away and thereby totally disrupt Southern agriculture. Moreover, the escaped slaves were anxious to aid the Northern armies. Eventually about 150,000 slaves became Union soldiers, while several hundred thousand aided the federal armies as laborers. The first Emancipation Proclamation of 1863 was thus primarily a military, rather than a humanitarian, gesture. Du Bois contended that the blacks who joined the Union forces were crucial in shifting the tide of war in favor of the North.

Meanwhile, white labor in the North was confused and resentful during the war. Many workers gladly joined the Union armies, but fear of labor competition, intensified by racist Democratic propaganda, soured the enthusiasm of others, especially the unskilled.[15] Still other white workers regarded the war as a conflict between the industrial rulers of the North and the agrarian master class of the South. To them, the common man was represented by neither party in the strife. By and large Northern white workers took no cognizance of the slaves' role in aiding the Northern war effort. On the contrary, it was all too easy for many of them to treat blacks as the prime cause of the war and the troubles it brought.

For example, the existence of a discriminatory conscription law inflamed the white working classes. The law made it possible for the wealthy to evade military service by providing a substitute or paying a $300 fee. Some labor leaders such as William Sylvis, while supporting conscription, attacked the class discrimination inherent in the law. The anti-administration press was not so judicious. It pandered to the fears and prejudices of the white workers and urged them to make known their views on the subject. Roused to anger, workers unleashed a three-day insurrection in New York City in 1863. White workers, mostly unskilled Irish laborers, ransacked the main recruiting station, wrecked shipyards, railroads and streetcar lines. But what began as a class conflict turned into an ugly race riot. Blaming black people as the cause of the war and conscription, the white mob destroyed homes and murdered every black person they could lay their hands on. The black population of New York was terrorized, and many fled the city. Similar race riots occurred in other parts of New York State, as well as Pennsylvania, Ohio, Indiana and Wisconsin.

Thus, while the Civil War and the activities of the slaves compelled the abolition of the practice of holding slaves as property and transformed slaves into "free" workers, at the same time white workers were highly agitated and increasingly worried about how to protect their jobs and status. This small-property mentality can be traced to the early trade or craft unions whose members regarded their skills as a kind of property, to be protected from interlopers and passed on to a chosen heir in the form of an apprenticeship. Following the Civil War the defense of trades and jobs as so much property—reflecting the hegemony of bourgeois ideology—was to be a central underlying theme in the manifestations of racism in the labor movement. Some of these concrete manifestations in the trade unions and their contribution to altering the status of black labor will now be investigated.

Discrimination in the Trade Unions

After the Civil War a variety of methods developed in the trade unions for discriminating against newly emancipated black workers. Over a period of time these became more elaborate and sophisticated, especially as some of the cruder forms of discrimination came under attack and had to be modified. Such discrimination, not only in the trade unions but throughout the labor movement, aided in forcing black workers out of a central role in the Southern economy into a marginal, but essential, role in the Northern, and later, national economy.

If emancipation and Reconstruction gave black people a brief taste of political freedom and power, the joint actions of prejudiced employers and exclusionist craft unions severely eroded the economic position of black labor. At the conclusion of the war the vast majority of black workers were unskilled laborers and consequently automatically excluded from the growing unions which sought to organize the skilled trades. Furthermore, skilled black craftsmen (who constituted 80% of the South's skilled mechanics in 1865) were excluded from the trade unions on purely racial grounds. White workers were determined to monopolize trades in which blacks were once active. It was common practice for trade unions, especially in the burgeoning transportation industry, to insert a clause in their constitutions that specifically prohibited non-white membership. The history of the railroad unions is an unrelieved story of strikes, treachery and violence aimed at completely eliminating blacks from any but menial positions on the railways and in the shops and yards. As late as 1930 there were still at least 26 national unions that formally excluded black workers.[16]

Other trade unions managed to exclude blacks through informal methods. Ray Marshall states that these included "agreements not to sponsor Negroes for membership; refusal to admit Negroes into apprenticeship programs or to accept their applications, or simply to ignore their applications; general 'understandings' to vote against Negroes if they are proposed (for example, as few as three members of some locals can bar applicants for membership); refusal of journeyman status to Negroes by means of examinations which either are not given to whites or are rigged so that Negroes cannot pass them; exertion of political pressure on governmental licensing agencies to ensure the Negroes fail the tests; and restriction of membership to sons, nephews, or other relatives of members."[17] Trade unions that have employed such devious informal techniques of exclusion include the building trades, plumbers and electricians unions.

Where black workers were not excluded outright they were usually organized into segregated locals. These segregated locals were then placed under the control of a white local or the national union. According to Spero and Harris, where segregation was the official policy of a national union, one or all of the following discriminations usually occurred: "(1) Negroes are organized in auxiliary locals usually in subordination to the nearest white local; (2)

they may not transfer to white locals; (3) they are not eligible for promotion to skilled work; (4) they may not hold office; and (5) they are represented in conventions or conferences only by white men."[18] Some years later A. Philip Randolph would argue that segregated auxiliary locals were like the "colonies of colored people" established by the "empire systems," and which enjoyed "none of the rights that the white population in the mother country enjoy, except the right to be taxed."[19]

While not all craft unions excluded or segregated black workers, investigation revealed that several unions that claimed full acceptance of black membership in fact practiced preferential placement in the employment of whites, thus discriminating against the black union member.[20]

Around the turn of the century the American Federation of Labor initiated a policy of chartering federal locals to black workers who were denied admittance to the white unions in their trades. These federal labor unions yielded good public relations material for the AFL, since their existence lent credence to the impression that the federation was genuinely interested in the welfare of black workers. However, as Bernard Mandel observed: "These bodies were completely ineffective to protect the interests of their members, for they were detached locals with no national head, and their standards were theoretically to be protected by the very internationals which claimed jurisdiction over their work but refused to admit them to membership."[21] The weakness of the segregated federal locals was attested by the fact that they were among the first unions to be destroyed when the AFL went into a decline after 1920.[22]

All in all, the policy of segregated locals and federal unions proved a very effective complement to the policy of racial exclusion. Organizing black workers into powerless, segregated locals brought them under the thumb of the white unions. Their freedom of movement and wages were in the hands of the white union, while at the same time segregation ensured that their grievances and demands would not be fairly met. In a word, under this policy black workers were organized, segregated and then ignored.

Union discrimination, as a reflection of white supremacy, was not limited to black workers. The majority of organized labor consistently opposed the immigration of Asian and Mexican workers and did little, if anything, to organize them. In California leaders of the white working class were the initiators and mainstay of the Chinese and Japanese exclusion movements.[23] White workers either actively discriminated against and many times excluded nonwhite workers from the mines of California and the Southwest, or acquiesced in the employers'practice of using different wage scales for white and nonwhite workers and holding certain skilled jobs for whites only. Asian and especially Mexican agricultural workers worked many times in jobs considered beneath whites, but even in agriculture organized white labor tried to push out nonwhite workers.[24]

Employers in California and the Southwest actively sought immigrant labor in order to obtain a cheap, docile labor force. In addition, they deliberately kept the immigrant groups isolated to ensure that the workers would not integrate into American society and transfer to better paying jobs. Organized labor cooperated fully in isolating nonwhite workers, leaving them vulnerable to extreme exploitation. Yet organization among agricultural workers did occur and many strikes took place, especially among the Mexican workers in the 1930's. The extreme racism of the white populace of the West and Southwest contributed to the employers' repression of this independent labor organizing. In addition, in most of these strikes the strikers were not aided by organized labor but left to their own devices. This made the Mexican workers particularly vulnerable as leaders would be arrested and deported as undesirables.[25]

Impact of Labor Racism

The impact of organized labor's racist policies on nonwhite workers was disastrous. Instead of being brought into the mainstream of organized labor the nonwhite work force before the Great Depression was excluded and degraded. The terrible consequences of these policies were graphically demonstrated in the case of black labor. When combined with other trends in the Southern and national economics, trade union discrimination acted to reduce black labor in the South to an impoverished subproletariat—a vast reserve army of unorganized labor which employers could draw upon to break strikes called by white workers. The racism practiced by white unions thus came full circle and was forcibly turned against them by the owners and managers of the new industries.

Several steps were involved in this process. In the first place, the class of black craftsmen, a product of the slave system, was virtually eliminated. Historian Charles Wesley estimated that at the conclusion of the Civil War 100,000 out of a total of 120,000 craftsmen in the South were black.[26] Between 1865 and 1900, however, the proportion of black artisans declined sharply due to the differential advantage accruing to white skilled workers as a result of trade union exclusion. Since craft unions control employment opportunities, unlike industrial unions, highly skilled black workers—masons, carpenters, plasterers, tailors, shoemakers, cabinet makers, painters, seamstresses, etc.—were forced to abandon their trades to become sharecroppers, agricultural workers or common laborers. They simply had no alternative.

As black craftsmen were being eliminated the rural black population was reduced to semi-slavery under the sharecropping system. Kept in perpetual debt by the landlord-merchant, the black sharecropper could eke out only the most miserable existence on his small patch of land. But even this state of affairs was highly unstable, and large numbers of black people were forced off the land and into the towns and cities, first in the South and later the North. The chief causes of this migration were (1) the widespread anti-black terrorism that began during Reconstruction; (2) the agricultural depression of the 1870's which hit small farmers and sharecroppers with special severity; (3) the capitulation of Populism to white supremacy which further isolated and undermined blacks in the South; (4) the beginning mechanization of agriculture which eliminated more farm jobs; and (5) the opening up of jobs in the North due to labor shortages created by World War I.

As blacks left the land they went into the Southern cities where Northern capital was already making great inroads. The expansion of the railroads opened the way to exploiting the South's rich natural resources. Northern capital poured into the lumber industry, buying up huge stretches of timber land, expanding the sawmills and multiplying many times over the value of Southern lumber output. Coal and iron deposits were developed, and Birmingham started on the road to becoming a major steel-producing center. A rapid expansion in cotton and tobacco manufacturing also took place.

Black workers were brought in at the lowest levels in many of the new industries, although some, such as textile manufacturing, virtually excluded the black worker. These workers were paid one-third to one-half the wages they would earn for the same work in the North. The working period in industry varied from 60 to more than 80 hours per week; and of course the largely unorganized black workers had no say as far as wages and working conditions were concerned. At the same time most of the skilled and better paying jobs went to white workers—a practice which became institutionalized with the passage of time. Even in older Southern industries, such as tobacco manufacturing where blacks once held a virtual job monopoly, the introduction of machinery provided a rationale for excluding black workers from skilled occupations.

Until World War I, industrial work in the North and Midwest was the province of white workers. The greatly feared flood of ex-slaves did not materialize after the Civil War, and the few who did make their way North were kept out of skilled occupations by rigid discrimination. Instead, rapidly expanding Northern industry was furnished with a constant supply of cheap labor by the steady stream of European immigration. The 13 million immigrants who arrived in this country between 1870 and 1900 were anxious to find decent employment in the promised land. But nativism and Anglo-Saxonism combined to make life difficult for the newcomers. Most of the immigrants, who were mainly unskilled and unorganized, went to work in Northern industries where employers skillfully used ethnic stereotypes to isolate and divide the national groupings, thereby checking pressure for wage increases by inflaming an already highly competitive situation. Ironically, one of the few things that united the various white ethnic groups was that almost all of them soon adopted the American prejudice against black people. What is more, the European immigrants also pushed blacks out of the personal service occupations in the North. Willing and able to provide the same services at the same price, the immigrants enjoyed the distinct advantage of being white in a white-supremacist society. Thus, in an area of the Northern economy where blacks had made some gains by providing personal services to white customers, they were undercut by European immigrants.

Employers in the North largely disregarded black workers as a source of industrial labor, except during periods of acute labor shortage as occurred during World War I, and, of course, during strikes. Northern employers had occasionally drawn upon the Southern reserve of black farmers and sharecroppers to help them break strikes, but it was not until the 1880's, as blacks were being forced off the land and the white labor movement was gaining ground, that this became a regular and frequent practice.

The majority of the black migrants coming North took low-paid, unskilled jobs in mass-production industries: steel mills, automobile plants, foundries and meat-packing houses. But the move North was marred by frequent strife and violence. Many of the blacks who first entered these industries came as strikebreakers. Discrimination by both employers and trade unions led the black worker to accept eagerly any sort of job that gave him a foothold in Northern industry, even if at the expense of a white worker out on strike. With few exceptions class solidarity was prevented from growing by institutionalized white supremacy. Seeing his opportunities curtailed by employers and his fellow white workers, the black worker sometimes concluded that strikebreaking offered his only chance of smashing through the barriers of job discrimination. However, strikebreaking by unorganized black workers only increased the determination of white workers to exclude blacks from labor organizations. Blinded by their own racism the white workers piously asserted that a black who scabbed was not worthy of being admitted to a union; conveniently forgetting that exclusion left the black worker few options: He could starve or he could take a job in disregard of labor principles which were not intended to include him. Such a discordant situation inevitably led to violence, as happened in the terrible anti-black riots that repeatedly shook Chicago between 1894 and 1919.[27] The pattern of the Civil War riots was repeated as blacks became the victims of a class struggle between whites. Neither white employers nor white workers regarded blacks as anything more than passive, faceless beings, barely human, to be manipulated at will and destroyed if they evidenced too much independence.

The net result of the process described in the last few pages was a radical transformation of the black work force. During the decades of capitalist accumulation prior to the Civil War, black slave workers were essential to the development of the American economy, providing the nation with much of its early wealth. As industrial capitalism matured into monopoly capital, however, black workers were reduced to a reserve of cheap labor which could be manipulated, excluded and degraded at the whim of employers and trade unions. Blacks were cast in the role of "shock absorbers" of American economic and class conflicts: few enough to be disregarded in times of recession, yet numerous enough to make a marginal difference in times of military or economic need. In effect, black workers provided an essential subproletariat which added elasticity to the national labor pool, and which—because of its insecure status— could also be pitted economically against other sectors of the labor pool. Thus, blacks were forced to absorb a disproportionately heavy share of the economic stresses and conflicts inherent in a monopoly capitalist economy, with the side effect that class contradictions were obscured and often deflected into race conflicts.

Social and Economic Causes of Labor Racism

It is possible to identify certain specific factors that have fostered racism in the labor movement. Important among these is the prevailing racist social climate. There can be little doubt that rank-

and-file union members reflected and helped to propagate the racist attitudes and stereotypes common in white society. With notable exceptions only the most feeble and sporadic attempts were made by the established unions to educate their members away from racist thinking. The more common occurrence was for unions to implement racism in their practices and procedures, thus giving concrete form to the prevailing social ideas.

This was particularly true of those unions, such as the railroad brotherhoods, which also regarded themselves as fraternal and social organizations. It was a regular practice for such unions to sponsor dances, picnics and other social events in which the members were encouraged to take part. Since these unions were formed at a time when "social equality" was being loudly denounced, it comes as no surprise that they excluded blacks. Even after the turn of the century the social equality issue continued as a rationale for exclusion. Thus at the 1905 convention of the railway car workers a resolution in favor of black admission met with sharp attacks. "I don't think," one delegate declared with great emotion, "there is a member in this room that believes in taking the Negro in with him on social equality. I believe that God in his infinite mercy made the Negro but he never made him to be a car worker. I do not believe the time will ever come when he should come into a union along with carmen. . . . I want to tell you that I am a Northern man. . . . I was born with an abolitionist father; but when the time does come that I must sit down in social equality with the Negro. . . . I want to be carried to the nearest insane asylum."[28]

As already noted, the most common rationale for excluding blacks from trade unions was the notion that black workers were strikebreakers and therefore untrustworthy. This was little more than a thin disguise for racism. While it was true that black workers were used by employers in many industries to break strikes—with the active encouragement of some black community leaders—nevertheless race hatred caused (1) the prevalence of black strikebreaking to be exaggerated, and (2) its meaning to be distorted. Unbiased labor scholars have noted that the number of strikes disrupted by black labor does not begin to compare with the number broken by white scabs. Rather, race prejudice causes the black strikebreaker, even though he may be only a few among hundreds of white scabs, to be singled out for special slander and violence. Historically, the press, often pro-employer, has played a central role in provoking latent race hatreds on the picket lines.

A case in point would be the 1905 Teamster's strike in Chicago. Over a period of time some 5,800 strikebreakers were brought in to fill the places of 5,000 strikers. All but about 800 of the strikebreakers were white. Yet the press aroused racial animosities by printing stories that pictured hordes of blacks taking the jobs of the white strikers. In point of fact, it was white strikebreakers who were doing the cause greatest harm. Moreover, "even where Negro unionists have struck side by side with white, the introduction of Negro strike breakers has stirred up the same racial antipathies among white strikers as if they alone had been carrying the strike."[29]

Such thoroughly racist behavior prompted Booker T. Washington to complain: "Strikers seem to consider it a much greater crime for a Negro who had been denied the opportunity to work at his trade to take the place of a striking employee than for a white man to do the same thing. Not only have Negro strike breakers been savagely beaten and mobbed by strikers and their sympathizers, but in some instances every Negro, no matter what his occupation, who lived in the vicinity of the strike has found himself in danger."[30]

Strikebreaking had been distorted to seem as though it were a racial question. Actually it was a problem of economics, union organization and employer tactics. Black workers who were welcomed into the unions displayed no greater proclivity to scab than did white unionists. However, a group, of any race whatever, which is in an economically depressed condition and excluded from union membership can be readily manipulated by employers to the detriment of organized labor. Labor leaders have known this simple fact from earliest times, but many of them chose to ignore it and instead blamed black workers for their own victimization.

When the AFL was organized in the early 1880's its leader, Samuel Gompers, prodded by a black delegate, urged that all workingmen be organized irrespective of color.[31] This was both a matter of principle and practicality. Divisions in the labor movements only eased the employers' task of holding wages down. Gompers even recognized that white prejudice was the cause of black exclusion from the labor movement and this encouraged their use as strike-breakers. Yet within a few years Gompers yielded to racist forces within the labor movement and tried to shift the blame for strike-breaking to black workers themselves. "When asked [in 1896] why there were not more skilled Negro workers, he assigned two reasons for it," states Bernard Mandel. "First," he said, "Negro workers did not possess the required skill, but he did not mention the fact that most of the trade unions prevented them from acquiring that skill by refusing to accept them as apprentices. The second reason was that in many cases when white workers were on strike, Negroes took their places and thus helped the employers to tear down labor standards and destroy the unions. While he had previously argued that this was the inevitable result of the white workers' ignoring the organization of Negroes, he now stated: 'If workers will not organize to protect their own interests and the interests of their fellow workers, or if workmen are so lost to their own self respect and interests as to turn the weight of their influence on the side of the capitalists as against that of the workers, these men are enemies of progress, regardless of whether they be white or black, Caucasian or Mongolian.' "[32]

In 1899 Gompers told the United States Industrial Commission that organized labor discriminated against blacks not because of race prejudice but because they have "so conducted themselves as to be a continuous convenient whip placed in the hands of the employers to cow the white men and to compel them to accept abject conditions of labor." Six years later he asserted that "caucasians are not going to let their standard of living be destroyed by negroes, Chinamen, Japs, or any others."

Gompers and other labor leaders of his persuasion knew full well what they were doing. Although he originally opposed opening the doors of the AFL to unions that practiced racial exclusion, Gompers soon realized that many powerful craft unions were determined to preserve a racial monopoly of available jobs. Without the support of these unions the AFL was doomed to impotence. Thus, Gompers and other labor leaders abandoned the principle of labor solidarity and instead opportunistically embraced racial discrimination as an expedient method of uniting the privileged upper levels of white labor (around white supremacy), while entrenching themselves in positions of power. Following the lead of the Populists they accomplished this by a simple racist trick; viz., blame the victims for their own victimization and then use this as the reason for excluding them.

Ideological and Structural Contributors to Labor Racism

Looking back over labor history it is possible to discern three different forms of labor organizing which arose with the development of the U.S. political economy. These three represented quite different responses to the crisis presented to labor by industrialization and economic concentration.

The oldest is *craft unionism,* of course, which goes back to the eighteenth century when production was organized according to skilled trades which were passed from master to apprentice. By the late nineteenth century, craft or trade unionism sought to protect the interests of skilled craftsmen by monopolizing work and excluding competition from unskilled workers, a possibility which had developed with the growth of the industrial system. What monopoly is to business, craft unionism is to labor. Craft unionism advocates organization of only the skilled workers; the unskilled are automatically excluded. It further encourages exclusion by limiting opportunities for apprentices to join the union and learn the trade. A craft union is thereby able to establish a virtual monopoly over its trade, and control both work opportunities and wages. What is termed the "aristocracy of labor," the highly skilled and tightly organized craftsmen, benefited immensely from the monopoly and exclusion of the trade unions.

Most of the unions that came together in 1881 to form the AFL were craft unions, and their ideology was reflected in the structure of the organization they set up. The AFL was a confederation of autonomous national and international craft unions. Jealously guarding the autonomy that made possible the building of a protective wall around the jobs they controlled, the constituent unions granted only limited power to the federation, thus ensuring that the narrow and conservative policies of local unions could dominate the policies of the Federation. This fostered racism in the AFL. Federation officers were reluctant to use what power they had in enforcing racial equality because a strong stand might jeopardize their positions. Thus, craft unionism, once militant, became more conservative and racist as it incorporated itself into the structure of monopoly capitalism.

The second major form of labor organizing is *industrial unionism.* Mechanization and industrialization meant that many of the old skills and crafts were being replaced by unskilled or semi-skilled mass-production operations. Consequently, effective labor organizing increasingly demanded that unions organize all workers in a given industry—skilled and unskilled, black and white—rather than follow the old tradition of organization by crafts.

However, industrial unionism did not develop overnight. Its growth was hindered for many years by the entrenched position and conservative policies of the craft unions, which long were the dominant element in the labor movement, and it did not fully mature until the great labor struggles of the 1930's. Hence, industrial unionism went through an embryonic or experimental period when its character was not clearly defined. This is usually referred to as *reform unionism,* and was especially apparent in the two decades after the Civil War when industrial capitalism was beginning to mature into monopoly.

Reform unionism represented in part a continuation of the political reform activity that was pervasive in American society before the Civil War. As manifested in organized labor this reformism sought to abolish, or at least modify, the wage system through independent political action. In theory, reform unionism hoped to bring all wage earners into a great labor party. However, sharp differences in political orientation between the reformers and black labor leaders, combined with racial prejudice, forestalled the development of lasting black-white unity.

It would be accurate to conclude that craft unions have generally opted for racism not only because of the general social climate but also because racism was a logical extension of the exclusionism practiced by these unions; whereas the unions most friendly toward nonwhites have been those organized on the industrial principle of labor solidarity. While the discussion in the preceding pages would bear out the first part of this statement, it remains to examine the policies of the labor reformers and industrial unions.

Reform Unionism

After the Civil War the principle of labor solidarity without regard to race was advocated most strenuously by the radical reformers of the National Labor Union (NLU) and the Knights of Labor—organizations that also proposed producers' cooperatives and independent political action as instruments for the salvation of the working class. But even these exceptional unions were not without serious problems.

The NLU, formed in 1866, was the first trade union federation of the postwar era. From the outset important NLU leaders pushed the organization to follow an equalitarian racial policy, to make "no distinction of race or nationality," but the organization's course was marked by confusion and evasion of the issue, and further complicated by the leaders' inability to understand or support the freedmen's struggle for full political and civil rights.

At its second convention in 1867, a committee was appointed to study the question of racial cooperation. The committee came up with an evasive report. It pointed to "the danger in the future of competition in mechanical negro labor" and noted the diversity of opinion among the membership on the subject, finally concluding that the whole question should be postponed until the next meeting.

William Sylvis and other NLU leaders objected to postponing a decision. Predicting that the freedmen would "take possession of the shops if we have not taken possession of the negro," Sylvis declared, "If the workingmen of the white race do not conciliate the blacks, the black vote will be cast against them." The matter was referred to the committee but was dodged again when the committee reported simply that it "had come to the conclusion that the constitution already adopted prevented the necessity of reporting on the subject of negro labor."[33]

It was not until 1869, when confronted by a black labor delegation, that the NLU formally adopted a resolution urging that black workers be organized. Isaac Meyers, a black labor leader, praised this action but he observed that the real test would be whether the resolution was implemented by the affiliated unions. The NLU was a delegate organization with no powers of enforcement; hence Meyers' caution was well founded. In point of fact, only groups affiliated with the Marxist International Workingmen's Association in New York and, at the national level, the Cigar Makers and Carpenters and Joiners unions took any official steps to organize black labor. Most unions simply refused to take a stand or openly excluded black workers by constitutional provision.

The official air of cooperation between the NLU and black labor did not prevail for long. Black workers, increasingly under the sway of political leaders such as P.B.S. Pinchback of Louisiana and Frederick Douglass were greatly concerned with winning political equality and civil rights, and they regarded the Republican Party as the political instrument for achieving these goals. In addition, black labor conventions deprecated the notion of class struggle, thinking that education and cooperation would make such strife unnecessary.

The white leadership of the NLU, on the other hand, proposed to reform the monetary system, increase taxation on the rich and reduce the workday to eight hours. It hoped to achieve these reforms through the agency of an independent labor party. Furthermore, the NLU, identifying its enemies as the Northern industrialists, attacked the Radical Republicans, ridiculed Reconstruction programs such as the Freedmen's Bureau, and proposed in essence that political power be returned to the Southern planters.[34]

The tension between the black and white labor organizations came to a head at the 1870 convention of the NLU. The black delegates were outraged when two of their number were initially denied seats at the convention on the grounds that they were agents of the Republican Party.[35] After this meeting the blacks withdrew from the NLU. At its 1872 convention the National Black Labor Congress, which had been organized in 1869, denounced the NLU and reaffirmed its loyalty to the Republican Party. The black labor group carried out agitational and organizational work in the South, but over the next two years it lost much of its trade union character, becoming more of a political organization appended to the Republican Party. By 1874 it had ceased to exist.[36] Meanwhile, the NLU had also declined, torn between trade unionism and political activism while drifting ever closer to the Democratic Party.

The relationship between the NLU and black labor amply illustrated the manifold complexities of race, politics and economics during Reconstruction. Racial prejudice and fear of economic competition virtually nullified the NLU's official policy of racial cooperation. At the same time black political survival was, for the moment, dependent on an alliance with the Republican Party, which also represented Northern industrial capital. Leaders of the NLU, recognizing the class character of the Republicans, were drawn toward alliances with discontented farmers and middle-class reformers who were mainly Democrats. Thus, whatever common interests existed between the NLU and black labor were submerged in a whirlpool of conflicting currents. Furthermore, the pragmatic approach of both groups to economic and political problems emphasized short-term considerations at the expense of long-term objectives. Neither possessed an analytic framework from which to assess overall trends in the American political economy. Most blacks clung desperately to the Republican Party, failing to realize that the Republicans would champion black rights only so long as their class interests made it expedient to do so. On the other hand, craft unionists in the NLU gladly excluded black workers in order to gain immediate advantages for white craftsmen. They thus endorsed capitalism's self-serving ideology of race conflict; and thereby helped render unattainable reform unionism's long-term objectives, which could be achieved only by practicing a solidarity that crossed race lines. Early Marxist labor leaders, who at least possessed an independent ideology, exercised only limited influence in the labor movement as a whole. Moreover, the Marxists, drawing upon the European experience, tended to underestimate the importance of race in America, or they, too, simply succumbed to the prevailing prejudices.

The ideal of black-white labor solidarity advanced to a highwater mark in the nineteenth century during the heyday of the Knights of Labor. Organized as a secret society in 1869, the Knights, under the leadership of Uriah Stephens and Terence V. Powderly, stressed the ideal of industrial brotherhood and attempted to educate the trade unions away from their exclusionist practices. Recognizing the dangers posed by black-white competition and lack of organization, the Knights officially welcomed all workers into the fold, skilled and unskilled, black and white.[37]

The Knights reached their maximum strength during the period of labor unrest in the 1880's. It was during this time that large numbers of black workers were recruited into the organization. At its peak in 1886 the Knights claimed between 60,000 and 95,000 black members out of a total membership of 700,000.[38] If these figures are accurate, the Knights had a larger percentage of black members than either the AFL or CIO could claim as late as 1945. Most of the black members were organized into some 400 all-black locals. The first of the black locals was set up in Iowa in 1881. In some areas, including the South, black workers were integrated into the white locals. During its existence several independent black unions affiliated with the Knights, including a black teamsters union in Louisville and hod carriers unions in St. Louis and Washington, D.C. Also, several of the organizers and leaders of the Knights were black workers.

Throughout the country, but especially in the South, the Knights faced stiff opposition in their campaign to organize black workers.

Blacks were intimidated, imprisoned and murdered if they dared to join the organization. In South Carolina the legislature appropriated money to increase its militia, and it very nearly passed a bill "extending the conspiracy laws of the state with the avowed purpose of preventing the Negroes from organizing into local assemblies."[39] Eventually the Knights in South Carolina were compelled to go underground.

Blacklisting, terrorism and frame-ups were freely employed to weaken and finally destroy the Knights of Labor. In addition, the organization was beset by internal dissension stirred up by the trade unions. Trade unionists were hostile to its reform goals and especially the Knights' flirtation with Populism. Despite the official policies of the Knights, many of these unions continued to exclude black workers, and they agitated for a "pure and simple" unionism that would concern itself only with increasing wages and tightening union control over jobs. These were the chief interests of the skilled white workers, and soon the trade unions withdrew from the Knights to join the AFL.

The withdrawal of the trade unions speeded the dissolution of the Knights. Unfortunately, the organization drew much of its power from the well-organized and rapidly growing trade unions; and consequently their defection constituted the final blow to the "Noble Order."

The most radical form of revolutionary idealism in the labor movement's subsequent history was represented by the IWW. Founded in 1905 in opposition to the conservative and exclusionist trade union policies of the AFL, the Wobblies, as members of the IWW called themselves, did much to popularize the concept of industrial unionism, although in the end they failed to build a lasting labor organization. Opposed to segregation of any sort within the labor movement, they opened their membership and leadership to anyone who was a wage worker, regardless of race, nationality or sex, purposely keeping initiation fees and dues low so that everyone could join. Committed both to building an industrial union capable of fighting the everyday battles of labor and to acting as a revolutionary cadre promoting class consciousness and socialism, they

were destroyed by employers' repressive tactics and systematic persecution by the federal government during and after World War I.[40]

To Wobblies the basic conflict in society was between employers
and workers. They rejected the "business unionism" of the AFL
which espoused a partnership of interests between the two groups,
and for this reason they were reluctant even to sign formal contracts
with employers. Preaching the need for the overthrow of capitalism
and the establishment of a new social order with the working class
in control of production and distribution, their volatile rhetoric created hysteria among the respectable classes and earned them the un-
dying hatred of employers who used every method in their power—
from smear campaigns to mass arrests, deportations and open violence—to destroy the IWW. Working hand-in-hand with the businessmen, the national leadership of the AFL helped employers plan
strategy, provided strikebreakers, publicly maligned the Wobblies
and even forbade affiliated unions to support IWW strikes, although
this latter directive was not always followed.[41]

The Wobblies believed that increased concentration of ownership
and solidarity among employers necessitated a unified working
class. Their dedication to the class struggle meant that they conceived the problem of racism in simplistic class terms. To them race
prejudice was simply manufactured by employers to keep workers
divided against themselves. They had little knowledge of the involved history of racism and only a limited appreciation of the extent to which it had become embedded in the entire American social
fabric. Within their organization and activities they were consistent
in promoting racial solidarity and brought Japanese, Chinese, Mexican and black workers into their organization. In their denunciation of Jim Crow, lynching, disfranchisement and the exclusion
movement on the West Coast, they in effect challenged white supremacy. However, this challenge was weakened by their insistence
that there was no "race problems," only the class struggle. Consequently, they lacked any concrete program to alleviate the racial
oppression of nonwhites, and this limited their appeal. They did
not, for example, actively support the black struggle for the vote.[42]

Within the IWW, organization of black workers, who may have comprised as much as 10 per cent of its membership,[43] was strongest among the dock workers and longshoremen in Philadelphia, Baltimore and Norfolk, Virginia, and in the lumber mills of Texas and Louisiana. The Philadelphia Marine Transport Workers, of whom half were black, was an exception to the general inability of the IWW to organize stable unions. The leaders of the dock workers concentrated more on building a union according to the principles of industrial unionism and devoted less energy to promoting revolutionary syndicalism. Affiliating with the IWW in 1913, this union exercised job control on the docks and gave industrial equality to black workers under the leadership of both blacks and whites, including the foremost black IWW organizer, Ben Fletcher. Unable to win a strike called in 1920, although solidarity among the workers was maintained, the Marine Transport Workers declined in 1923 due to competition from other unions, disagreements with the new IWW leadership and the failure of yet another strike.[44]

The lumber workers of Texas and Louisiana organized the Brotherhood of Timber Workers in 1910 with segregated locals and power vested in the white locals. But upon seeking membership in the IWW in 1912 they were told by organizer Bill Haywood to integrate their meetings. According to Spero and Harris, integrated meetings became the policy except in cases where local authorities intimidated black workers into meeting separately. Destroyed by the repression of employers who were determined to block union organizing, the Brotherhood did achieve racial solidarity among not only its own members but also among blacks, Mexicans and foreign whites who were brought in as strikebreakers.[45]

Although their membership shot up with each strike, the IWW was unable to sustain a large, stable membership, especially in the East among the industrial workers. Moreover, with the exception of the Lawrence textile strike of 1912, most of its strikes were not fully successful due to the repressive tactics of employers and government and lack of support from the main body of organized labor. The IWW's main strength came from the migrant workers of the

West, the homeless and despised "unorganizable" groups who were forced to drift from place to place seeking work. Here the IWW found ready recruits, for it offered the despised respect, the hopeless hope and the exploited an understanding of the causes of their condition and a course of action.[46]

Aside from repression, failure to consolidate their gains stemmed in part from the IWW's dual purpose of being at the same time a union and a revolutionary propaganda group. It was much more successful in the latter role. In addition, tensions existed between the Eastern and Western locals regarding the concept of leadership and centralization. But most important of the disagreements within the IWW was a dispute over political action as a method of achieving its goals. Unlike the NLU and the Knights, many Wobblies believed that corruption and the influence of Big Business in American politics removed the possibility of achieving socialism through political action. Rejecting the government as a tool of the capitalists, these Wobblies believed that only direct action on the part of the workers would bring about the new social order. This position was solidified at the 1908 convention under the leadership of Vincent St. John, William Troutmann, and the Western delegates, causing a large loss of membership and outside support. At a time when progressive reformers were turning to political action as a panacea for social ills, the Wobblies' position seemed incomprehensible. But many of the members of the IWW were disfranchised—the foreign-born, floating workers, nonwhite workers and women—and for them electoral politics was something less than a real option.[47] In addition, Philip Foner has observed, "as a syndicalist organization, [the IWW] opposed political action at the ballot box as a waste of energy, and put its faith primarily in industrial organization and the general strike."[48] All options were closed, however, as business and government conspired to eliminate the Wobblies and their organization.

With the destruction of the IWW the vision of a radically new society, the hope of labor reformers and revolutionaries, all but died. Unable to infuse their ideals into the labor movement as a whole, rejected by their own and persecuted by their class enemies, the labor visionaries faded into obscurity. Yet their incessant agitation and propaganda, coupled with the dynamics of a maturing industrial capitalist economy, pointed the way to a new form of unionism that was to take hold of the American working class.

Industrial Unionism and the CIO Era

Early industrial unions, such as the United Mine Workers (UMW) and the International Ladies Garments Workers Union (ILGWU), demonstrated that the problem of strikebreaking could be solved not by exclusion but by better labor organization. Put into practice, this simple insight—long advocated by labor leaders—was an important advance in overcoming racial prejudice in parts of the labor movement. As events turned out, however, this first step was followed by many reversals and other developments which hardly bode well for black labor.

In order to organize in the central competitive mining area—Ohio, Indiana, Illinois and western Pennsylvania—it was necessary to eliminate the possibility of miners being brought from the coal fields of the South to act as scabs. When the UMW was organized in 1890 its leaders concluded that rather than excluding potential strikebreakers the union should organize them—and since a large percentage of the miners in the South were black this meant that they, too, should be organized. Black miners were brought into the union not only as rank-and-file members but also as organizers and leaders.

However, union leaders' efforts were hampered by the attitudes of many Northern white miners who "often refused to work with Negroes, and in some places have struck or threatened to strike if they were employed."[49] Further, although the locals in the South were organized on an interracial basis, seating arrangements at meetings often were segregated. Despite these problems, the UMW succeeded in bringing a great measure of interracial labor solidarity to parts of the South.[50]

The UMW unfortunately failed to remember the lesson of its own history. In 1922 the union made the near-fatal mistake of blacklisting a racially mixed group of nonunion miners who had aided it in a strike. The UMW's desertion of these miners eventually precipitated a revolt in its ranks led by Communists who accused the union of racism. This revolt, plus the fact that many black miners were disillusioned and leaving the union, led to the defeat and virtual collapse of the UMW in 1927.[51]

The International Ladies Garment Workers Union (ILGWU) faced a similar problem with strikebreakers being brought into the shops from the South, and it decided to organize these workers who were mostly black women. This positive attitude was reinforced by the union's experience in organizing the diverse nationalities seeking employment in the garment industry. But ethnic competition still marred the ILGWU's record. The union was so structured that as late as 1965, although its membership was heavily black and Puerto Rican, its leadership and the better jobs were in the hands of the children of the white immigrants who flooded into the union decades ago.[52]

The hardships of the Great Depression inspired a new wave of reform activities, including a vigorous organizing drive aimed at bringing workers in the mass-production industries into the unions. The drive was spearheaded by industrial unionists in the AFL under the leadership of United Mine Workers personnel and assorted labor radicals, including Communists. This organizing effort was resisted by the craft union leaders of the AFL and in 1937, when the industrial organizers were expelled, they formed the Congress of Industrial Organizations.

Because of the CIO's interest in organizing and protecting the unskilled mass-production workers it became an active lobbyist for New Deal social welfare legislation. The federal government, concerned that widespread labor unrest might result in a revolutionary situation, passed laws that facilitated labor organizing, but these laws also brought organized labor under closer scrutiny of government agencies.

The CIO was more favorably regarded in the black community than the AFL because of the former's avowedly friendly attitude toward black labor. The CIO organized black workers both as a matter of principle and out of necessity. The industrial principle of labor solidarity and, perhaps more important, the evident fact that black workers had made tremendous inroads in the mass-production industries since World War I meant that these workers could not be ignored. The CIO brought black workers into leadership positions; it won equal wages for black and white workers; and it tried with considerable success, especially in the North, to eliminate social segregation among its membership. The CIO also established a civil rights committee which carried on active propaganda, both within and outside the labor movement, against race prejudice.

It further sought the good will of the black community by making financial contributions to the NAACP and other organizations, and it provided personnel to work in some of these groups. In return, NAACP leaders actively campaigned for CIO unions. By 1945 black workers comprised almost seven per cent of the CIO's membership, as compared with 3.4 per cent for the AFL. The CIO made its greatest gains among black workers in the automobile, steel, shipbuilding, electrical and packinghouse industries of the North.[53]

Although the CIO leadership initiated an aggressive campaign against racial discrimination, the limits of its capabilities soon became apparent. During World War II white CIO members struck several times to prevent the hiring or upgrading of black workers, with the result that black workers were confined largely to unskilled work in CIO unions. In Illinois white workers even went on strike to maintain segregated toilets. CIO leaders opposed these strikes but the leadership itself was becoming less militant on the question of racial equality.

The leadership's retreat on the race question coincided with the launching of its Southern organizing drive in 1946 and the rise of the anti-communist hysteria that gripped the nation following the war. As soon as the CIO began moving into the South it was met with a barrage of accusations. The press and Southern industrialists charged that union organizers were Communists, subversives, carpetbaggers, nigger lovers, etc. The AFL, fearing that its hegemony in the South might be threatened, opportunistically joined in the attacks.[54] The attacks reached hysterical pitch, and the CIO leadership, instead of maintaining its stance and viewing the attacks

as indicative of its strength, gave in to the pressure. Attempting
to placate its sworn enemies, it appointed regional directors who
were more in accord with the racism and anti-communism of the
Southern industrialists. Its Southern drive became a campaign to
organize white workers first, with black workers often relegated to
segregated locals. In an effort to present itself as 100% American,
the CIO also purged its ranks of members and unions suspected
of being pro-Communist, and in the process it eliminated many of
the radical reformers who were most committed to racial equality.
Its civil rights committee became a watchdog to keep Communists
out of the labor movement and out of the black community.

In the postwar years the CIO in effect purged itself of the vision
of reform and labor solidarity that had inspired its formation. By
the beginning of the 1950's the CIO was well along the road toward
the kind of political conservatism and bureaucracy which characterized the AFL. The final step in this process was taken in 1955
with the merger of the two. Although blacks were represented in
the leadership of the new group, Ray Marshall pointed out that
"a number of features of the merger caused Negroes to become increasingly skeptical of the federation's civil rights program. Some
Negro leaders noted that unions could be expelled for corruption
and communism but not for civil rights violations. . . . Relations
between the AFL-CIO and the Negro community were also influenced by the fact that two-thirds of the official positions of the
merged organization, including the presidency, went to the
AFL. . . . Furthermore, the AFL-CIO Executive Council admitted
two unions—The Brotherhood of Locomotive Firemen and the
Brotherhood of Railway Trainmen—to the merged organization
even though they still had race bars in their constitutions."[55]

On paper the AFL-CIO was committed to racial equality, but
its bureaucratic structure and political conservatism acted to vitiate
this commitment. The intense black-white labor strife that occurred
in the years after the merger and the recurring necessity for black
workers to resort to litigation in order to break down race barriers
clearly indicated that the AFL-CIO leadership, for all its resolutions

and rhetoric, had little desire to mount a serious drive to eliminate white racism from the labor movement.

The Black Community and Black Unionists

Considering the pronounced hostility of the bulk of the labor movement during most of its history, it is remarkable that the black community has not with one voice rejected unionism outright. There has indeed been a strain in that direction but this has been countered by the economic realities of black community life. The overwhelming majority of the black population are members of the working class—until relatively recently the professional and business classes were minuscule. Consequently, the black community has long displayed an active interest in labor principles despite the unfriendliness of much of white labor. To be more precise, at least four different responses to labor organizing have been manifested at various times in black history. These are (1) anti-unionism, (2) adaptation to segregation within the union movement, (3) militant protests to challenge racist practices in the unions, and (4) independent labor organizing activities.

The prevalence of racism in so much of the trade union movement provoked many black community leaders to adopt an anti-union, pro-employer attitude. Booker T. Washington summarized this view in an article that was published in *Atlantic Monthly* in 1913: "The average Negro who comes to town does not understand the necessity or advantage of a labor organization which stands between him and his employer and aims apparently to make a monopoly of the opportunity for labor." The black worker is "more accustomed to work for persons than for wages," he contended. "When he gets a job, therefore, he is inclined to consider the source from which it comes." The black worker regards his employer as his friend, Washington said, and "does not understand and does not like an organization which seems to be founded on a sort of impersonal enmity to the man by whom he is employed." Washington, who in his youth had been a coal miner in West Virginia and a member of the Knights of Labor, said that discrimination caused black workers to become "very willing strike-breakers." He concluded that trade unions would continue their policy of racial discrimination so long as this worked to the advantage of the white members, but he held out the hope that labor leaders might change these practices for the very reason that discrimination in organized labor only served "to produce among the Negroes a prejudice and fear of union labor such as to create in this country a race of strike-breakers."

Marcus Garvey also advised black workers to beware of the white labor movement. "It seems strange and a paradox," Garvey wrote, "but the only convenient friend the Negro worker or laborer has in America at the present time is the white capitalist. The capitalist being selfish—seeking only the largest profit out of labor—is willing and glad to use Negro labor wherever possible on a scale 'reasonably' below the standard union wage. . . but, if the Negro unionizes himself to the level of the white worker, the choice and preference of employment is given to the white worker." Garvey concluded with the advice that the black worker should "organize by himself and always keep his scale of wage a little lower than the whites until he is able to become, through proper leadership, his own employer; by doing so he will keep the good will of the white employer and live a little longer under the present scheme of things."[56] Both Garvey and Washington believed that the ultimate salvation of the black worker lay in the establishment of a separate black economy and the creation of a class of black capitalists. Then the worker could become his own employer ideally; or he could seek work from a black capitalist who presumably would not discriminate.[57] The combined trends toward bigness and economic concentration in the general economy, however, ensured that this hope would never be more than a dream.

Black social welfare agencies have been ambivalent in their approach to organized labor. At various times and places the Urban League, for example, has been openly hostile toward labor. Urban League chapters sometimes actively encouraged strikebreaking by black workers. In addition some chapters provided employers with social workers whose duties included espionage and informing on the off-duty activities of black employees, indoctrinating black workers against unionism, and operating social clubs financed by employers as a way of pacifying labor unrest.[58] However, it must also be noted that other Urban League chapters were friendly and helpful to organized labor, especially after the advent of the CIO; and as early as 1918 the National Urban League and the NAACP together approached the AFL in an attempt to get it to change the discriminatory practices of its member unions.

The anti-union attitude of some black community leaders and organizations cannot be attributed entirely to the racial practices of white unions. In point of fact, black leaders have also been hostile toward black labor groups. In the 1920's when A. Philip Randolph was organizing his all-black Brotherhood of Sleeping Car Porters union, he was attacked by black politicians and newspaper editors. Randolph was accused of being communist-influenced and of misleading the black workers in his union.[59] Although much of this opposition was engineered by the Pullman Company, it was symptomatic of an underlying antagonism toward the principles of labor organizing that went far beyond the question of racism in white unions.

Two black researchers, Horace Cayton and George Mitchell, attempted to analyze this phenomenon in terms of the ideology that characterized many of the leaders of the black community. Reporting their findings in a book, *Black Workers and the New Unions* published in 1939, they observed that a small elite group had grown up in the black community. Composed of businessmen, professionals, newspaper editors and religious leaders, this elite made its living by furnishing goods and services that the segregated black community was prevented from obtaining in the white world. Segregation and discrimination thus created a separate economic base that made possible the development of a black elite; and these factors also shaped its ideology. According to Cayton and Mitchell:

> The educated upper class Negro does not, now that he has found a comfortable place, care to champion doctrines which purport to help

the black worker by changing the social system. . . that has given him a position of advantage within his group. In addition to the fact that he is complacent and respectable, or perhaps because he is complacent and respectable, the upper class Negro is economically conservative. His primary interest tends to be in that which protects the differential between himself and the Negro masses, rather than in an effort to improve the conditions of the majority of his group in a manner which almost necessarily endangers his own position. The Negro masses have accepted the leadership of this handful of upper class persons. Since black workers have been isolated from the influence of the white working class, the talented, educated members of their group appeared as their natural leaders. Race consciousness had built up a semblance of solidarity between the classes which has benefitted the Negro elite by providing its members with a tenable social position and has benefitted the blacks by giving them leaders who have symbolized to them their possibilities as persons if conditions but allowed. The Negro upper class depends on this racial solidarity to maintain and enable it to exploit the market for professional and business services which racial prejudice has tended to create.[60]

The petty bourgeois black elite therefore opposed labor organizing not only because of racism in the union movement, but also because labor organizing by black workers threatened to create an alternative leadership to the established community leaders. Moreover, the radicalism of some black labor leaders raised questions as to the viability of the capitalist system; a system in which black businessmen were anxiously seeking to participate more fully. Du Bois' Talented Tenth thus found labor organizing and economic radicalism offensive to its newly found social status and its vested economic interests.

Black workers and labor leaders responded to union racism in several different ways. Some simply adapted to segregation and attempted to make the best of the situation. For example, Southern locals of the International Longshoremen's Association maintained a rigid structure of job and union segregation, with special work-sharing arrangements elaborated between black and white locals. In exchange for the job-sharing arrangements black longshoremen supported the ILA in bargaining with employers and aided it in resisting the organizing efforts of the International Longshoremen's and Warehousemen's Union. These reciprocal agreements resulted in blacks rising to positions of considerable power within the ILA. The leaders of the black longshoremen thus successfully used segregation to acquire a power base within the union and to obtain certain benefits for the black members. This attempt to convert a liability into an asset was not at all unusual in situations where black workers had to function within a segregated white union.[61]

A more widespread response among black workers was to protest the racism of the union movement and to demand full and equal admission to all levels of the labor movement. As early as 1869 black labor leaders confronted the National Labor Union with this demand, and black spokesmen have continued to press the matter ever since. The urgency of black labor needs moved the Urban League and the NAACP to make similar overtures to the AFL in 1918, 1920, 1924 and 1929. Within the AFL the most tireless fighter against discrimination was A. Philip Randolph. Literally for decades at every AFL convention, Randolph used his position as president of the sleeping car porters union to attack racial discrimination. For the most part, however, his complaints and proposals were ignored. Randolph also took his protest to the federal government. In 1941 he threatened to launch a massive black march on Washington unless President Roosevelt called a halt to discrimination in defense plants. Roosevelt issued an executive order establishing a federal Fair Employment Practices Commission, and he prohibited racial and religious discrimination in the war industries, government training programs and other government industries. Since that time blacks have with greater or lesser success prodded the federal government to pass anti-discrimination legislation and to bring pressure to bear on organized labor. In 1960 Randolph and other black labor leaders formed the Negro American Labor Council which sought to wage an organized fight against discrimination from within the labor movement.

Along with protest activity, black workers reacted to the racism of organized labor by establishing independent labor unions. As early as 1868 the first state and local conventions of black workers were held and in January, 1869, the first national black labor congress took place in Washington, D.C. In many areas where black workers were excluded from the white unions they organized their own unions. By 1929 there were at least 13 such independent unions with a reported membership of between 15,000 and 20,000.[62] In 1919 an attempt had been made to federate all of the black unions into an organization called the National Brotherhood Workers of America. For a time the Brotherhood Workers achieved considerable strength among shipyard and dock workers in Virginia. The organization embraced socialism and Randolph's magazine, *The Messenger,* became its official organ. Significantly, the Brotherhood Workers also saw the necessity of organizing black agricultural workers in the South. It was on the West Coast, however, that organization among agricultural workers first took hold. Shortly after the turn of the century Mexican agricultural workers attempted to organize. In 1910, along with Japanese workers, they called a strike in the sugar beet fields at Ventura, Calif. The first stable organization of Mexican workers was the Confederacion de Uniones Obreras Mexicanas in Southern California in 1927.[63] This group was a forerunner of Caesar Chavez' organization of Mexican-American farm workers.

The most famous of the independent black unions was Randolph's Brotherhood of Sleeping Car Porters. First organized in 1925, after a decade of jurisdictional disputes with AFL unions, it was finally chartered as a national union by the AFL in 1936.

More recently there has been an upsurge of independent organizing among black and other nonwhite workers. A good example of the contemporary movement was seen in the League of Revolutionary Black Workers, organized among auto workers in Detroit. Formation of the League began in May, 1968, around the issue of racial discrimination in the auto plants and the acquiescence of the United Auto Workers union in these practices. In some plants blacks reportedly made up as much as 70 per cent of the work force, but because of discrimination they were restricted to the hardest, lowest-paying and least-skilled jobs. The UAW, one of the pioneering CIO unions, made little effort to halt this practice. After some experience with wildcat strikes the black workers, with the help of black community groups and students, started to build their organization, gradually spreading it to other plants and even other cities.

For the most part the early independent unions of nonwhite workers were not notably successful. They were not strong enough to protect their members in the face of powerful employers, and by and large they had to accept work standards and wage scales set by the dominant white unions. It is only in those areas where nonwhite workers have made up all or a very substantial portion of the work force—such as the Pullman porters, or in the Detroit auto plants, or in California agriculture—that independent minority unions have enjoyed a greater measure of success. The future of the minority unions, and newly formed minority caucuses within predominantly white unions, is very uncertain, but, aside from protest groups and falling back upon the good will of a federal government that is itself part of the structure of racism, they appear to offer the only serious challenge to white supremacy in organized labor.

CHAPTER VII:
Socialists, Communists, and Self-Determination

The great crisis in the American political economy that catapulted middle-class reformers into the Progressive movement also propelled a segment of American intellectuals into leadership positions in the fledgling socialist movement.[1] The birth of American imperialism combined with the growth of monopolistic concentrations in the economy unsettled the independent middle classes and professionals as nothing had since the Civil War. For these alienated strata, a socialist critique of society provided an explanation that gave meaning to their troubled situation and pointed out a course of remedial action. Many were consequently attracted to the early Socialist Party.

The economic dislocations of the period also spurred many workers toward socialism, especially unskilled workers whose lives were very insecure. A large number of dispossessed workers enlisted in the syndicalist IWW. The left wing of the Socialist Party flirted with the IWW but no firm alliance developed, in part because simultaneously the party's right wing was courting the AFL, a fact which incensed the IWW leadership. The bulk of organized labor was to be found in the AFL, but industrial expansion and monopoly practices gave skilled workers an advantageous position with increasing rewards which made them deaf to socialist pleas, particularly after World War I. Consequently, the disintegration of the IWW and the growing complacency of the AFL meant that the potential organized mass base for a socialist movement was seriously undermined, at least until the Great Depression. The early Socialist Party therefore was overly influenced by intellectuals who were not rooted in the working class, and its efforts to establish ties with the AFL encouraged opportunistic and conservative influences within the party.

These were not the only problems that afflicted the socialist movement and influenced its perceptions and understanding of racism. Of equal importance were two other factors: (1) the effects of European social democracy on American socialism, and (2) the lack of ideological independence and initiative on the part of American socialists. Taken together, these factors led most American socialists to dismiss or over-simplify the role of racial antagonism in U.S. society. Lacking ideological clarity about racism, the socialist parties generally related to black people in an opportunistic and dogmatic manner, resulting in much conflict and bitterness on both sides.*

Social Democracy

Just as the rise of imperialism had a conservatizing influence on parts of the labor movement, so did it have a similar effect on the European socialist parties. The consolidation of powerful capitalist democracies in Europe and the codification of liberalism as the ideology of the bourgeoise in the latter part of the nineteenth century prompted some socialist intellectuals to revise Marx's analysis of the development and decline of the capitalist order. Deceived by the formal machinery of bourgeois democracy, these Socialists concluded that in the advanced capitalist countries peaceful, evolutionary transition to socialism was possible.[2] They argued that there

---

* Although in theory socialist parties aim to achieve state power, in practice those examined in this chapter have been mainly concerned with protest activity or struggling for certain concrete reforms or specific changes in government policy. Hence their inclusion in these case studies.

was no longer an irreconcilable conflict of class interests, and that violent revolution and the dictatorship of the proletariat were not necessary to achieve socialism. They believed that the development of democracy in Europe, based on industrial capitalism, allowed peaceful reforms and the incorporation of the working class into the political power of the bourgeois social order. This was to be achieved by building mass socialist parties, under the leadership of the radical intellectuals, that would fight to widen the franchise and open the way for a transition to socialism through parliamentary methods. Hence, the social democrats became lobbyists for reforms instead of agents of revolutionary change. They soon degenerated into bureaucrats in the "loyal opposition" in the European countries.

Social democratic revisionism, which became particularly evident with the disintegration of the Second International (which had been formed to unite the various socialist parties), not only contributed to opportunism, but also laid the basis for social chauvinism. Marx had envisioned the overthrow of the bourgeois order as a task to be accomplished by the industrial workers in the advanced capitalist countries. He took note of the struggles of suppressed nationalities in Europe and Asia and he opposed black slavery because it threatened to degrade the white working class in America, but he never doubted the vanguard role of European workers in the expected revolution. These views were subsequently crystallized into a rigid dogma by social democrats. If colonized nonwhite peoples were considered at all, they were told they would have to fall in line behind the leadership of white workers and intellectuals. The practical consequences of this chauvinism would become clear with the development of the American Socialist Party, in which European immigrants were very active.

It is understandable that modern socialist thought emerged first among those intellectuals located in the very heart of world capitalism. Being in the best position to observe the internal workings of capitalism, Western intellectual critics were led logically to analyze its structure and phases of development. However, the radicalized intellegentsia were not immune to the influence of racism and cultural chauvinism—ideological offspring of Western imperialism—and this distorted and narrowed their perception of the problem. Modern capitalism was regarded as only incidentally—rather than intrinsically—connected with colonialism and imperialism. Consequently, "true" socialism was regarded as possible only within the "advanced" cultural mileux of Europe and the U.S. Socialism thereby was restricted in applicability to the industrially advanced nations, as the radical Western intellectuals in effect claimed Marxism as their private ideological property and used this claim to elevate themselves to the role of guardians of the ideological purity of the socialist movements.

This further exposed the social chauvinism of the Western social democratic intellectuals which precluded their perceiving the relationship between the rise of imperialism and the encrusting of underdevelopment in the colonized world, and the consequent vanguard role assumed by national liberation struggles in the world movement. Lenin's theses on imperialism and national liberation, growing out of the experience of revolutionary struggle in a backward, multi-national country, greatly enriched socialist theory by placing the class struggle in an international context. For Lenin, capitalism was no mere European phenomenon incidently exploiting a few colonies, but a worldwide system of monopoly that had to be viewed in its totality to be understood. Moreover, national-racial oppression no longer could be dismissed as a minor side-effect of capitalism but was an intrinsic component of capitalist colonialism and imperialism.

Two important conclusions flowed from this analysis. In the first place, imperialist oppression tended to generate strong oppositional forces in the colonized world. Summarizing Lenin, historian Wilson Record observed that imperialism

> led to resistance among these peoples. A national consciousness emerged, and was followed by movements for national liberation. While the capitalist countries had exploited the backward areas, they had also laid the groundwork within them for a new bourgeois class anxious to free itself and develop independently its own economic institutions. These two forces combined to offer increasing resistance to exploitation, and colonies sought to establish their independence at an opportune time.

Any movement of national liberation, although it might be led by the bourgeois elements within the country, tended to weaken the grip of monopoly capitalism.[3]

Lenin concluded, therefore, that it was imperative for Socialists in the capitalist nations to support the right of oppressed nations to political self-determination. Otherwise, Socialists would find themselves pitted against one of the most powerful forces opposing the sway of monopoly capital. At the same time, Lenin insisted that Socialists in the oppressed nations must struggle against their national bourgeoisie constantly and maintain international proletarian solidarity.[4] Implicit in this statement was the notion that Socialists in the oppressed nations must organize independent revolutionary political parties to fight for both national liberation and socialist revolution.[5]

A second conclusion drawn from Lenin's analysis was the fact that imperialism laid the basis for opportunism and racism among the workers of the imperialist nations. Imperialist exploitation of the colonized nonwhite world was crucial in contributing to the growing affluence of segments of the white working class in Europe and America, beginning in the latter part of the nineteenth century. Lenin warned that imperialism thereby tends "to create privileged sections. . . among the workers, and to detach them from the broad masses of the proletariat."[6] He noted further that "as the result of a far-reaching colonial policy the European proletariat has partly reached a situation where it is not its work that maintains the whole of society but that of the people of the colonies who are practically enslaved. . . . In certain countries these circumstances create the material and economic basis for infecting the proletariat of one country or another with colonial chauvinism."[7] Thus, the resulting racism and chauvinism among white workers were much more than mere diversionary tactics introduced by conniving capitalists to divide the world working class; on the contrary, these ideological manifestations were firmly grounded in the dynamics of imperialist development. Consequently, Lenin insisted that "the fight against imperialism is a sham and humbug unless it is inseparably bound up with the fight against opportunism."[8]

Lenin's warnings came too late, however, to influence the ideo-logical formation of the American Socialist Party, which for many years was the largest and most influential socialist organization in the United States.

The Socialist Party

The pro-white bias of social democracy gave form to the racial out-look and practices of the early Socialist Party (SP). Organized in 1901, the SP had little or nothing to offer black and other nonwhite workers. At its founding convention the SP reluctantly adopted—at the insistence of black delegates—a resolution expressing "sym-pathy" for the black workers and inviting them to join the party. However, until the 1920's and 1930's, when it faced sharp competi-tion from the Communists, the SP did nothing as an organization to oppose lynching and disfranchisement, or otherwise address itself to the special problems confronting black workers as the result of racism. On the contrary, Socialist leader Eugene Debs insisted that "We have nothing special to offer the Negro, and we cannot make separate appeals to all the races." Debs even thought that the mild resolution of 1901 went too far toward being a special racial appeal and he urged that it be repealed.[9]

Branches of the party did, however, make special appeals to white racism. The Louisiana locals meeting in 1903 adopted a plat-form advocating racial segregation as a tactic for discrediting the Democrats' charge that Socialists favored social equality.[10] This pol-icy was rejected by the national office with the advice that the mat-ter of segregation could be discussed after socialism was achieved. Despite national policy statements, many locals of the SP, especially in the deep South, practiced segregation both out of fear of racist authorities and from a desire not to antagonize white members. In the upper South and Southwest, party locals were much less com-mitted to defending, and sometimes even opposed, the Southern Code.

Before World War I the national office of the SP generally avoided actively interfering with the racial practices of local branches. For example, in 1913 the national office conducted a survey of black membership that revealed segregationist practices in many branches. Yet, as Sally Miller has observed, the national leadership "refrained from initiating measures on behalf of its now formally recognized Negro membership or from seeking to alter the status quo in any way. The Socialist Party had been led to its inquiry but it had no interest in exploring the ramifications further."[11]

Several prominent figures in the SP were aggressive racists. Victor Berger, editor of the *Social Democratic Herald,* announced that there was "no doubt that the Negroes and mulattoes constitute a lower race." Socialist author Jack London flatly stated that he was "first of all a white man and only then a Socialist." The socialist paper, *Appeal to Reason,* rejected any thought of social equality. "Socialists do not believe in a mixture of the races," the *Appeal* said. "Socialists believe in justice to the Negro, not in social, but in economic equality. . . . . Socialism will separate the races."[12]

In the light of such extreme sentiments and the more general reluctance of the SP to do anything about racial oppression, it is difficult to understand what Socialists meant when they spoke of "justice" for the Negro. The SP regarded black oppression as perhaps more extreme but certainly in no way different from the class oppression of white workers. Further, to early Socialists racial conflict and racist thinking were groundless and artificial tactics introduced by employers in an effort to prevent working class solidarity. For example, in 1912 the Tennessee SP adopted a plank declaring that "the question of race superiority" was "injected into the mind of the white wage-worker" merely as a "tactical method" used by the "capitalist class to keep the workers divided on the economic field."[13] Proceeding from this social democratic ideology inherited from European intellectuals, SP leaders apparently never considered that racism might be grounded in Western imperialism. Moreover, since black workers were only a minority, their needs were definitely subordinate to the interests of the larger white working class. The result, according to Sally Miller, was that "Marxist ideology, instead of leading Socialists to seek out the Negro as the worker with absolutely nothing to lose but his chains, reinforced the existing national tendency to overlook his comprehensive exploitation."[14] Added to all of this was the desire of SP leaders not to alienate the established white trade unions in the AFL which they were courting assiduously. This further compromised their interest in racial justice in organized labor.[15]

Even the SP boast that it was the party of "the whole working class of the world" had definite racial implications. Most American Socialists adopted an enlightened position on the immigration of European workers to the U.S., but they made no secret of their opposition to Asian immigration. However, it was necessary to reconcile this latter sentiment with their official espousal of international working class solidarity. Between 1908 and 1910 the SP worked out an expedient compromise in the form of a resolution that favored "all legislative measures tending to prevent the immigration of strikebreakers and contract laborers, and the mass importation of workers from foreign countries, brought by the employing classes for the purpose of weakening the organization of American labor, and of lowering the standard of life of American workers." The second part of the resolution opposed "the exclusion of any immigrants on account of their race or nationality."[16] The SP thus neatly straddled the fence by passing a resolution that couched racism in patriotic, pro-American labor language.

Here and there individual Socialists demurred from the racism that characterized the dominant wing of the party. Mary White Ovington, William English Walling and Charles Edward Russell, for example, were among the founders of the NAACP. Involved in many of the social reform activities that marked the Progressive Era, these Socialists and others were nevertheless unable to swing the SP toward a more enlightened position on race.

Not surprisingly, the SP attracted very little black support in its early years. W.E.B. Du Bois made a brief foray into its ranks in 1911 only to resign a year later in disillusionment. Du Bois criticized the SP for "failure to face fairly the Negro problem and make a straightforward declaration that they regard Negroes as men in the same sense that other persons are."[17] Ironically, he left the SP to support Woodrow Wilson in the 1912 election. As to general black participation in the SP, David Shannon concludes:

> How many Negroes there were in the prewar Socialist Party and exactly what role they played in the organization cannot be ascertained. But some things are certain: they were not important in the party, the party made no special effort to attract Negro members, and the party was generally disinterested in, if not actually hostile to, the effort of Negroes to improve their position in American capitalist society.[18]

After World War I, the SP was plagued by factionalism and went through a period of decline. Chief among the disagreements was whether to support the Russian Revolution. The anti-Bolshevik moderates retained control of the party, but more than two-thirds of the membership drifted out of the party or joined forces with the leftists. Several of the left-wing splinter groups that broke with the SP eventually formed the Communist Party in the years 1919-1923. Even earlier, many of the middle-class radicals who dominated the party were frightened off by the "alien ideology" label being pinned to socialism, while others gave up the idea of an independent radical party and opted for trying to influence the established capitalist parties.[19] The Red Scare of 1919-1920 contributed further to the decimation and virtual destruction of the SP.

In the 1920's, faced with vigorous competition from the newly organized Communists, the SP began to look for ways to recruit black workers. Toward the end of the war, the party had attracted Chandler Owen and A. Philip Randolph, editors of *The Messenger,* into its ranks, and during the postwar period they used their magazine, which had an impressive circulation of over 40,000, as a forum for socialist thought. Repeatedly the two black editors called upon progressive blacks to join the SP. At its 1923 convention the SP broke with its past tradition of acquiescence in the face of labor racism and urged white workers to oppose prejudice and discrimination in the labor movement. Under the leadership of Norman Thomas in the 1930's, the SP endorsed anti-lynching legislation and opposed all forms of racial discrimination. In the South it organized an interracial—but not integrated—tenant farmers' union that attempted to expose the failure of the New Deal to meet the needs of Southern farmers.[20]

These actions did not make the SP more palatable to black workers nor check its decline. The appeal to black workers and farmers was grafted onto the SP program almost as an afterthought. Unlike the Communists, the SP was never pushed by external forces to seek black support. The Socialists were classic social democratic Marxists who looked to the white workers and intellectuals of the West as the vanguard of world revolution. Others might be "invited" to join the struggle, but the leadership and overall objectives were predetermined by the party's ideology. Given this orientation, the failure of early white Socialists to oppose racism actively was a logical consequence of their being both Americans and inheritors of an ideology shaped by European radical intellectuals.

The Communist Party

The Communist Party (CP) has left a lasting imprint on the struggle for racial equality. Despite the generally negative image of the party conveyed in the popular media and standard history texts, the Communist Party in its heyday probably did more than any other predominantly white political group to promote racial equality in American life. Unfortunately, the party's inflexible adherence to the Communist International's ever-changing political line often placed it on a collision course with other groups seeking racial betterment. Further, the party's aggressive insistence that only it was in possession of the "correct" political strategy at any given moment made it a continuous opponent of black political independence, even though officially the party endorsed black self-determination.

At the height of its influence during the 1930's, the party could point to many accomplishments in the field of race relations. Its long-standing interest in industrial unionism enabled party organizers to play a crucial role in the organizing drives of the CIO. The progressive racial policies of the CIO in its early years are at least in part attributable to the influence of political radicals.[21] Capitalizing on the hardships of the Depression, Communists established interracial Unemployed Councils around the country and brought thousands of jobless workers into the streets to participate in "hunger marches."[22] A young black Communist organizer, Angelo Herndon, led one of these marches in Atlanta, Georgia. Herndon was imprisoned for "attempting to incite to insurrection," but was later freed after an immense national campaign. His lawyer, Benjamin Davis, who later became a top-ranking black Communist official, was eventually elected, as a Communist, to the New York City Council.[23]

The party's influence in organized labor and its control of the Unemployed Councils secured an important place for it in the New Deal. Officially the party was alternately hostile or friendly to the New Deal, depending on the current "line." However, the demands the Communists raised in organized labor and the Unemployed Councils, combined with the evident revolutionary threat reflected by the growth of the party, contributed to the pressure for New Deal labor and social welfare measures.[24] The Communists also gained considerable influence in some New Deal programs such as those of the Works Projects Administration.[25] They were able to use the WPA projects in some areas to extend their influence among black workers and intellectuals.

Other areas of American life also felt the effects of Communist activity. In the South the party organized a predominantly black Sharecroppers' Union in 1931 that eventually included several thousand members.[26] Although the union met with severe repression from local authorities and was finally dissolved in 1936, a contemporary observer noted that its existence revealed "the presence of a will to organize and a tenacity hardly short of heroic on the part of the impoverished Negro tenants."[27] The party's intervention in the Scottsboro case, in which nine black youths were accused of raping two white women, gave it an opportunity to expose American racial practices to world scrutiny.[28] However, the party's role in the case created animosity between it and the NAACP, which sought to conduct the defense along more conventional lines.[29]

The Communist Party's attitude toward the black middle class and moderate reform groups varied with its changing political line. At times, the party denounced these elements as petty bourgeois manipulators under the control of the dominant white economic interest. During other periods, it sought to conciliate them and win their support for the party's current campaigns. Nevertheless, the party's overall impact on the moderate groups, whether intended or not, was not entirely negative. In 1951, Wilson Record concluded:

> The growing identification of the NAACP with the labor movement, which dates back to the early 1930s, can be viewed as partly the result of Communist pressure. The greater concern of the National Urban League for educating Negro workers about trade union membership as well as for specific occupations also falls in this category. The growth of internal democracy within the NAACP has been in part a gratuitous by-product of the Communist threat to the existing administration. The Communists have sought to discredit the incumbent national leadership in order that the Party might capture local branches and, ultimately, the national organization. This threat has tended to increase the responsiveness of the NAACP officialdom to the rank and file.[30]

The party's strong opposition to segregation and "white chauvinism," its open espousal of social equality, and its elevation of blacks to positions of leadership within its own structure and the organizations it controlled—all made the party attractive to many black workers and intellectuals. In the 1930's literally thousands of blacks were recruited into the party,[31] although just about as many defected from the ranks, completely disillusioned by the party's shifting tactics, at the end of the decade. After studying the Communist impact on Chicago's black community, Drake and Cayton concluded that the Communists "won the admiration of the Negro masses by default. They were the only white people who seemed really to care what happened to the Negro. Yet few Negro sympathizers were without reservations. Some thought Communists were 'using Negroes.' Others felt that 'if they ever gain power they'll be just like the other crackers.' Many regarded the interracial picnics and dances as 'bait.' But Negroes are realists. They take 'friends' and allies where they can find them."[32] Party leaders themselves eventually admitted that "Negro workers come into our Party primarily because of the Party's position on the Negro question and not the class struggle," but the leadership insisted that "unless our Party comrades are imbued with a perspective of socialism and see in this the ultimate solution of the Negro question there is no basis for sustained Party membership."[33]

While the party recruited many blacks into its ranks, there remained a serious degree of alienation between it and the black community. This was indicated by the party's frequent and often vicious conflicts with a wide range of black moderate, nationalist and religious groups, and its inability to stabilize its black membership. There is no way of knowing how many of the blacks whom the party recruited or influenced were imbued with a "perspective" of socialism, yet it is clear that hostility to socialism was not the chief cause of the party's failure to establish itself as "the party of the Negro people." The party's history reveals that its actual behavior, rather than its professed goals, was its chief liability. The party sought to use black people not to build socialism in the United States, but to advance the foreign policy interests of the Soviet Union. At times this overriding concern coincided with the main thrust of the struggle for racial equality, and sometimes it ran counter to the struggle. Aside from its subservience to the Communist International, other liabilities limited its success: its continuing effort to subjugate black groups to its policy (and failing this to discredit or disrupt them), its mechanical application of Lenin's theory of self-determination without regard to the particular history of black people in the U.S., its oversimplified view of racism and consequent failure to eradicate "white chauvinism" from its own ranks, and its paternalistic attitude toward black Communists.

It is impossible to understand the history of the American Communist Party without placing it in an international context. In particular, the party's relationship with the Soviet Union, via the Communist International, was of paramount significance. "Whatever has changed from time to time," Theodore Draper has written in *American Communism and Soviet Russia,* "one thing has never changed—the relation of American Communism to Soviet Russia.

This relation has expressed itself in different ways, sometimes glaring and strident, sometimes masked and muted. But it has always been the determining factor, the essential element." The American Communist Party has gone through several periods in its history and all of these were linked to changes in the policy of the Communist International, itself dominated by the Soviet Communist Party.

Of course, the CP's total commitment to the defense of the Soviet Union must be viewed in historical context. The Soviet Union, the world's first socialist state, was confronted by hostile capitalist nations that desired nothing less than its total obliteration. It was therefore incumbent upon all Communist parties to rally to its aid. Nevertheless, for the American party the result of this commitment was a complete lack of independence and flexibility in achieving its avowed goal of building socialism in the U.S.

Erratic swings from "left" to "right" and vice versa sharply affected the party's tactical approach to other groups and organizations. In "left" periods it followed the tactic of "revolutionary dual organization," which involved the establishment of rival trade unions and ethnic organizations to compete against existing "bourgeois" groups. At such times the party loudly denounced black professionals, ministers, intellectuals—the black middle class generally—as "traitors to the race," while also castigating moderate reform groups as agents of white capitalists. Nationalists such as Garvey and independent labor leaders such as Randolph were equally charged with being "misleaders."

In "right" periods the party did an abrupt about-face, muting its criticism of individuals and organizations with whom it now sought to form alliances. Adopting "united front" and "boring from within" tactics, party leaders soft-pedaled their own ideology while trying to win friends and influence within already established organizations.[34]

Although the tactics changed from one period to another the party's basic strategy remained the same: to gain control of the black movement and bring it in line with the current policy of the Communist International. The history of the National Negro Congress (NNC) and A. Philip Randolph's March on Washington movement vividly confirm this assertion. In 1935 a conference at Howard University proposed the idea of a National Negro Congress to bring unity to the black movement by embracing black labor unions, religious, reform, fraternal and civic groups.[35] Some 800 delegates answered the call and organized the NNC in Chicago in February, 1936. The Communists, then trying to unify all antifascist forces in the U.S. against the threat of Nazism, were active in the organization from the beginning, although they did not initially control it. The Congress adopted a long list of resolutions covering a wide range of problems affecting black people. Since blacks were becoming increasingly aware of the dangers posed by Nazism, a resolution opposing fascism was among those passed. Naturally, this met with the wholehearted approval of the Communists.

Concentrating on immediate issues and grievances, the NNC, with the help of party organizers, set up local and regional councils around the country. Within a few years the NNC became one of the more important black organizations of national stature. This success was short-lived, however. The political unity that the NNC had fostered was irreparably disrupted following the Russo-German pact of 1939. The alliance between Stalin and Hitler suddenly compelled the American CP to reverse its previous policies. Opposition to fascism was transformed into opposition to the U.S. defense effort: the U.S. must be kept out of the war at all costs. Assuming an anti-war posture, the party informed black people that they had no stake in the European war. Blacks who could not accept this flip-flop were castigated and reviled as traitors to the race. Seeking to impose its new line on the NNC, the party succeeded only in decimating the ranks of this once-promising organization.[36]

A. Philip Randolph was among those who left the NNC rather than kowtow to the new line. Randolph, always the activist, proceeded to organize the March on Washington movement as a new vehicle for demanding an end to discrimination in the defense industries. The new movement had the misfortune of straddling two periods of CP history; thus, it was attacked by the party for reasons which were diametric opposites from one year to the next! Before the 1941 Nazi attack on the Soviet Union, Randolph's movement was vilified because it did not vigorously oppose the "imperialist" foreign policy of the Roosevelt administration. After 1941 the party, now pro-war and loudly patriotic, accused Randolph and his movement of "sabotaging" the war effort.[37] Party leaders explained this remarkable reversal by noting that the "objective" situation had changed. This was in part true; but what had changed were the foreign policy needs of the Soviet Union, not the domestic needs of black people. Protestations to the contrary, the party's practices in fact reduced black people to the role of passive objects to be manipulated in accordance with priorities that had little or nothing to do with the economic and political objectives of black workers themselves.

Throughout most of its history the party advanced two main slogans related to black people: equality and the right of self-determination. The slogans were formalized by resolutions passed by the Communist International in 1928 and 1930.[38] The equal rights slogan was applied to all blacks, North and South, while self-determination was to be the "main slogan" in the Southern Black Belt. Here is the beginning of a basic confusion which was to render the Communist espousal of self-determination virtually meaningless. The self-determination slogan was based on Lenin's analysis of black people in the U.S. as an "oppressed nation." According to Lenin, an oppressed nation has a right to self-determination, which means the right of self-government and even political separation from the oppressor nation.[39] Stalin's definition of a nation which, among other things, insisted that a true nation possesses a common territory,[40] necessarily limited the right of self-determination to the Southern Black Belt—the only area where black people could be said to possess a common territory. In mechanically following Stalin's definition the American CP (1) failed to heed Lenin's injunction to avoid abstract definitions and instead study the actual development of national movements, and (2) thus closed itself off from understanding Northern and urban black nationalism as a manifestation of self-determination. Both Lenin's and Stalin's understanding of self-determination was based primarily on the European and Russian experience. Neither had direct knowledge of the struggles of black people in the U.S. If they had they might have realized that the struggle for self-determination among blacks was only occasionally linked to the land. Black people were not a nation oppressed on its own land by foreign rule. Blacks had been ripped from their homeland and oppressed by the social organization of white America and its dehumanizing ideology of white supremacy. Consequently, chief themes in the struggle for black self-determination have been the demand for organizational and ideological independence. Sometimes these themes were manifested in specifically separatist movements. At other periods even integrationists insisted that blacks must organize independently to define the meaning of equality and to press for integration. The American CP, saddled with definitions and concepts drawn from the European experience, could not begin to understand the black experience in America. Its bizarre attempt to limit and control self-determination (a contradiction on its face), and its misreading of the full meaning of black nationalism[41] resulted from its uncritical acceptance of a political ideology that had been nurtured in a very different social environment.

The party never attempted an objective investigation of how self-determination might be related to the historical experience and strivings of the black liberation movement. Instead, it imposed a ready-made formula complete with maps of the "Negro nation" and an elaborate rationale.[42] The problem was not that the party advocated the right of self-determination, but that it sought to define and restrict this right without taking cognizance of the dynamics of black history. Consequently, the party found itself burdened with an unrealistic program of black liberation that advocated nationhood without nationalism, on one hand, and racial integration without ideological independence on the other. At different times the party pushed one or the other side of this program, but always it was moving against the tide of black militancy which had long insisted on independence, whether expressed in nationalist or integrationist terms. After wavering for decades, the party officially dropped the concept of self-determination in the 1950's following the advent of the era of "peaceful coexistence."[43]

In the pre-World War II era, another consequence of the party's ideological inheritance was its oversimplified view of racism, and the history of racial antagonism. If racism was simply a device used by the capitalist ruling class to divide the workers, then it followed that the workers have no material stake in the maintenance of racism. Once apprised of their true interests the workers could be expected to join the forces opposing racism. Such has not yet been the case, as the history of the labor movement amply illustrates. Yet Communist writers insisted upon regarding the white working class as the bearer of true enlightenment and fraternity; at the very minimum they contended that if only the workers would accept Marxism-Leninism *then* racial antagonisms would fade away. These contentions ignored the ideological impact of the very real material advantages that have accrued to white workers as a result of racial discrimination at home and racist imperialism abroad. Further, racism as an ideology became so deeply ingrained in American life that, as Ernest Kaiser observed, it became a social-psychological force, shaping and directing behavior, not merely reflecting it.[44] While Communist historical writers did much to outline the full dimensions of black history, they did not display a similar diligence in examining the ideology of white supremacy.[45] Instead, they for the most part simply accepted the social democrats' faith that class struggle led by white workers and revolutionary intellectuals would resolve race conflict in the U.S.

In this, the Communist writers were little different from other white comrades. It required prodding by militant black Communists to get the party to deal with race prejudice. All too often, however, the party's response was aimed at placating the black members and gaining itself a proper, progressive image rather than actually eradicating "white chauvinism." Between 1931 and 1933 the party conducted a series of white chauvinism trials and expelled several members accused of this offense.[46] Apparently these efforts did little to abate racial prejudice and discrimination within the party. In 1949, *Political Affairs,* the party's theoretical journal, devoted a special issue (June, 1949) to the problem of white chauvinism. Pettis Perry, a black member of the Negro Work Commission of the Communist Party exposed what he considered several instances of blatant prejudice and discrimination within the party's ranks and among the leadership. Perry rejected the tactic of holding show trials to "prove" the party's sincerity in opposing racism. He called instead for an ideological and political struggle within the party to "destroy the virus of white chauvinism."

The party's treatment of black women was particularly revealing. Party oganizations routinely included demands for economic, political and social equality for black women in their platforms. However, within the party itself black women were often ignored or treated in a condescending manner. Sometimes party members who were criticized for relating to black women as inferiors attempted to cast blame on black women themselves for being too "subjective." Yet black women were ignored both socially and politically, according to Claudia Jones, and in addition it was known that some party members who employed black domestics refused to hire them through the Domestic Workers Union or to help expand the union.[47] The practice of white party members using domestic help might explain part of the tendency to regard black women as inferior recruits; Claudia Jones asserted that party employers were little different from other whites of their class in the contempt with which they treated domestic workers.

The party officially advocated equality in social relations between the races, but in practice this exposed further discrimination against black women. Insofar as there were interracial contacts in the social life of party members, black women often were ignored or snubbed by the white comrades of both sexes. The racism and sexism of American society found curious reflections in the social behavior of party members.[48]

In response to demands by Perry, Jones and others, the party launched another campaign against chauvinism that resulted in more expulsions, but still fell short of the desired goal. Subsequent reports and articles by Perry revealed that chauvinism, paternalism and discrimination continued to plague the party and hindered its organizing efforts among black people.[49] The failure lay in the fact that the party responded to racism organizationally instead of ideologically. Individuals were purged but the "virus of white chauvinism"—an ideological phenomenon—was not attacked.

The party's paternalism and its failings in the area of race relations were due to several factors. In the first place, there were no blacks in the CP when it was organized, and only a handful were drawn into the party before the great influx of the 1930's.[50] Consequently, the party's basic ideology, which was formulated in these early years, did not reflect much interest in or understanding of the black struggle. Indeed, Lenin's intervention was required in 1921 before the party undertook organizational work among black people.[51] Second, the 1928 and 1930 resolutions on race only confirmed the party's habit of grafting ideological interpretations onto the black experience, instead of using that experience as a basis for theoretical extrapolations. Third, paternalism was further reinforced in the 1930-1950 period by a sharply increased flow of middle-class intellectuals into the party, and by intra-party ethnic conflict which often redounded to the disadvantage of the black community.[52]

Thus, by the beginning of the 1950's, the Communist Party had revealed itself as a highly unstable ally of black freedom: alternately embracing and rejecting black reformers, sometimes abandoning the black struggle altogether, and then reacting with breast-beating campaigns against white chauvinism that disrupted its own organization more than it diminished prejudice among the members.[53] The party had certainly made positive contributions to the struggle for racial equality, but its erratic behavior and compulsion to dominate the black movement lost it many friends. In the end, however, it was government persecution during the McCarthyite hysteria that virtually destroyed the party, eliminating what remaining influence it had in the black community. It would be more than a decade before the party showed signs of recovering some of its former strength.

The Socialist Workers Party

Aside from the Socialists and Communists, another major tendency in American Marxist movements was represented by the Trotskyist Socialist Workers Party (SWP). In some regards the SWP appeared to have learned much from the history of other radical groups concerning black liberation, but it may have been due equally to lack of opportunity that the Trotskyists managed to avoid repeating some of the old mistakes in the period before 1950. They were a much smaller group and had only limited contact with black organizations.

Founded in 1928 as a result of an ideological split between Stalin and Trotsky,[54] the small Trotskyist splinter group struggled along for ten years before formally organizing itself into a party. During these lean years the Trotskyists functioned mainly as a propaganda and agitational group espousing Trotsky's political line and engaging in a running battle with the American CP, which was under the influence of Stalin.[55]

In the Trotskyists' ideological feuds with the Stalinist CP the question of the black struggle did not figure prominently, although the Trotskyists tended to play down the idea of black self-determination because, according to George Breitman, "they did not believe that it was the issue around which Negroes could be mobilized for struggle."[56] As was the case with the CP, it was the intervention of a Russian revolutionary, in this instance Trotsky, that would shape the basic political line on racial matters of his followers in the U.S. However, Trotsky had been purged from the Soviet power structure and consequently was under no compulsion to use the international Communist movement as a weapon for defending the Soviet Union.

In 1929 Trotsky, then in exile in Turkey, sent a letter to his handful of American followers who had by then organized themselves into the Communist League of America (CLA). In the letter he warned them not to be infected by the "aristocratic prejudices of the upper strata of the workers," telling them that instead they must "find the road to the most deprived, to the darkest strata of the proletariat, beginning with the Negro. . . who must learn to see in us his revolutionary brothers." Trotsky observed that the possibility of this latter point being realized "depends wholly on our energy and devotion to the work."[57]

It was not until 1933 that Trotsky offered more concrete ideas on black liberation and the relationship between black and white workers. In the meantime, the CLA had generally accepted the need to fight for racial equality within the context of class struggle, although the group was too small to accomplish anything significant. It still had considerable trouble with the Stalinist slogan of self-determination. Was it valid to apply this concept to the black struggle?

In February, 1933, Arne Swabeck, a member of the CLA, visited Trotsky to discuss the matter. Swabeck presented the CLA view that black people did not comprise an oppressed nationality and therefore the main slogan should be "social, political and economic equality for the Negroes," instead of the nationalist slogan of self-determination. Swabeck added that the self-determination slogan "tends to lead the Negroes away from the class basis and more in the direction of the racial basis" of struggle.[58]

Although Trotsky was not especially familiar with the situation of U.S. blacks, he felt that on the basis of "general considerations" he was competent to make some comments. He pointed out that he was certainly not opposed to the equality slogan, but he didn't believe self-determination should be jettisoned. His argument for self-determination contained three basic points. First, he said, a nation is not based on abstract definitions but develops in accordance with the "historical consciousness" of the people in question. He believed that the "suppression of the Negroes pushes them toward a political and national unity," but ultimately the question of black nationality would depend on the consciousness developed by black people themselves. Second, he said that if and when black people demand self-determination it should be actively supported by Socialists, because the struggle for national self-determination necessarily leads to class struggle. Trotsky based this latter assertion on two arguments. He observed that the demand for autonomy would place blacks in a "position hostile toward American imperialism." Implicit in this statement was the view that black nationalists thereby would be thrown into the struggle against monopoly capital. He further contended that since the black petty bourgeoisie "can get nowhere" in the struggle for self-determination, a class struggle would ensue in which the black proletariat would move to the forefront of leadership in the black community. Consequently, if Trotsky's theory was correct, the struggle for self-determination would force the black community into the class struggle on two fronts: externally (against the dominant white capitalists) and internally (against the black petty bourgeoisie).

Finally, Trotsky's third major point was that to oppose self-determination was to yield to the reactionary ideology of white workers who believe that the American state belongs solely to whites. The corollary of this line of reasoning was that white workers must lead the class struggle and that black nationalism was a divisive tactic. Trotsky contended that, on the contrary, it was possible for blacks to assume leadership of the class struggle as backward Russians had assumed leadership of the socialist struggle in Europe. "It is very possible," he said, "that the Negroes also through self-determination will proceed to the proletarian dictatorship in a couple of giant strides, ahead of the great block of white workers. They will then furnish the vanguard." On the basis of this reasoning he concluded that Socialists should struggle "not against the supposed national prepossessions of the Negroes but against the colossal prejudices of the white workers."[59]

Perhaps realizing that his approach to the race question might have confounded his American followers, Trotsky suggested that they undertake "serious discussion" of the matter in an internal bulletin.

Such a "serious discussion" was postponed, however, by Trotskyist efforts in the mid-1930's to penetrate the Socialist Party, an action that disrupted and contributed to the further weakening of the SP.[60] In 1938 the expelled Trotskyist faction officially constituted itself as the Socialist Workers Party, and in April, 1939, a delegation was dispatched to Mexico to confer again with Trotsky concerning the party's attitude toward black people.

Essentially, Trotsky repeated the main points of his 1933 argument for socialist support of the right of black self-determination. However, having reviewed the experience of the Communist Party, Trotsky added that the CP's "attitude of making an imperative slogan" of self-determination was false, and contributed to the idea that white socialists were advocating segregation. "I do not propose for the party to advocate, I do not propose to inject, but only to proclaim our obligation to support the struggle for self-determination if the Negroes themselves want it," Trotsky said.[61]

As for organizational tactics, SWP delegates proposed, and Trotsky accepted, the idea of establishing a mass organization to fight for black equality. The question of whether the proposed organization would be a front group, similar to CP organizations, was discussed but left unresolved. However, Trotsky himself took the position that the SWP must "take the initiative" in "awakening the Negro masses." Running through these discussions was the idea that an elite cadre must lead the backward masses along the proper socialist course, as the Trotskyists had tried to do in the SP.[62]

Following these discussions, the SWP at its July, 1939 convention passed resolutions supporting the right of black self-determination and calling upon its black members to "take the initiative and collaborate with other militant Negroes in the formation of a Negro mass organization devoted to the struggle for Negro rights." However, the resolution specifically denied that the proposed group would be a front controlled by the SWP. Instead, the resolution stated that the proposed organization would elaborate its own program with the "participation" of black SWP members.[63]

World War II and internal dissension within the party prevented the SWP from implementing its organizational plan. Instead, the SWP was limited to a secondary role, supporting the March on Washington movement and other independent black struggles.[64] Despite its small size and restricted influence, the SWP did succeed in recruiting black members, so much so that by 1946, according to SWP writers, the party's membership was one-fifth black.[65] Even earlier the SWP had recruited the noted black historian C.L.R. James, who did much to shape the party's ideology and its understanding of the independent black movement. James, however, left the party later to become involved in the Pan-African and African nationalist movements.

The SWP again turned to the question of black liberation during its 1948 and 1950 conventions. In a resolution, the SWP attacked the "revisionist" argument that "the Negro movement is in essence helpless and useless unless directly led by the organized labor movement or the Marxist party," and suggested that this argument led to "an underestimation of the revolutionary tendencies of the Negro movement." The SWP contended instead that the logic and history of the independent black movement revealed that "at critical periods in this country's history, the Negroes have allied themselves with the revolutionary forces," both as followers and leaders. Undoubtedly, this analysis reflected the influence of C.L.R. James. Yet the SWP could not relinquish its own claims to leadership and the resolution concluded by urging the unification of the labor and black struggles under the guidance of "the revolutionary party."[66]

All in all, in the decades before 1950 the influence of the SWP was much more circumscribed than either the Socialist Party or the Communist Party. With a few exceptions, such as the Minneapolis truck-drivers strikes of 1934, the Trotskyists exercised relatively little influence in the labor movement; nor did they have much impact on the independent black movement. However, beginning in the 1960's the SWP's favorable attitude toward nationalism enabled it to align itself with Malcolm X and certain elements of the black nationalist movement. These actions have precipitated a heated and continuing debate as to whether the SWP has been "principled" or "opportunistic" in its relations with black nationalists.[67]

Socialism, Black Nationalism and Pan-Africanism

Before the beginning of the twentieth century, few black leaders espoused socialism. A notable exception was Peter H. Clark, who in 1877 joined the Workingmen's Party and became a vocal advocate of democratic socialism. Clark is regarded by historian Herbert G. Gutman as probably the first black socialist in the U.S.[68]

Black militancy in the nineteenth century was usually couched in racial terms, although it was not unknown for racial radicalism to spill over into economic radicalism. More than one black leader noted that emancipation had simply meant exchanging one form of servitude for another, and that there was an economic basis for unity between black and white workers.[69] The racism of organized white labor, however, largely precluded formation of a viable alliance.

After the turn of the century, a whole generation of young black leaders seriously examined socialist thought, and several of them became active proponents of socialism. Better known among them were such figures as W.E.B. Du Bois, Cyril V. Briggs, Chandler Owen and A. Philip Randolph. Despite their espousal of socialism, however, none of these leaders established a black socialist party, preferring instead to work with white socialists or to build independent black organizations that were only incidentally, if at all, concerned with socialism. Many black radicals at the beginning of the new century were not hostile to classic socialist ideology, even with its insistent blindness to the meaning of racism. Yet their own daily experiences underscored the shallowness of this ideology and compelled them, to a greater or lesser extent, to search for a synthesis between nationalism and socialism.

As early as 1904 Du Bois had become convinced that economic discrimination was the root of racial oppression, and in succeeding years he wrote favorably of socialism.[70] Always an internationalist, Du Bois believed that the black struggle might somehow be linked to the worldwide socialist movement. He flirted briefly with the Socialist Party, became a partisan of the Russian Revolution and a staunch advocate of labor solidarity. However, the unrelenting racism of organized labor coupled with constant Communist Party attacks on him and the NAACP left Du Bois frustrated and embittered.[71] He turned his energies instead to organizing a Pan-African movement, which for many years did not concern itself in the least with socialism.

Cyril Briggs was a West Indian who came to the U.S. as a youth in 1905. An early advocate of black self-determination, he established a monthly magazine, *The Crusader,* in 1918. The magazine eventually reached a circulation of 36,000.[72] In 1919 Briggs helped organize the African Blood Brotherhood (ABB), a revolutionary nationalist group. The ABB proposed a "worldwide federation" of black organizations and the creation of a "great Pan-African army" that would drive the imperialist powers out of Africa. On the domestic front the ABB called for armed self-defense of black communities against white mobs, black labor organization and rapprochement with "class-conscious revolutionary white workers." At its height, the ABB had between three and five thousand members, most of whom were ex-servicemen.[73]

Briggs later reported that his interest in socialism was "derived from the enlightened attitude of the Russian Bolsheviks toward national minorities."[74] National liberation was his greatest concern, over and above purely economic struggles. Nevertheless, Briggs believed that the "salvation of all Negroes (as well as other oppressed people)" depended upon establishing a "Universal Socialist Co-operative commonwealth."[75]

Briggs' deep interest in nationalism and Pan-Africanism led him to attempt to forge an alliance between the ABB and Garvey's Universal Negro Improvement Association (UNIA). Mutual suspicions between the two groups, however, forestalled any alliance. Theodore Vincent, a student of the Garvey movement, believes that had the proposed alliance been culminated it would have significantly affected the development of Garveyism by combining a mass nationalist base with revolutionary militancy.[76]

Rebuffed by the UNIA, the ABB's leadership drifted into the Communist Party, and the prospects for an independent black socialist organization declined as the group disintegrated.

Like Briggs, Owen and Randolph initially had no organized black base, only *The Messenger*. They used the magazine to promote labor unionism and socialism among blacks. According to Spero and Harris, *The Messenger* contended that "in an individualistic economic system, competition for jobs and the profitableness of race prejudice to the capitalist class were incentives to race conflict. Therefore the removal of the motive for creating racial strife was conditioned upon the socialization of industry and the nationalization of land, in short, upon the elimination of economic individualism and competition through social revolution."[77] They soon began organizing black workers in New York and later affiliated themselves with the National Brotherhood Workers of America, a short-lived black labor federation.

Owen and Randolph also supported the Socialist Party with Randolph himself running on the socialist ticket in New York in 1920 and 1921. By the late 1920's, however, Owen had become disillusioned with socialism and denounced all forms of radicalism. Randolph by this time was busy organizing the Pullman porters and had retreated from some of his earlier radical positions, although he never turned his back on the Socialist Party.

Thus, in the first quarter of the twentieth century, a number of militant blacks were torn between socialism and nationalism. Eventually, each of these black activists opted for one position or the other, or attempted an uneasy compromise, but none were able to effect a synthesis of the two positions.

The contending claims of nationalism and communism were also apparent in the Communist Party and were vividly revealed in the career of Richard Wright. Wright was never able to choose fully one or the other, nor could he reconcile the two ideologies. In the end he was alienated from both, spending the latter part of his life in self-imposed exile in Europe where he flirted with existentialism. Wright certainly tried to bridge the gap between black cultural nationalism and the Communist Party, but his effort was in vain. The party distrusted all "petty bourgeois" nationalists whom it said substituted the false notion of race conflict for the true reality of class conflict. Conversely, nationalists were irritated when the party insisted that race was really of secondary importance: such a view made little sense given the concrete reality of social conditions in the United States. Wright, the son of a Mississippi tenant farmer, had a deep appreciation of the cultural roots of black nationalism, which he traced to the folk traditions and independent social institutions of black people in the South.[78] He recognized, however, that nationalism had both progressive and reactionary components: it could provide the individual building blocks for international unity among oppressed peoples or it could degenerate into a rigid and ultimately self-defeating hatred of the white race.[79]

Indeed, as Wright became more knowledgeable of the world he was fascinated to discover that oppressed people reacted in similar ways to oppression.[80] He came to see the reactive element of nationalism in a wider perspective. At the same time, his early contact with the Communist Party in Chicago left him awed at the prospect of the world's dispossessed and despised masses uniting to end their oppression.[81]

Wright interpreted these new insights as a direct challenge to his literary talent. "I wanted to reveal the vast physical and spiritual ravages of Negro life," he later wrote, "the profundity latent in these rejected people, the dramas as old as man and the sun and the mountains and the seas that were taking place in the poverty of black America."[82] For Wright this meant that the black writer must attempt to describe what he sees, but from the perspective of the new social possibilities created by communism.

This he tried to do in his famous novel, *Native Son*. The hero of the novel, Bigger Thomas, is presented as a neurotic personification of black oppression. In him are seen the psychological results of lack of self-determination. He is caught between two worlds— denied the possibility of participating in the dominant culture, and unable to conceive of creating a viable and strong culture among his own people. His response takes the form of reactionary nationalism. He fears and hates the whites, but he cannot reach out to blacks because of his own self-hatred. He achieves a sense of freedom only after accidently killing a white woman, but this new-found sensation dissipates long before he is captured. It remains for his lawyer, a white Communist, to explain the significance of the social role into which Bigger was forced by oppression. But this is the least convincing portion of the novel. The reader is left with the impression that while Wright may agree intellectually with the lawyer's social analysis, he cannot make this an organic part of his artistic vision. Nationalism and communism meet in the pages of this book, but they do not interact, and they part almost total strangers.

Wright's novel was received with mixed feelings in Communist circles. Samuel Sillen, who initially gave the book a rave review in *New Masses*, soon began backtracking as party leaders questioned its value.[83] Was Bigger Thomas a valid symbol of the Negro people? Why were there no black characters in the book who were identified with the labor movement? Why was the Communist lawyer's speech so overdrawn and implausible? Underlying these questions was an anxious concern that Bigger Thomas was far from being an example of the black proletarian engaged in heroic struggle; in fact, he was no hero at all but an anti-hero. He did not overcome circumstances; he was overcome by them. Worse still, although the white Communists in the book were portrayed as selfless individuals, Wright nonetheless made it clear that it was partly the paternalism of the Communists that precipitated Bigger's crime. This implication was flatly rejected by Communist critics who could not conceive of a Communist character acting other than as a Communist *ought* to act.

Richard Wright's years in the Communist Party were marked by tension, mistrust and frequent strife. A strong individualist, he was unable to accept party discipline or adjust easily to the Communists' shifting political line. The party's apparent desertion of the black cause during World War II combined with party members' criticism of *Native Son* moved Wright to break with the party in the early 1940's.[84]

Wright's departure from the party was duly noted and critiqued by Samuel Sillen who pointed out, with appropriate quotes from Earl Browder, the obvious flaws in Wright's charge that the party had regressed on the question of black rights.[85] Ironically, several years later, after more political twists, the party's leadership in essence confirmed the truth of Wright's accusation.[86]

As has been suggested, a long-standing tension has existed between socialists (especially Communists), on the one hand, and black nationalists (including Pan-Africanists), on the other. This may seem strange if one recalls Lenin's and Stalin's many articles on the national question and self-determination. It might have been expected that Communists would favor black nationalism and its logical extension, Pan-Africanism. Such has not been the case for several reasons. In the first place, the political demands placed by the Soviet Union on the international Communist movement have changed frequently depending on how it was thought the survival of the Soviet Union could best be assured. In periods of rapprochement with the West the Communist movement abandoned the national liberation movements in the colonies and played down the grievances of oppressed national minorities in order not to embarrass new-found imperialist friends. In addition, the Communist movement opposed nationalism and Pan-Africanism because these apparently stressed racial/national strategies at the expense of the class struggle. Finally, Communists (and other Socialists) feared that nationalist movements might be captured by petty bourgeois intellectuals, politicians and businessmen who would be pro-capitalist in their sentiments. In the U.S. this fear was translated into active and vociferous opposition to all independent black nationalist groups, while at the same time the CP was suspicious of any nationalist manifestations within its own ranks.[87] The upshot was a rigid and mutually debilitating opposition between socialism and nationalism that has yet to be fully resolved.

A better understanding of this dispute can be obtained from a brief review of the history of Pan-Africanism. W.E.B. Du Bois is often called the father of Pan-Africanism, but this is an oversimplification. Du Bois was an important figure at the first Pan-African conference held in London in 1900, but the conference was actually organized by Henry Sylvester Williams, a West Indian barrister.[88] Even earlier, Edward Blyden, a West Indian who had settled in New York, emigrated to Liberia in 1850 where he became a leading politician and early theorist of the concept of an "African personality." Blyden played an important part in laying the basis for the concept of Negritude and contemporary forms of black cultural nationalism. He traveled back and forth between the U.S. and Africa eleven times on speaking tours, and he was one of the first people to voice the idea of "Africa for the Africans."[89] This idea subsequently became an integral part of Pan-Africanist thinking, and it contributed significantly to the development of African nationalism. Martin R. Delaney was another early exponent of African nationalism.

Thus, the roots of African nationalism can be traced partly to alienated black intellectuals in the West. In their search for an identity that had been shorn from them during slavery, these children of Africa forged a black cultural/racial consciousness that, after more than half a century, would contribute to the emergence of national consciousness in Africa.

Throughout the first half of the twentieth century, a host of American and West Indian blacks expressed a deep interest in Africa. These included Du Bois, Marcus Garvey and George Padmore, who were the chief catalysts and organizers of the Pan-African movement; and also a number of black scholars and creative writers who gave shape to the cultural aspects of Pan-Africanism. All of these men were responding to a common challenge—the challenge implicit in the racist statement that Africans, unlike other nationalities, had made no collective contribution to human history. This was a commonly held belief at the time among white intellectuals and the white population in general. It was part of the general racist justification for degrading and exploiting black people. Two responses to this challenge were possible. One was to dig up the African past and expose the cultural and artistic achievements of African people. This was the course chosen, for example, by Carter Woodson, a black historian who proposed the idea of Negro History Week. The other response involved organizational and political activity aimed at laying the basis for African nationalism and some form of contemporary collective achievement.[90] It was the intermingling of these two responses that defined the first phases of the Pan-Africanist movement.

The organizational response culminated in a series of Pan-African congresses, the first held in 1900. Du Bois was largely responsible for organizing the later congresses in 1919, 1921, 1923, 1927, and 1945. The early Pan-African congresses were held in the capital cities of the imperialist powers, and essentially they resulted in appeals to the imperialist governments for better treatment of the subject African peoples. They called for the recognition of the dignity and humanity of the black race, a demand which corresponded with the cultural concepts of Negritude and African personality which were evolving during this same period. Politically, the early Pan-African congress did not demand independence but only called for giving the Africans a voice in the colonial governments.[91] (It was not until the 1945 conference that the movement began to address itself to colonial subjects as well as the colonial powers, and to demand political independence for the African colonies.)

The early congresses equivocated on the question of imperialism, with some delegates favoring a critical approach while others desired accommodation to the status quo. Du Bois himself was far from clear on the matter at that time. For example, he attacked Marcus Garvey because he said Garvey alienated the British imperialists by his tactlessness, and Du Bois believed the help of Great Britain was required in any international trade arrangements. Garvey responded by ridiculing the leaders of the Pan-African congress because they invited white representatives of the imperialist powers to attend their meetings.[92]

Garvey is important to Pan-Africanism because his organization had as one of its aims the liberation of Africa. He proposed that American blacks return to Africa both to escape racial oppression in this country and to fight for African independence. He succeeded in building one of the largest mass movements this country has ever seen, a movement that enjoyed the active support of millions of black people.

The bitter clashes between Garvey and Du Bois and between Garvey and the Communist Party throw much light on the early development of Pan-Africanism. Du Bois assailed Garvey for his "dictatorial" and anti-democratic tendencies. Garvey spoke of founding a democratic African republic, but his critics charged that he was really a demagogic empire builder. Garvey did, however, build a nationalist movement based on the masses of black people, something Du Bois never accomplished. In fact, Du Bois was very much an elitist. He believed that a black aristocracy—a Talented Tenth—would have to undertake the task of liberating the ignorant black masses. He did not have the concept of leadership arising out of the masses of people engaged in struggle. Garvey in turn attacked Du Bois for snubbing the masses and believing in what Garvey called a "bastard aristocracy."[93]

Garvey sharply criticized the white labor movement because of its well-known racism. But he went further than that. He dismissed the idea of class struggle by declaring that "the fundamental issue of life is the appeal of race to race, of clan to clan, the appeal of tribe to tribe. . . ."[94] For him race conflict was more important to worry about than class conflict. Garvey took this line of thought to its logical conclusion when he argued that the "only convenient friend" of the black workers is the white capitalist because he "is willing and glad to use Negro labor wherever possible on a scale 'reasonably' below the standard white union wage." Garvey urged black workers to keep the goodwill of the white capitalists by keeping their wages lower than white workers. Needless to say, such statements were sharply attacked by black labor leaders such as A. Philip Randolph.[95]

Nevertheless, Garvey's sentiments combined with Du Bois' elitism to produce an early tendency within Pan-Africanism to view oppression primarily in terms of race and to discount the notion of class struggle. Indeed, Pan-Africanism initially was chiefly a racial ideology stressing independent activity by black American and West Indian intellectuals aimed at (1) establishing cultural and trade relations with Africa, (2) opposing racial discrimination on an international basis, (3) enabling blacks in the diaspora to return to Africa to join in—and possibly lead—the nation-building process, and (4) uniting people of African descent throughout the world. This initial tendency to view problems purely in terms of race conflict and to discount class conflict combined with the elitism of the Pan-African congress organized by Du Bois caused many Socialists (including black Socialists) to regard the movement with suspicion.

But there were additional reasons for hostility between Socialists and Pan-Africanists. Garvey, for example, was strongly anti-Communist. He believed that white Communists and Socialists were just as racist as white workers. The history of the socialist movements of that time provided ample evidence to support Garvey's claim. But again Garvey went to the opposite political extreme. In 1937 after Italy had overrun Ethiopia, Garvey boasted that he had been the first prophet of fascism. "We were the first Fascists," he told a friend. "We had disciplined men, women, and children in training for the liberation of Africa. The black masses saw that in this extreme nationalism lay their only hope and readily supported it. Mussolini copied Fascism from me."[96]

The Communist Party was fascinated by Garvey's mass appeal and the spontaneous upsurge of black unrest which his movement represented. Futile attempts were made by the party to gain control of Garvey's organization or to win Garvey over to the Communist side.[97] All of these efforts ended in failure, and finally the *Daily Worker* charged Garvey with collaborating with the Ku Klux Klan[98] and of building up a "petty bourgeois circle of 'leaders' with a vested interest in subduing the class struggle in America."[99] The party dismissed Garveyism as nothing more than a black version of Zionism.

C.L.R. James has tried to sum up Garvey's impact from the perspective of a Pan-Africanist and Socialist:

> Despite his militancy. . . Garvey was confused. He attacked imperialism, but he was ready to propound the doctrine that the Negro must be loyal to all flags under which he lives. He viciously attacked Communism and advised the Negro workers against linking up with white workers in industrial struggles. He negotiated with the Ku Klux Klan for the repatriation of Negroes to Liberia. . . . He indulged in some unsound business schemes. . . . One thing Garvey did do. He made the American Negro conscious of his African origin and created for the first time a feeling of international solidarity among Africans and people of African descent. In so far as this is directed against oppression it is a progressive step.[100]

The sixth Pan-African Congress held in 1945 marked the beginning of a second period in the Pan-African movement. The movement began to concern itself more with speaking to the colonial subjects than to the imperialist powers. For the first time African trade unionists as well as intellectuals attended the meeting, and there was evidence of growing ideological differences between the African workers and the African intellectuals and middle classes.[101] During this new period, the Pan-African movement took on a more political tone and started demanding formal independence for the African colonies.[102] Following this meeting, the scene of Pan-Africanist activity began shifting from Europe to the organizational stage in Africa, and nationalist leaders such as Kwame Nkrumah and Jomo Kenyatta made their appearance.

It was also during this period that George Padmore emerged as a leading ideologist of the Pan-African movement. Padmore was born in Trinidad, attended school in the U.S., and then traveled to Europe where he became active in the Communist International. For several years Padmore was the Communist International's expert on African and Afro-American affairs. However, in the 1930's Padmore left the Communist movement because, in his view, the new "people's front" diplomatic policy of the Soviet government caused it "to put a brake upon the anti-imperialist work of [the Communist International] and thereby sacrifice the young national liberation movements in Asia and Africa. This I considered to be a betrayal of the fundamental interest of my people."[103] The Communist International accused Padmore of being a petty bourgeois nationalist and of working for black unity on race rather than class lines. The hostility was mutual. Padmore had nothing but contempt for the Communists whom he felt were betraying the national liberation movements of nonwhite peoples. Nevertheless, in his public writings he continued to support the Russian Revolution, and he continued to regard himself as a Marxist.[104] For a number of years he organized and worked in various anti-colonialist and reform groups, and he gradually became involved in the Pan-African movement. It was in this movement that Padmore met Nkrumah in London. The two men became political allies, and Padmore eventually became a chief advisor to Nkrumah, a position that gave him great influence over the developing ideology of Pan-Africanism.

With the independence of Ghana in 1957, Pan-Africanism achieved a base of operation within Africa. The first All-African

Peoples Conference was held in Accra in 1958. Nkrumah spoke at the conference and paid homage to both Du Bois and Garvey as pioneers, but he made it clear that hence forward Pan-Africanism would have a continental focus and the leaders would be Africans. Meanwhile, the ideology of Pan-Africanism had been taking clearer shape. The Pan-Africanism of that period favored a federation of African states, was nonviolent, advocated "communal" or "African socialism," and espoused nonalignment in the Cold War. Pan-Africanism sought a neutral position vis-à-vis the imperialist powers (although anti-imperialist rhetoric was not lacking), and there was a pronounced hostility toward international communism, even though it favored some form of socialism.[105] This latter attitude probably reflected the views of Padmore.

But here a distinction is necessary. Padmore is sometimes pictured as a simple anti-Socialist or anti-Communist, but according to his recently published biography he was not so much anti-Communist as he was anti-Stalinist.[106] He believed that the Stalinist parties—firmly bound to Soviet foreign policy—were not to be trusted because of their resulting manipulative practices and hostility toward national liberation movements. Thus, by the late 1950's, Pan-Africanism had moved beyond the out-and-out anti-communism of Marcus Garvey to a more sophisticated pro-socialist but anti-Stalinist position.

But still there were problems, and these became evident in the decade of the 1960's. In the first place, the course of history soon proved that it was impossible to maintain a neutral position in the face of Western imperialism. The murder of Lumumba, the ouster of Nkrumah in 1966 and the overthrow of various other African governments established this brutal fact beyond the shadow of a doubt. It also became clear that the class struggle could not be ignored within Africa. Frantz Fanon was among the first to point this out in his book, *Wretched of the Earth,* published in 1963. Fanon argued that opportunist and bourgeois elements were conspiring to sabotage the African revolution. Nkrumah discovered this fact for himself when the military, civil service, business and professional elites within Ghana collaborated with the imperialists in ousting him from power. Class struggle, based on the masses of workers and peasants, had now become an obvious imperative in Africa. Further, it became evident that bureaucratic forms of socialism that do not involve the popular masses in active, on-going struggle were in the long run self-defeating. This was certainly the lesson of Ghana and Algeria. Elitism and bureaucracy were exposed as, in fact, the enemies of socialism.

Thus, the objective situation forced some Pan-Africanist thinking into a third stage of development that emphasizes active anti-imperialism, stresses the necessity for class struggle as well as the struggle for national liberation, and foresees the need for a form of socialism based on mass participation. The recent writings of Nkrumah, who was the leading contemporary spokesman of Pan-Africanism, provide ample evidence of this ideological development.[107] Indeed, Nkrumah concluded that the African revolution may be a prelude to a worldwide socialist revolution.

Nkrumah's thinking incidentally provides a useful yardstick for examining the views of his American followers. For example, a reader of Stokely Carmichael's recent book, *Stokely Speaks: Black Power to Pan Africanism,* is left with the impression that Carmichael's political thinking has matured, and that he is beginning to resolve some of the contradictions and misconceptions of his past positions.[108] Carmichael was living in Guinea where he reports he studied under Nkrumah. However, those familiar with the writings of his mentor will realize that, although Carmichael has progressed, he appears confused as to his conception of socialism. At one point in the book he speaks of scientific socialism, but elsewhere he refers to a socialism "which has its roots in [African] communalism."[109] This latter is the definition of "African socialism," which Nkrumah has denounced as a myth which is "used to deny the class struggle, and to obscure genuine socialist commitment."[110] Again, Carmichael continued to advocate a vague, apolitical unity for blacks in the U.S. This at a time when Nkrumah was arguing that unity can be achieved only through struggle and must be based on commitment to a revolutionary program. Finally, Carmichael, in his American speaking tour in 1971, continued to uphold cultural nationalism.

Again it was Nkrumah who wrote that Negritude, the prototype of contemporary cultural nationalism, was "irrational, racist and non-revolutionary."[111]

Thus, among its more advanced spokesmen, Pan-Africanist thought was manifesting a new revolutionary content. What began primarily as a racial ideology was compelled by the rise of neo-colonialism in Africa to view matters from the standpoint of a worldwide class struggle against imperialism. This is the kind of thinking that is evident, for example, among the leaders of the advancing liberation struggles in southern Africa.

In retrospect it becomes apparent that the Communists were correct to criticize bourgeois tendencies in the Pan-African movement. However, these criticisms were divorced from an analysis of the material conditions of blacks in the U.S. and Africa and how these conditions would affect the developmental dynamics of Pan-Africanism. Hence, the criticisms were reduced to derogatory labeling and outright attacks that played no useful part in the development of revolutionary Pan-African solidarity and anti-imperialist consciousness.

As for the charges of manipulation leveled by Padmore and others, this problem has been resolved by the more advanced liberation struggles in Africa without falling into the trap of simple-minded anti-communism. By developing truly independent, mass-based liberation organizations, African freedom fighters have taken charge of their own destiny and, at the same time, are able to have beneficial relations with the socialist nations and Communist parties on the basis of equality and mutual respect.

Organizational independence and political struggle based on clear analysis of the problems in their own countries were the keys to forging a unity of national and socialist consciousness in the advanced African liberation struggles. Forging the unity of racial and socialist consciousness is a task still confronting the revolutionary movements in the United States.

CHAPTER VIII:

Capitalism, Racism and Reform

The preceding chapters have examined the ways in which racism has affected the ideologies and practices of six major American social reform movements. While both a wide variety and a fairly lengthy time span are represented by these six, still two basic and important factors immediately stand out when these case histories are reviewed. In the first place, it is apparent that virtually all of these movements (with certain limited exceptions) have either advocated, capitulated before, or otherwise failed to oppose racism at one or more critical junctures in their history. These predominantly white reform movements thereby aligned themselves with the racial thinking of the dominant society, even when the reforms they sought to institute appeared to demand forthright opposition to racism. Instead of opposition, the reformers all too often developed paternalistic attitudes that merely confirmed, rather than challenged, the prevailing racial ideology of white society. Secondly, but equally striking, constant efforts were made by black reformers to get their white co-workers to reject and oppose racism, both within the reform movements themselves and throughout society in general. In each of the six movements blacks were actively involved, although the degree and success of their involvement varied considerably. In each case, the reformers struggled to have blacks included both as supporters and beneficiaries of reformism, since black people in fact needed the proposed reforms as much as whites.

The movements covered in this study include practically all social, ideological and organizational groupings found in white society. The whole span of social classes is represented, from poor and working-class whites through middle- and upper-class whites. Also included as distinct variables are urban-rural, male-female and regional divisions; yet, as with class, none of these variables can be identified as clear correlates of antiracist thinking. Our case histories include movements with no significant ideology beyond a few demands, as well as some with elaborate and fully articulated doctrines. While it is suggested that reform movements with a broad or universal approach to social change, such as the Garrisonian abolitionists, are more amenable to antiracist views than movements which propound a narrow or single-issue approach—such as the female suffragists at the turn of the century—still no hard and fast distinction between the two is warranted, as demonstrated by the early history of the Socialist Party, which had a broad ideology but little positive interest in blacks. Similarly, it is not certain that we can make a sharp distinction in racial attitudes between movements that were loosely organized versus those that were tightly and hierarchically organized; although it does seem that movements that aim to build a broad organizational base are more friendly toward nonwhites than those based on exclusionist principles, as illustrated by the history of the labor movement. Lastly, if we compare those reformers who sought to function primarily as agitators with those who grasped for conventional political power as the road to social change, we again find it impossible to draw a firm line of demarcation between the two. Certainly, politically oriented Populists and Progressives were opportunistic in espousing white supremacy, but was this fundamentally different from the manner in which Communist agitators sought first to exploit and then later abandoned the black cause? No rule of thumb is revealed for predicting the relative incidence of opportunism and adherence to principle in the racial practices of white reformers. Indeed, this entire discussion has raised serious doubts as to the suitability of merely a simple comparative method in attempting to understand the impact of racism on social reform movements. Some other analytic framework is needed.

Similar problems confront us when we attempt to compare the attitudes and practices of blacks who were active in the six social reform movements. Black reformers disagreed among themselves over how best to counter the racism of their white fellow workers. Some advocated separate organizations, while others insisted that individual blacks must merge with white reform groups. However, it is significant that even among the latter we consistently find efforts to maintain an independent black press, as was the case, for instance, with Douglass in relation to white abolitionists, Du Bois in relation to white progressives, and Randolph in relation to white Socialists. The tactical dispute among black reformers was reflective of the fact that while both black and white reformers operated in the ideological realm, the latter often had potential access to the levers of real power, which was almost never true of the blacks. Hence, black reformers were compelled to function solely in the ideological sphere, and the question became whether maximum ideological influence could be exerted organizationally or individually. A related problem confronting black reformers—who tended to be middle class—was the question of their relationship to the black community as a whole. The reformers were articulate but they were also always a minority of the total black community; hence, they could be co-opted, isolated or repressed by whites with relative ease. Obviously problems such as these are complex and require something more than simple comparisons.

In American reform movements, we note a continuous clash between black and white reformers over the question of race. Both groups were equally determined to do what they believed was best, but both were also clearly unbalanced in terms of actual or potential power. Black reformers—even when organized independently—almost always operated from a position of relative weakness, yet the vigor of their assault indicated a firm and deep commitment to attack racism with whatever tools were at hand. On the other hand, the hesitant and shifting attitudes of most white reformers revealed the extent of their own allegiance to racism and, paradoxically, also showed that racism, although always present, was not a monolithic and unchanging ideology. For example, the attitudes of militant abolitionists, social welfare progressives and radical CIO organizers toward the matter of black economic integration suggest that these reformers were responding to or reflecting differing racial ideologies. Among abolitionists the question of black economic integration was hardly discussed before the outbreak of the Civil War. Social welfare progressives aided black migrants in squeezing into the lowest levels of the industrial economy, while the CIO and other labor radicals advocated that blacks be fully integrated into all levels of the work force. The differences pointed up here were not incidental; they were barometers of the racial atmosphere of the times.

To understand the relationship between black and white reformers and the ideological development of the reform movements themselves it is necessary to extend our analysis beyond the internal dynamics of these movements. At this juncture a general historical analysis of racism, brief though it must be, is more useful for our purposes than further microanalysis of social reformism. Such an analysis will enable us to locate the ideologies and practices of social reform movements in broader perspective.

In the span of American history covered by this study—ranging from the beginning of the nineteenth century through the middle of the twentieth—it is possible to isolate three broad periods in the development of racial ideologies: the simple biological racism associated with slavery, the more sophisticated, but no less oppresive, racism which accompanied the rise of monopoly capital and imperialism, and finally the racial attitudes which have increasingly come to the fore since World War I. As with all attempts at historical periodization, no sharp and fast boundaries can be drawn between these three, nor should we be surprised if we find occasional proponents of one racial ideology voicing their opinions in a period that we have characterized by another racial ideology. Our task here is to attempt to define that elusive quality which historians have termed the spirit of an age, not simply to inventory all ideas expressed during a given year or decade. Some overlap and interweaving of specific themes from one period to the next, while making our task more difficult, is to be normally expected.

We should also observe that racism is not a phenomenon limited to the United States; indeed, no adequate understanding of racial ideology can be obtained without placing its genesis and development in an international context. Hence, before proceeding to discuss the three periods it is first necessary to set the international stage on which the drama of racism was to be played.

Capitalism and Colonialism

Modern racism originated with European colonial expansion. While occasional expressions of racial sentiments are recorded in the history of some ancient societies, it is nonetheless clear that the systematization of racist ideologies did not occur before the advent of the modern epoch of world history, beginning about 500 years ago.[1] Racism did not emerge as a full-blown theory; it developed gradually as Europeans came in contact with and attempted to subjugate other peoples of the world. Its full articulation had to await the beginning of the attack on slavery, for capitalist slavery represented the institutional basis of the most degrading forms of racism, as became evident in the defenses mustered by apologists for the slave system.

It should be observed that racism was not a quality inherent in white Europeans, nor is it somehow an innate feature of human nature. If the former were so, then we would expect the historical record to reveal continuous indications of European pretensions to superiority. In fact, Europeans evidenced a kind of inferiority complex in their initial contacts with Eastern cultures. Only a few steps removed from barbarism, they hardly felt equal to the civilized peoples they encountered. As for the second assertion, it certainly appears that ethnocentrism is generally distributed among human cultures, but ethnocentrism refers only to a socially shared feeling of in-group solidarity. It is not necessarily a racial phenomenon, and it certainly does not imply the development of institutional and ideological forms of oppression based on race. At worst, ethnocentrism is a form of inward-looking narrow-mindedness; whereas racism involves an outward-facing hierarchical ordering of human beings for purposes of racial oppression. The former may or may not be a universal facet of human nature, but the latter is definitely socially conditioned. The two should not be confused.

Similarly it is important to recognize that while it was the rise of commercial capitalism in western Europe and the subsequent spread of capitalist colonialism to virtually all parts of the world that gave shape to the modern historical epoch, this process need not be attributed to any supposed racial or cultural "superiority" of Europeans. Paul A. Baran has argued cogently that three basic conditions were prerequisite for capitalist development: (1) a steady increase in agricultural output accompanied by massive displacements of the traditional peasant population, thereby creating a potential industrial labor force; (2) society-wide propagation of a division of labor resulting in the emergence of a class of artisans and traders (incipient bourgeoisie), accompanied by the growth of towns as economic centers; and (3) massive accumulation of capital in the hands of the developing merchant class. It was the convergence of these historically conditioned processes that precipitated capitalist development. The first two processes were maturing in many parts of the world during the pre-capitalist era, but it was the spectacular development of the third process in Europe that marked all subsequent history. We may say that the first two conditions were *necessary* but by themselves they were *not sufficient,* since without massive capital accumulations large-scale capitalist manufacture for the market could not have been organized.

Mercantile capitalist accumulations were rapidly acquired in western Europe because (1) the geographical location of many European countries gave them the opportunity to develop maritime and river navigation and trade at an early date, and (2) such trade was stimulated paradoxically by Europe's relative lack of economic development and paucity of valued natural resources.[2] Thus, Europe's easy access to potential river trade routes and natural seaports, combined with its location near a crossroads of trade routes between more economically developed civilizations and countries more richly endowed with natural resources, stimulated an explosive advance of trade and capitalist accumulation by European merchants. Moreover, the requirements of long-range navigation and trade fostered rapid development of scientific knowledge and a weapons technology that enabled Europe to begin the colonial plunder and subjugation of other areas.

Oliver C. Cox has pointed out that colonialism and plunder were the logical consequences of the expansionism of the developing capitalist system.[3] Indeed, the first areas to be plundered were not Africa or Asia but the rural hinterlands of Europe itself. The growing capitalist cities became centers of an early colonial empire in Europe. However, as capitalist culture spread over Europe the expanding system launched the "age of exploration," and the focus of the colonial quest shifted to other parts of the world.

Wherever it penetrated, capitalism brought about basic changes in social life. At the most fundamental level it completely altered the process of production. Capitalism "socialized" the production process by (1) replacing the individual producer of pre-capitalist societies with an organized social work force, and (2) replacing individual tools with social tools (e.g., plantations, machinery, factories, etc.). This revolutionary reorganization of production brought about a tremendous increase in the productive powers of human societies. It liberated untapped potentials of human organization. At the same time, however, since capitalist production was for sale on the market instead of for immediate use, the developing capitalist classes assured their control over this production by imposing the concept of capitalist private property. This made possible individual ownership of a process that was inherently social in nature. This was the fundamental contradiction of capitalism, and to it are traceable a wide range of conflicts (including racial antagonism). The alienation of the European worker from the land and the means of production via capitalist property relations, combined with the money-wage system, made the capitalist class—always a small minority—the dominant class in the political economy of capitalism. The worker, compelled to sell his labor power in order to live, was correspondingly reduced to a mere cog in the capitalist social order. Hence, the fundamental contradiction of capitalism expressed itself in terms of a class conflict between workers and capitalists.

However, it is imperative to realize that the class conflict in the European heartland of capitalism took place in the larger context of colonialism and imperialism. Internationally the emergence of commercial capitalism resulted in the concentration of capital in a small part of the world—western Europe, and later North America. The colonial plunder of the non-European world provided a global base for fantastic accumulations of capital in Europe. In turn, these accumulations fostered industrial and cultural development. The development of the steam engine, much heavy industry, ship-building and many modern financial institutions, for example, were all underwritten directly or indirectly by the colonial slave trade and other forms of colonial exploitation. Indeed, it is no exaggeration to suggest that the Industrial Revolution, which enabled Europe and North America to leap far ahead of the rest of the world in material welfare, would have been delayed, possibly by many generations, were it not for the capital yielded by colonialism.

For the peoples of the colonial world capitalist penetration was disastrous. They were bequeathed all the evils of capitalism and none of the benefits. Their wealth was mercilessly plundered by European pirates, disguised as traders. Moreover, colonialism disrupted their traditional agricultural economies, forced them to grow exportable commercial crops, and thereby undermined the self-sufficiency of the colonized societies. European colonialism was much more than a mere repeat of the conquests of ancient history. It was based on the new capitalist principle of production of exportable commodities for sale on the home market. Hence, European colonizers did not simply demand tribute from the conquered peoples; instead, the colonized societies were completely reorganized. Whole populations were uprooted and turned into a vast colonial work force to man the plantations and mines. Those who would not work, or sought to resist the invaders, were brutalized and murdered. Outright slavery was resorted to in many instances. In areas such as North America, where the indigenous population was relatively sparse, a slave labor force was imported from elsewhere. African slaves thereby became the colonial work force of North America. Thus, the colonized societies were forcibly brought into the worldwide system of commodity circulation, contributing their economic "surplus" to the growing capital of Europe. Their economies were distorted by the demands of colonialism, and their traditional industries and handicrafts were destroyed by competition from European manufacturers. Consequently, they were forced onto the path leading to economic underdevelopment.

Colonialism, Slavery and Racism

Illegally confiscated land and forced labor were the cornerstones of capitalist colonialism. Initially, colonial activity was rationalized on religious grounds; by contributing their land and labor to the Christian invaders it was argued that the heathen natives were bringing themselves closer to the redeeming forces of Christendom. However, implicit in this theory was the notion of eventual religious conversion and assimilation—an idea which posed a dilemma for the colonizers and slaveholders. If the heathens were converted, previous claims to their land and labor might be vitiated. Therefore, beginning in the sixteenth century serious arguments were made that Indians, for example, could have their lands taken and be enslaved not merely because they were heathens but more fundamentally they were considered less than human, on the same plane as animals. Consequently, such beings were incapable of conversion and their subservient status was permanently fixed. These conjectures provoked a heated dispute in the Catholic church in Spain, eventually culminating in a ruling in favor of the Indians.

In northern Europe and North America the moderating ideological influence of the Catholic church was largely missing; its place taken by an aggressive Protestantism that embodied the very spirit of capitalism.[4] More important, the North American colonies were true settler colonies, involving migration and settlement of entire families of colonists rather than the patriarchal pattern of adventurers-conquistadors more characteristic of Latin America, and the emerging northern ruling class was more bourgeois and rigidly property-oriented than its semi-feudal South American counterpart.[5] The result was the evolution of a rigid two-category system in North America that relegated Indians and slaves to the ideological status of sub-men. The "savage Indian brutes" could thus be cheerfully cheated, forcibly relieved of their land and very nearly exterminated by aggressive Protestant settlers. Slaves fared little better. Capitalist slavery in fact totally dehumanized the slave; it reduced a human being to the status of a draft animal—chattel. Consequently, the ideology of North American slavery asserted a biological inequality of the races; that black slaves were either an entirely different species—polygenesis—or a transitional group located somewhere between apes and white men. Since virtually all slaves in North America were black and the overwhelming majority of the black population were slaves it is not surprising that the evolving racist ideology increasingly recognized no significant distinction between slaves and free blacks. The latter were a small minority who were eventually engulfed by the tide of white racism.

Although elements of color prejudice may have predated slavery, Africans were not enslaved in North America because they were black. The developing colonial agricultural system in the southern colonies of North America—based on production of exportable commercial crops—demanded a *large and fixed* labor force. Without such a work force it would have been impossible to sustain the plantation economy. The labor demands of the mercantile plantation system fell first on Indians and white indentured servants. The former proved unsatisfactory as a labor source for several reasons: their limited numbers (the main concentration of North American Indians was on the West Coast), their susceptibility to the white man's diseases due to recent contact between the two groups, and the fact that they could escape from servitude with relative ease since they knew the land better than the white settlers. White servants also presented problems, since their contracts specified a time limit for service. At the same time, whites could not be enslaved because this would provoke political repercussions in Europe and very likely stem the tide of white immigration across the Atlantic; white slavery would thus be self-defeating. Asians, if considered, were too far away; the transportation costs would be prohibitive and the likelihood of successfully completing such a long and dangerous sea voyage, given the state of seafaring technology, was highly questionable. South American Indians were already claimed by the Spanish and Portuguese.

Fortunately for the North American colonists, the Spanish and Portuguese had already led the way in tapping a virtually bottomless reservoir of labor: the peoples of the west coast of Africa. Indeed, the first blacks to arrive in North America in 1619 were probably victims of the Iberian slave trade. Africans provided an ideal source of labor for the English colonies: the west coast of Africa was relatively near the Caribbean, there were never any complicating questions of voluntary migration or political repercussions, many Africans were agriculturalists who quickly grasped the demands of agricultural labor on the plantations, the long contact between Europe and Africa meant that Africans were not so easily decimated by the white man's diseases—they had built up a resistance—and, finally, unlike Indians, Africans were unfamiliar with the new land and thus found it more difficult to escape and successfully avoid capture. Therefore, Africa became the hunting ground of the European slave powers. The development and specific labor requirements of the capitalist colonial plantation system, not race, marked Africans as the chief victims of slavery. However, once this process was set in motion, the institutionalization of capitalist slavery promoted the elaboration of a justificatory racist ideology.[6] Unlike ancient slavery, modern capitalist slavery demanded a permanent, nonassimilable labor force to produce the agricultural commodities which were salable on the home market in the mother countries. Capitalist plantations, existing in a vast land of immense opportunity, could maintain their labor force only through the mechanism of slavery buttressed by a trenchant racism that totally denied the possibility that slave workers might assimilate into the general population, to seek their fortune on equal footing with the white settlers.

Slavery degraded human beings to the level of brute animals who must be "domesticated," forced to work and constantly supervised. The elaboration and articulation of an ideological rationalization accompanied the institutionalization of slavery, and reached its apex as the slave system entered its final crisis in the nineteenth century. Beginning in the seventeenth century, we note a steady shift in ideological perspective from religion to race as the prime justification for slavery. Racism proved to be an ideal ideology for slavery. For unlike attempts at justification on religious grounds alone, there was no possibility of *racial* conversion, although there was no lack of speculation along this line. Also the ideological unity of the white population was assured by the economic and psychological advantages which accrued to them purely on the basis of their whiteness. This avoided the ideological disunity that afflicted Latin whites who tried to construct a rigidly religious rationalization for slavery and colonization.

The ideological influence of developing racism was widespread due to the economic structure of North American society. The slave system was essential to the development of the Southern plantation economy, and initially it provided a strong stimulus to Northern industry and shipping (thereby ironically aiding the North in building an industrial society that by the mid-nineteenth century would clash with the South). Not only did capitalists and plantation owners gain from slavery but also many of the white workers who immigrated to the New World. As James Boggs has observed, initially even whites at the very bottom of colonial society benefited from African slavery: "First, the expanding industry made possible by the profits of slave trafficking created jobs at an expanding rate. Second, white indentured servants were able to escape from the dehumanization of plantation servitude only because of the seemingly inexhaustible supply of constantly imported slaves to take their place. . . . For the individual white indentured servant or laborer,

African slavery meant the opportunity to rise above the status of slave and become farmer or free laborer.''[7]

During this early period, slavery and colonialism also brought numerous economic rewards to all segments of the population in the colonizing societies.[8] Thus, virtually all elements of the white population embraced the racist ideology of slavery. It was only the rapacious spread of cotton plantations and the maturation of industrialism in the nineteenth century that made slavery a threat to some segments of white farmers and workers. The nineteenth century was a time of turmoil and crisis for the colonial slave system throughout the world. On the one hand, colonialism and slavery had underwritten the development of a great industrial system that made Great Britain the most powerful European nation. At the same time, industrial capitalism made the old-style colonialism and slavery obsolete. Unlike commercial or mercantile capitalism, which had required that nations and people be kept in direct political bondage to facilitate channeling of economic surpluses to Europe, industrial capitalism—with its monopoly on industrial production established—was no longer dependent solely on direct political or military methods to bind colonial people to its service. The process of capitalist trade itself increasingly became the binding link. With their economic development halted or distorted by colonialism, the colonized peoples of the world were compelled to trade with European capitalists (which, given the terms of trade, meant in effect they were working *for* the European capitalists) not because of physical coercion but due to economic compulsion; only thus could they gain access to the manufactured goods associated with a higher standard of life. Indeed, in some instances the economic life of the colonized societies had been so crippled that their very survival depended on continued trade with the Europeans.

This process was accompanied by efforts of some of the colonies to break free of bondage. The United States had led the way and was seeking to become an industrial capitalist nation, employing a "free" labor force based on economic rather than political or physical compulsion. However, U.S. society exhibited a dual character due to the existence of a slave-plantation South which was still linked in semi-colonial fashion to England. In the United States a growing industrial capitalism existed side by side with a mercantilist slave economy, but not without severe political and economic strains which eventually culminated in the Civil War.

Thus, internationally and domestically the transition to industrial capitalism set in motion the social forces that brought about the abolition of slavery. Anti-slavery thought had been around as long as slavery, but it did not become a socially compelling ideology until economic transformations were making slavery itself anachronistic. This was not a simple process. As the new industrial society was taking shape in the North following the war for independence, abolitionism flourished and slavery was outlawed in several Northern states. However, the rejuvenation of the Southern plantation system that followed the invention of the cotton gin strengthened slavery, resulting in a temporary lull in abolitionist activity. But the conflict between the political-economic organizing principles of two stages of capitalist development was not long to be repressed. By 1830 the debate between pro- and anti-slavery forces had resumed with a new vehemence, the former elaborating a systematic ideology of black degradation and inherent inferiority. The debate was highly involved, but resting at its core was the concept of the fundamental non-humanness of blacks.[9] For the first time, the full ideological ramifications of slavery were spelled out and exposed to public view.

Abolitionists centered their attack around the assertion that black people were in fact human beings, and therefore it was morally indefensible to subject them to slavery. They admitted that blacks were degraded by slavery, but this was a fate that could befall any race subjected to such brutal oppression. The question of black humanity thus became the touchstone of antebellum ideological contention.

Although white abolitionists championed black humanity, they did not necessarily advocate equality. At various times pro-abolition voices advocated the removal (colonization) of the black population as the only way to solve the race question. Other abolitionists fell into a kind of paternalistic, romantic racism that was simply a liberal version of biological racism. Abolitionists urged that black people, as human beings, should be free, but they were confused and often reactionary on the matter of racial equality.

This ideological confusion was manifested in other ways. Although white abolitionists reflected the individualist and moral-religious ideas of developing industrial capitalism, they exhibited virtually no understanding of economics. Unlike some black abolitionists, they did not call for black economic integration into the new industrial society. A counterpart of this peculiar failure was also to be found among anti-slavery white workers, who opposed slavery but also opposed movement of black workers into the free territories.

How are we to explain this anomaly of a social system that produced intense opposition to slavery but no ideology of incorporating the emancipated black workers into its economy? The answer probably lies in the particular method by which the Northern industrial working class was formed, namely, European immigration. With a steady stream of skilled and unskilled workers from Europe— a stream which swelled into a torrent after the great crisis that gripped Europe in the 1840's—there simply was no need for bringing blacks into the Northern industrial system. The labor needs of the North were already being met. Consequently, all segments of the Northern white population displayed a pronounced lack of interest in black economic integration. Indeed, many in the North who supported the anti-slavery cause nevertheless cherished the hope of a future industrial America that would be all white in racial composition. The ideology of racism, although grounded in social organization, was taking on a life and direction of its own, actually shaping white behavior, not merely reflecting it.

Black abolitionists, although embroiled often in internal tactical disputes, were generally agreed on the ideological necessity of supporting white abolitionist activities. Debates centered around the interrelated questions of how best to do so, and how best to attack the racial prejudices of the white reformers. In point of fact, these questions were answered in practice. Between 1817 and the outbreak of the Civil War thousands of blacks organized and participated in an independent black abolitionist movement with its own independent press. Even blacks such as Frederick Douglass, who believed that individual blacks should integrate into white reform organizations, were compelled to modify their position. Douglass found himself hemmed in by his Garrisonian friends, and he split with them precisely over the question of ideological independence. When Douglass determined to found his own newspaper, he was seeking an institutional vehicle that would enable him to exert ideological leadership.

The existence of an independent black movement enabled black abolitionists to exert considerable influence on abolitionism in general. Local, state and regional organizations, firmly rooted in the black community, provided the institutional support necessary for developing and propagating a black ideology. Consequently, black abolitionists did much more than simply welcome and endorse white reformers' advocacy of black humanity. Backed by their own organizations and press, militant blacks asserted their ideological leadership by (1) demanding black economic (and political) integration, and (2) insisting that black people were fully equal to whites (i.e., capable of self-development) and fully independent (i.e., capable of self-direction). Thus, when white abolitionism hesitated and became confused, black leaders, representing the victims of slavery and racism, stepped in and took up the ideological assault on both slavery and racism.

The limits to the success of black militancy were imposed by the powerlessness of blacks in post-bellum America. Black people were emancipated from slavery, but not from economic and political dependency. The refusal of the white rulers to undertake radical agrarian reform after the Civil War meant that black people could not achieve economic independence in the South, while at the same time the racism of employers and labor unions denied them economic integration in the North. The sharecropping system kept blacks in slave-like economic bondage while the machinations of the Republican Party assured their political bondage.

Blacks did succeed in steering white abolitionists away from colonization schemes and in confronting them with other questions concerning racism; and black workers, by going on strike during the war, promoted the immediate abolition of slavery without compensation to slaveholders by demonstrating that it was in the military interest of the North to do so. But once these struggles were over, black people found themselves at the mercy of an ascendant Northern bourgeoisie whose first concern was to consolidate its political hegemony over the Southern rebels. Denied both economic independence and economic integration, black people became the wards of a triumphant but insecure Republican Party. While at the state level black leaders were able to effect many reforms during Reconstruction, their days were numbered by their economic and political dependency and the consequent inability of black leadership to break free of an ever-more-opportunistic Republican Party.

The Racial Ideology of Monoply Capital and Imperialism

The biological racism of slavery underwent a serious modification as international capitalism advanced to the monopoly and imperialist phase. Where slavery denied humanity, the new ideology admitted that nonwhites were human beings but maintained that they were inferior races which must be guided and ruled by a master race of whites that supposedly had demonstrated its superior civilized virtues in the course of centuries of struggle for world domination.

This ideological shift accompanied structural changes in the political economy of capitalism. In the latter half of the nineteenth century the "free enterprise" system gave way to gigantic monopolies as the dominant mode of economic organization. Unregulated capitalist competition played out to its logical conclusion; smaller, weaker firms—e.g., family ownerships and partnerships—were elbowed aside by the massive economic concentrations made possible by joint stock companies and corporations. The very structure of the latter encouraged capital concentration and centralization on a scale never before seen. The process of monopolization proceeded apace among both industrial firms and financial institutions, and subsequent linkages between these two culminated in an oligopolistic system of cartels, syndicates and trusts.

Monopoly not only concentrated capital but also exhibited a tendency to generate new surplus capital at a rapid rate.[10] The accumulation of economic surplus posed a serious problem, since its nonabsorption had a depressive and destabilizing effect on the larger economy. Several basic methods were evolved in the advanced capitalist nations for easing this structural problem. First, tremendous amounts of social energy were diverted from production to salesmanship and advertising. A large section of the work force was gradually shifted into staffing and managing the new white-collar jobs related to artifically stimulating a demand for the commodities of monopoly capital. Increased consumption meant increased production, which in turn opened up new areas for investment of surplus capital. Second, technological progress created still another avenue of investment. In particular, railroads and the automobile absorbed huge amounts of capital and created whole new industries, such as steel, oil and chemicals, which meant still more opportunities for investment. Finally, imperialism and militarism laid the basis for increased foreign sales and investment and the expenditure of surplus capital through building and arming a large military establishment. Obviously, these two phenomena went hand in hand and required active coordination by the national governments of the imperialist powers. Despite all of these avenues for absorbing surplus capital, the problem still remained, since all of these methods—with the sole exception of militarism—resulted in even more economic concentration and the accumulation of still more surplus. Consequently, it is not surprising that the economically inspired reformism in the waning years of the nineteenth century and the beginning of the twentieth increasingly demanded government regulation of the economy as the only way—short of social revolution—of stabilizing and rationalizing a chronically unbalanced system.

The transition from competitive capitalism to monopoly capitalism was beginning in the United States by the end of Reconstruction. With this transition, uncertainty about the future role of black labor was also resolved. Where blacks had been the main productive labor force of antebellum Southern agriculture, they were now to become a subproletariat, the "shock absorbers," of monopoly capital. The structural instability of the monopoly system meant that workers at the very bottom of the economic ladder were confronted not only by low wages but also extreme economic insecurity. The slightest gyration in the monopoly economy meant that thousands upon thousands of workers at its bottom levels would lose their jobs. So long as Western settlement was possible and European immigrants were available, the subproletariat remained white. Wave after wave of white immigrants arrived to take unskilled jobs in industry and then began climbing up the economic ladder by acquiring land or being bolstered by the next wave of immigration. But between the closing of the frontier toward the end of the nineteenth century and the outbreak of World War I, which cut off European immigration, a method had to evolve for supplying a new subproletariat and for keeping the new group permanently at the bottom of the economic heap. The latter requirement was made necessary by the fact that the maturation of monopoly plus the ending of westward expansion meant that opportunities for upward social mobility were being severely curtailed. The class structure of U.S. society, previously obscured by frontier individualism and seemingly unlimited opportunities for economic advancement, was now revealing itself with a severity that could not go unrecognized. In reaction, the attitude of the embattled small-property owner became the ideological stance of vast sectors of the white population, including millions who owned nothing but their own labor power.

The ideological racism left over from slavery, combined with the institutionalization of racism that followed Reconstruction, condemned black people to the role of scavengers of monopoly capital. Politically inspired disfranchisement and segregation reduced blacks to a virtual pariah caste in the South; while Southern violence and the beginning mechanization of agriculture, combined with the ending of European immigration, spurred a massive migration of black workers into the Northern industrial slums. Black workers were emancipated from slavery but their exploitation continued. Indeed, by converting black workers into a racially stigmatized category of "wage slaves" it was now possible to exploit them even more mercilessly. With blacks thrown on their own as individuals, instead of being the collective economic responsibility of the white master class, they could be used as a permanent subproletariat to increase the margin of profitability of monopoly industrial capitalism—dispensable in times of recession, available to work at low wages whenever required.

Furthermore, the advent of imperialism had opened whole new areas of the world to recruitment of a domestic colonial work force that, like blacks, could be stigmatized and subordinated on the basis of racial distinction. Already on the West Coast, Chinese contract labor used in railroad construction was proving the value of a semi-enslaved but ostensibly "free" labor force.

The specific ideological concepts of this period can be traced to two immediate sources. The Republican effort to impose Northern political hegemony through manipulation of the newly enfranchised black electorate raised howls of protest in the white South. Southern ideologues defended the necessity of "white supremacy" in the face of the supposed dire threat of "black domination," and their demands were backed up by organized terrorism. The gradual penetration of Northern capital into the South during and after Reconstruction built a foundation for closer integration of the two regions, but the attempted interracial rebellion of middle- and lower-class Southern farmers against the encroachments of monopoly could only be broken up by hysterically fanning the flames of white supremacy. Thus, Northern capital's drive to assert its political and economic control over the South provoked ideological reactions which contributed to the formulation of a new racist conception.

A second immediate source of the new racism was aggressive U.S. expansion into the Pacific and Caribbean areas in search of markets and materials. American imperialism, like its European counterpart, represented a new stage in the history of colonialism. Where the old colonialism plundered nations and disrupted their traditional economies, economic imperialism aimed to block the accumulation of capital and the creation of an industrial base in the colonies and semi-colonies. Increasingly, sophisticated economic exploitation replaced outright plunder as the modus operandi of colonialism. Consequently, economic development and underdevelopment were institutionalized as opposite sides of the same imperialist coin, as the underdeveloped countries became appended to the monopoly economies of the imperialist powers.

The success of imperialism necessitated a serious attempt to root capitalist economic and political institutions more firmly in the colonial areas, for it was only through such institutions (the market, private property, banking system, wage labor) that capitalist investment and domination could be secured. Thus, implicit in the new arrangement were the two ideas that the colonized were to continue to be dominated by the imperialists, but at the same time were to undergo a period of tutelage or "elevation" that supposedly would educate them to the value of bourgeois institutions, without, of course, raising any embarrassing questions about their assigned place in the imperialist order.[11] In racial terms, the new ideology found its most elaborate expression in Social Darwinism.

That Social Darwinism came to epitomize the new racist ideology is readily explained. In the first place, Social Darwinism, with its emphasis on vicious competition and unrelenting struggle of one against all, accurately reflected the economic dynamics leading to the rise of monopoly capital. Second, its categorization of blacks and other nonwhites as inferior races, not subhuman species, cleared away the older ideological baggage that these groups were incapable of performing industrial labor. Indeed, low-level industrial education of black workers was now heartily approved of by whites both in the South and the North. So long as it was understood that blacks would remain at the lowest levels of industry and be supervised by whites there was no disagreement. Third, despite occasional demurrers, Social Darwinism defined imperial expansion as a positive good which both expressed the so-called manifest destiny of the white race to dominate, and established contacts making possible the eventual "uplift" of the inferior colored races. Social Darwinism thus rationalized severe racial oppression on the grounds of a "natural" and unchanging racial hierarchy, and paternalistic philanthropy on the assumption that moral and intellectual "evolution" of inferior races was possible. This seeming contradiction was a source of some ideological confusion, but it presented no fundamental problem. The new racist ideology asserted not so much the irreversible bestial degradation of the nonwhite races, but affirmed primarily the determination of white rulers and ideologists to maintain the supremacy of the white race in the nation and the world. Exaggerated fear of inundation by nonwhites thereby was revitalized as a major theme of the new period of white racist thinking.

Social Darwinism was not the only way in which the new ideology found expression. Anglo-Saxonism, master race ideas, the concept of the white man's burden—all were evident during the period under consideration, but in terms of content they were largely variations on ideas that were more systematically manifest in Social Darwinism.[12]

If the fifty years between 1870 and 1920 witnessed the consolidation of monopoly capital and the rise of American imperialism, one effect of these developments was to undermine the old independent middle classes of small businessmen, professionals and small farmers which, until then, had been the economic backbone of white America. The growth of giant corporations intimidated and dislocated the old petty bourgeoisie. Entrenched monopoly bore down oppressively on unskilled black and other dispossessed workers, at the same time offering concessions to those elements of organized labor which accepted monopoly principles and racism. The result of all these tendencies was a proliferation of reform movements, led mainly by the middle classes and labor bureaucrats, aimed at confronting, regulating or imitating monopoly capital.

The Southern Populist revolt of small and poor farmers (many of whom were black) against the Bourbons and Northern capitalists represented an assault on monopoly capital which, in the South, functioned through the Democratic Party. White Populists organized black political support, which they needed to win state elections, and they propounded the theory of common economic interests of black and white farmers, but they failed to attack the white supremacist ideology inherited from the aftermath of Reconstruction. Consequently, charges of fostering "black domination" struck directly at the Achilles heel of populism in the South. Themselves thoroughly infected with racism, white Populists fell back in disarray and eventually joined their former enemies in affirming white solidarity. Black Populists, lacking an independent organization and press, were unable to affect these developments in any significant way. If anything, populism demonstrated that once established, an ideology does not merely reflect but is also capable of actually guiding social behavior, especially when there is no external ideological counterbalance.

Progressivism was an urban response to the same fundamental structural changes that motivated populism. However, the class basis of progressivism was undergoing a basic transformation at the very time that the movement was gaining momentum. The continuous and unrelenting incorporation of the old middle class into the new white-collar private and public bureaucracies of monopoly capital changed progressivism from a revolt against the system into an attempt to regulate it, the success of which established still more bureaucracies as the partnership between government and big business was institutionalized. Ideologically, progressivism exhibited a dual character but increasingly shifted toward corporate liberalism and welfare statism. As to the matter of race, progressives varied from the virulent white supremacy of many political progressives to what George Frederickson has termed accommodationist racism,[13] which was more characteristic of social welfare progressives. Both groups could agree, however, on a paternalistic approach to race relations which sought to accommodate blacks and other ethnic minorities to the labor demands of the new industrial order.

In the South Booker T. Washington, totally dependent on the philanthropy of monopoly capital, became a spokesman for the accommodationist racism of progressives. Although his hope for blacks to achieve economic independence under capitalism had already been defeated in the wake of the Civil War, his program to create a docile, apolitical industrial labor force meshed smoothly with the current interests of the captains of industry, North and South.

In the North a handful of middle-class black militants desperately tried to halt the spread of violent white racism, which they feared might engulf even the educated, exceptional members of the race. They founded newspapers and organizations for this purpose. However, the organizations were elitist; they represented the Talented Tenth and were largely divorced from the masses of black people. As a result, the militant organizations tended to be weak and constantly on the verge of financial collapse and thus could be co-opted by the well-heeled white progressives who organized the NAACP. Moreover, they failed to perceive that racial antagonism was assuming new guises in accordance with changes in the political economy. Yet, despite their weaknesses, the independent black organizations succeeded in formulating and propagating an anti-racist program which was to gain more and more adherents among both the white and black populations as the twentieth century progressed.

Industrialization and urbanization also prompted a large reform movement among middle-class white women, who began to demand the same rights and privileges as the men of their class. Although bourgeois feminism started as a multi-issue movement associated with abolitionism, it gradually narrowed to a single-issue movement with no significant ideology of its own. Consequently, its ideological proclivities were identical with those of the dominant society. Indeed, feminist leaders opportunistically embraced white supremacy as a way of asserting their own allegiance to white domination in hopes that this would establish their qualifications for exercising the franchise. White women totally betrayed their black sisters in the name of white solidarity. They were rewarded with the vote.

Middle-class black women also organized independently to work for race betterment and to demand their rights. Unfortunately, the concern with bourgeois respectability and proper decorum absorbed much of the women's agitational energy and deflected their direct assault on racism. Instead, they concentrated on organizing separate black institutions which were basically conservative in nature, much as the black church had done in the South. Even so, the black women's stress on self-help and their influence on progressivism conditioned the emergence of social welfare agencies such as the National Urban League.

The more radical and alienated of middle-class intellectuals found in socialism a congenial movement. Socialism also appealed to many elements of labor, but the concessions which the more skilled and privileged workers won from monopoly capital, combined with severe repression of the radical labor groups, soon removed this base of socialist support. White Socialists espoused egalitarianism but their social democratic inheritance and the influence of American racism made them something less than champions of racial equality, at least before World War I. In fact, for early Socialists, racism was a diversionary issue conjured up by calculating capitalists. They totally failed to understand that racism might be deeply ingrained in the historical development of capitalist culture and could not be written off as a mere capitalist conspiracy to divide the workers. In any event, in practice white Socialists largely ignored or even discriminated against black workers. The most active black Socialists of this period, A. Philip Randolph and Chandler Owen, were individual militants who had no organized base of support in the black community until after World War I. Thus, socialism, although like other reform movements in not being inherently racist, nevertheless absorbed a strong dose of racism from the European and American societies in which it made its first appearance.

The dominant trend in organized labor at the beginning of this century was a movement toward exclusionism and racism. The decades after the Civil War had been an era of uncertainty for unionism. Differing goals, tactics and organizing principles were openly debated. But with the overthrow of Reconstruction and the birth of monopoly and imperialism, organized labor's vision began to narrow. Indeed, a "labor aristocracy" developed within the working class. This privileged stratum understood that its favored status was based upon close articulation of the needs of monopoly capital and imperialism. In fact, it represented a monopoly within a monopoly, and hence proceeded to reproduce the ideologies of monopoly and racism within its ranks.[14] It was no accident that trade unions among skilled workers attempted to monopolize job opportunities by excluding other workers, especially members of subjugated racial groups. By doing so, they helped institutionalize a permanent black subproletariat as a base upon which white workers could-stand, thereby gaining the last chance of *upward social mobility* in a system that was becoming ever more rigid. Of course, monopoly capital's use of blacks as strikebreakers exposed the chimerical quality of organized white labor's privileges, but ironically this only reinforced labor racism.

Numerous attempts were made to build independent black labor unions, some of which achieved a measure of success. By and large, however, the limits of black labor organizing were defined by the role assigned black workers in the monopoly economy. Black labor organizing meant organizing the lowest paid and economically most insecure members of the working class, an extremely difficult task with little assurance of success. In all likelihood, it is those black workers who have moved into better paying and more secure jobs who will be most amenable to unionizing efforts, as proved to be true of the sleeping car porters in the 1920's.

All in all, the upsurge of reformism at the turn of the century did not halt the advance of monopoly capital nor abate racism. Instead, it helped to launch a process that was to culminate in the creation of modern corporate liberal society with its host of white-collar salaried employees and well-paid skilled workers. For blacks, this process hardly represented a blessing, since it relegated most black workers to menial and marginal jobs of short duration with minimum pay. That the NAACP and National Urban League were born out of all this must be counted at least a qualified victory. But these two interracial groups were born of compromise, and they faced a sharply uphill struggle in carrying their message to the country at large.

Cultural Chauvinism and Liberal Imperialism

The years since World War I mark the transition to still a third period in the history of racist thinking. This new period is increasingly characterized by the ideology of cultural chauvinism, the myth that a unique and independent cultural heritage and development somehow accounts for the greater material advancement of western

Europe and North America compared with other areas of the world. Cultural chauvinism treats industrial advancement as the natural end-product of a supposedly superior "Western culture," conveniently obscuring the fact that it was capitalist exploitation of the colonial world that contributed to rapid and continuing material progress in Europe and North America. By separating culture from economics and history, cultural chauvinism regards culture as a metaphysical attribute of a people or nation. As such, it can be considered a sophisticated variation on the older idea of racial chauvinism. However, cultural chauvinism does not stigmatize nonwhite peoples as inherently inferior, instead they are merely "culturally deprived" or "culturally backward." Hence, assimilation to bourgeois "Western culture" steadily replaces race as the main criterion for admission to the white world. Obviously this ideological changeover is far from complete even today, and there are serious reasons to doubt that in practice it ever can be.[15] But clearly the rhetoric of racial integration and cultural assimilation has come into vogue to a much greater extent than ever was the case in the past.

Perhaps the best way of clarifying the concept of cultural chauvinism is to examine the forces that brought it into being. At the outset of such a discussion it should be observed that the new ideology does not spring from purely internal developments of capitalism or the dynamics of imperialist expansion. On the contrary, it is external developments—the birth and rapid spread of anti-colonial and socialist revolts throughout the colonized and economically backward areas of the world—that have forced a defensive ideological reaction in the capitalist-imperialist system. For the first time in modern history the capitalist world is in retreat, buffeted by revolutionary forces which its own previous expansion helped to create. Hence, cultural chauvinism must be analyzed within this context rather than regarded simply as an ideological outgrowth of systemic development and expansion.

Among the factors that contributed to the emergence of cultural chauvinism, four are particularly significant. First, of course, was the birth of the anti-colonial struggle in the nineteenth century and its subsequent development into a worldwide movement against imperialism. This was no accidental development but represented a dialectical response to imperialist domination. Eric R. Wolf, for example, in his study of peasant wars concludes that capitalist penetration of traditional societies created severe dislocations and at the same time cut these societies off from their past so that the final outcome could only be an anti-colonial and in some cases, socialist, revolt.[16] With more and more colonies in uproar and clamoring for independence, the imperialist powers were compelled to modify their tactics. Since the strategic aim of imperialism is economic domination it was possible, and even desirable, to grant formal political independence to colonies so long as imperialist economic control remained secure. The latter was accomplished in part by turning over the reins of political power to comprador classes which had a material stake in maintenance of capitalist property and social relations. Indirect control thereby replaced direct control, and neo-colonialism was born.

Ideologically, the "right" of these comprador classes to rule could not be based on alleged racial superiority since they were drawn from the same racial stock as the native masses. Hence, assimilation into Western culture replaced race as the yardstick for privilege in the neo-colonial world. Special efforts were made to see that potential colonial political leaders, civil servants and military personnel were educated and trained in the imperialist metropolises so that they would be ideologically suited for their new role as liaison agents between imperialism and the popular masses of the neo-colonies.

Second, the Bolshevik Revolution of 1917 shook the very foundations of capitalism and unsettled its elaborate ideological edifice. The subsequent linking of the socialist movement to the anti-imperialist struggle against colonialism and neo-colonialism, and the spread of Communist thought and activity to the United States prompted hysterical reaction in defense of "Western civilization" and "the American Way of Life." The Russian Revolution also had the effect of polarizing the white population since Slavs, Jews and immigrants generally were now being stereotyped as dangerous radicals.[17]

Third, conflicts between the imperialist nations over control of colonies led to wars and further fragmentation of white solidarity. The capitalist nations divided into liberal democratic and fascist camps with each accusing the other of having betrayed the civilizing mission of Western culture. Defense of Western culture became a unifying theme among both liberals and fascists. The rise of Japan as a major capitalist and imperialist power posed something of a dilemma for Europeans and white Americans, but this was resolved by classifying the Japanese as unusually adept "imitators" of Western culture.

The two world wars resulted in the emergence of the United States as the most powerful capitalist nation and the acknowledged leader of the rest. With its own population composed of an amalgam of national and ethnic groupings, and faced with hostile anti-imperialist and socialist movements, the U.S. power structure could hardly afford to revert, at least officially, to the old biological and Social Darwinist racial theories. Moreover, advances in scientific knowledge had largely discredited the evidence gathered in support of these theories. Clearly, a new ideology was urgently needed.

Final factors in the genesis of cultural chauvinism were the mass movements launched by black people, and the interaction between these movements and the anti-colonial revolt. The Garvey movement after World War I and the civil rights movement after World War II-Korea both represented a growing black awakening to the world situation. Garvey explicitly hoped to liberate blacks in any nation where they were oppressed. Unfortunately, Garvey's own racial chauvinism, a defense against the racism of the dominant society, sidetracked him into cultural mysticism and grandiose dreams of founding a black empire. Nevertheless, Garvey's movement showed as nothing before the determination of hundreds of thousands of black people to break free of racial oppression. Moreover, Garveyism and the Pan-African conferences organized by Du Bois played significant roles in promoting a nationalist consciousness in Africa.

The civil rights movement began as an independent black struggle, but it started declining partly because its middle-class leadership merged with white liberals and allowed them to define goals and tactics. The concept of "Black Power" as articulated in the sixties represented a reassertion of black independence. It did not reject tactical alliances with white reformers but insisted that black groups must maintain their organizational integrity and establish strong ties with the general black community. Further, African independence struggles and the Vietnam War made a deep impact on the political consciousness of black nationalists. The revolutionary implications of this became most apparent in the personality and thinking of Malcolm X.

The dangerous mixture of nationalism, anti-imperialism and socialism that some black radicals were beginning to advocate could not long be tolerated. Two ancient tactics were trundled out to meet this threat: repression of the radicals and concessions to the moderates. Additionally, efforts were made to recruit militant but acculturated members of the black middle class as liaison agents between monopoly capital and the rebellious black ghettos.[18] Thus, the specter of a massive black revolt veering toward political radicalism spurred the further development of cultural chauvinism as a defensive ideology.

In sum, in the era of imperialist crisis cultural chauvinism emerges as the ideological defense of the capitalist system, seeking to unify factionalized white populations in support of Western (capitalist) culture while offering to assimilate those members of oppressed national and ethnic groups who are willing to abide by the system's rules. The roots of cultural chauvinism can be traced to World War I, which should not be taken to mean that other forms of racism abated after that war. On the contrary, cultural chauvinism was simply one side of a dual defensive reaction, the other side of which was protofascism and revived Ku Klux Klanism. These two ideological strains openly confronted each other in World War II and fascism, at least for the time being, went down to defeat. Since then, we have seen the consolidation, not without setbacks, of cultural chauvinism as the racial ideology of the liberal imperialist state.

All of these developments were not without their effects on social reform movements. Chief among these was the increasing advocacy of racial integration of nonwhites into American life. This was a liberal reform version of cultural chauvinism, for it still assumed that integration of nonwhites would not challenge the foundations of American society. Thus, CIO organizers and New Deal progressives agreed that blacks and other nonwhites should be counted in. Yet the conservatism and complacency that settled over white America in the 1950's revealed the tenuous nature of integrationism. It required a massive civil rights movement and revolts in Africa to inject some substance into the integrationist rhetoric.

Communist and Trotskyist radicals of the inter-war years were caught in a curious dilemma by integrationism. On the one hand, they advocated full racial integration as a democratic demand, but the Russian revolutionaries to whom they looked for ideological leadership insistently talked about the right of self-determination. Since the Russians had only limited knowledge of American conditions and history, and the American radical Socialists had little understanding of self-determination, the result was a mass of confusion, opportunism and outright betrayal. Very few white Socialists identified self-determination with the repeated, independent black efforts to organize and struggle against racism.

Thousands of blacks were active in the labor and socialist movements in the 1930's, but with few exceptions they simply integrated as individuals into white-controlled organizations. The radical black groups that did exist tended to be fronts for white groups or they were eventually taken over by white organizations. Consequently, militant blacks possessed no independent base; they were simply dispersed in a sea of white confusion. The major exception was A. Philip Randolph, whose Brotherhood of Sleeping Car Porters not only sought to protect black porters but also provided Randolph with an independent base from which he continuously attacked the racism of the AFL.

Cultural chauvinism, by making a fetish of Western culture, has had still another effect on contemporary movements for social change; namely, it has fostered a reaction in the form of cultural nationalism among different ethnic groups. In turn this has led to cultural arrogance between various Third World groups in the U.S. Hence, there are numerous instances of cultural antagonism between blacks, Chicanos, Puerto Ricans, Indians, and Asian-Americans. The cultural chauvinism of the dominant society encourages ethnic organizations to react by focusing on their cultural differences rather than their common struggle against racism. Moreover, many nonwhites in the U.S. have unwittingly adopted cultural chauvinist attitudes toward Third World liberation struggles—assuming that Third World militants in the American stronghold of imperialism somehow *automatically* know what is the best course for anti-imperialist struggles in Africa, Asia and Latin America. This attitude is little different from social chauvinism of nineteenth century European intellectuals. As we have seen in the discussion of the early socialist movement, such arrogance only serves to undermine solidarity between different oppressed groups, thereby bolstering imperialism. Clearly, cultural chauvinism, like the racism of which it is an extension, has acted to confuse and weaken social change movements.

The preceding discussion suggests that as the social structure undergoes changes, whether due to its internal logic or external pressure, social reform movements arise which generally reflect the liberal aspects of the resulting ideological development. Social reformers, jarred into action by structural change, are to a greater or lesser extent alienated from and critical of the dominant social system, and by organizing movements they attempt to push the system in what they believe is a progressive direction. While it is true that these movements are not the underlying cause of social change, they can in fact influence the *specific direction* it takes, within the general limits set by structural readjustments. Reform movements, thus, are the ideological antennae of change.

As such, progressive reform movements are sensitive to and can be made to respond to organized social pressure from other groups in society. Throughout the history of the United States, militant blacks have tried to accomplish precisely this. The clash between black and white reformers forms an integral part of the ongoing drama of the advance and counterattack against racism. This drama in itself is an ideological and institutional manifestation of the expansion and forced retreat of capitalist imperialism. Indeed, it could be argued that just as imperialism created the external forces capable of rolling it back, so has it created an insistently independent internal ideological force committed to opposing imperialism's racist ideologies. White reformers, themselves largely unaffected by racism, generally fail to perceive its full ramifications and subtleties. This is why militant blacks and other nonwhites, who can't escape racial oppression, have so often taken the lead in promoting and consolidating opposition to racism.

This does not mean that no whites understood the importance of struggling against racism, nor that black leaders were always correct in their proposals and programs. It simply expresses a social dynamic that has recurred in the history of American reformism. White leadership is not automatically racist, nor black leadership automatically correct. Such mechanical formulas do not meet the test of practice. However, the continuance of this social dynamic around racism indicates a recurring problem or contradiction in the nature of reformism.

The foregoing analysis of the roots of racist ideology implies that ultimately the attack on racism must become a struggle with the bourgeois social order itself, since the two cannot be isolated one from the other. Bourgeois property relations and their ideological rationalizations in the popular mind of white America have repeatedly incited racial antagonisms. Unfortunately, black leaders themselves have not always understood this, some making a fetish of separatist and escapist fantasies while others vainly sought assimilation into a bourgeois order that could not but be racist.

The dynamics of U.S. historical development led black reformers to develop as an independent ideological force, but not a separate ideological force. That is, although having their own press, organizations, caucuses, and other concerted efforts, black social reformers were seeking to push general social reformism toward a broader struggle where it would confront racism. But this would mean these were no longer reform movements but revolutionary movements attacking a principal phenomenon of the bourgeois order.

This is the final dilemma of reformism. Reform movements have been consistently undermined by racism, but to resolve this problem demands that both the struggle for reforms and the struggle against racism be incorporated into a thoroughgoing process of revolutionary social transformation. Here reformism balks, for its aims are limited and highly specific. However, without transcending these limitations, social change movements will continue merely to react to problems—rather than taking the lead in rooting out causes of problems—and the problems themselves will simply recur in new forms. Like Sisyphus, reformism can expect neither final success nor rest, unless it fundamentally alters its conception of the task at hand.

Notes

Chapter I

1. The New Deal, it should be noted, is not included as a separate case study because it was not a movement. The New Deal represented a federal administration's response to a crisis presented by a catastrophic depression and the convergence of three reform movements (labor, socialist-communist, and the remnants of progressivism) which themselves were spurred to a new militancy by the same economic crisis. Consequently, the New Deal is discussed in the context of these reform movements.
2. For a discussion of ideology, see Karl Mannheim, *Ideology and Utopia: An Introduction to the Sociology of Knowledge,* Harcourt, Brace, Jovanovich, New York (New York: Harvest, 1936), pp. 55-59, 64-70; George Lichtheim, *The Concept of Ideology and Other Essays* (New York: Vintage, 1967), pp. 3-46; Peter L. Berger and Thomas Luckmann, *The Social Construction of Reality: A Treatise in the Sociology of Knowledge* (Garden City, N.Y.: Doubleday-Anchor, 1967), pp. 123-25.
3. Robert L. Allen, *Black Awakening in Capitalist America: An Analytic History* (Garden City, N.Y.: Doubleday-Anchor, 1970).

Chapter II

1. David Brion Davis, "The Emergence of Immediatism in British and American Antislavery Thought," *Mississippi Valley Historical Review,* Vol. 49, No. 2 (September, 1962), pp. 226-27.

2. Benjamin Quarles, *Black Abolitionists* (London and New York: Oxford University Press, 1969), p. 19.

3. Herbert Aptheker (ed.), *One Continual Cry: David Walker's Appeal to the Colored Citizens of the World* (New York: Humanities Press, 1965), p. 54.

4. *Ibid,* p. 63.

5. *Ibid,* p. 77.

6. *Ibid,* p. 89.

7. *Ibid,* p. 137.

8. Herbert Aptheker (ed.), *A Documentary History of the Negro People in the United States* (2 vols.; New York: Citadel Press, 1951), Vol. I, pp. 226-33.

9. Leon F. Litwack, *North of Slavery: The Negro in the Free States, 1790-1860* (Chicago and London: University of Chicago Press, 1961), p. 245.

10. Aptheker (ed.), *One Continual Cry,* pp. 126-28.

11. *Ibid,* p. 121. Walker seems to have believed that British abolition of the slave trade was inspired by humanitarian feeling. With the advantage of hindsight, historians have been less charitable in their assessment of British purposes. For example, W.E.B. Du Bois has observed: "When the American colonies won their independence, the Caribbean ceased to be a British sea and investment began to be transferred from the West to the East Indies. . . . Eventually Negro slavery and the slave trade were abandoned in favor of colonial imperialism, and the England which in the 18th century established modern slavery in America on a vast scale, appeared in the nineteenth century as the official emancipator of slaves and founder of a method of control of human labor and material which proved more profitable than slavery." See Du Bois, *The World and Africa* (New York, 1947), pp. 63-64. See also Eric Williams, *Capitalism and Slavery* (New York: Capricorn Books, 1966).

12. Over the preceding years blacks and Indians had developed close ties in parts of the South. Whites, fearing a joint rebellion by black slaves and dispossessed Indians, sought to create hostilities and racial animosity between the two exploited ethnic groups. The whites' worst fears were realized when blacks and Indians fought side by side in the Seminole Wars of 1817-18 and 1835-42. For a discussion of black-Indian relations in the South, see William S. Willis, "Divide and Rule: Red, White, and Black in the Southeast," *Journal of Negro History,* Vol. 48, No. 3 (July, 1963). Also, Kenneth W. Porter,

"Florida Slaves and Free Negroes in the Seminole War, 1835-1842," *Journal of Negro History,* Vol. XXVIII (October, 1943).

13. Truman Nelson (ed.), *Documents of Upheaval: Selections from William Lloyd Garrison's The Liberator, 1831-1865* (New York: Hill and Wang, 1966), pp. xv-xvi.

14. *Ibid,* p. 37.

15. Davis, "Emergence of Immediatism."

16. Philip S. Foner (ed.), *The Life and Writings of Frederick Douglass* (4 vols.; New York: International Publishers, 1950), I, p. 31.

17. Herbert Aptheker, *Essays in the History of the American Negro* (New York: International Publishers, 1945), pp. 145, 148-49.

18. In 1829 in Cincinnati racial strife developed out of job competition between black and white workers. The city fathers resorted to an old law requiring blacks who came into Ohio to post a bond as guarantee that they could support themselves. However, the amount of the bond was so large that it was beyond the reach of most workers of any race, and the law was in effect a means of keeping blacks out of the state. See Howard H. Bell, "Free Negroes of the North 1830-1835: A Study in National Cooperation," *The Journal of Negro Education,* Vol. 26, No. 4 (Fall, 1957).

19. Bella Gross, "The First National Negro Convention," *The Journal of Negro History,* Vol. XXI, No. 4 (October, 1946), p. 435.

20. Aptheker (ed.), *Documentary History,* I, p. 106.

21. Bell, "Free Negroes in the North," p. 452.

22. *Ibid,* p. 453.

23. Aptheker (ed.), *Documentary History,* I, pp. 363-66.

24. Litwack, *North of Slavery,* pp. 237-40.

25. Charles H. Wesley, "The Participation of Negroes in Anti-Slavery Political Parties," *The Journal of Negro History,* Vol. XXIX, No. 1 (January, 1944), p. 43-44.

26. Howard H. Bell, "National Negro Conventions of the Middle 1840s: Moral Suasion vs. Political Action," *The Journal of Negro History,* Vol. XLII, No. 4 (October, 1957), pp. 247-49.

27. *Ibid,* p. 253.

28. Quarles, *Black Abolitionists,* p. 11.

29. The tendency toward moral absolutism among some of the militants created problems when, for instance, in later years they mechanically trotted out this argument to oppose a fund being raised to purchase Frederick Douglass' freedom.

30. Louis Ruchames (ed.), *The Abolitionists: A Collection of Their Writ-

ings (New York: Capricorn Books, 1964), pp. 78-83.

31. Aileen S. Kraditor, *Means and Ends in American Abolitionism* (New York: Pantheon Books, 1969), p. 8.

32. Eleanor Flexner, *Century of Struggle: The Woman's Rights Movement in the United States* (New York: Atheneum, 1968), p. 42.

33. The Bible was the chief authority invoked by antebellum debators in discussions dealing with all manner of philosophical, social, scientific as well as purely religious subjects; although there was a growing awareness among some that the facility with which the Bible could be quoted in support of almost any side of any issue indicated that it yielded something less than absolute clarity on these matters. The Bible was also widely quoted by the apologists for slavery.

34. Benjamin Quarles, *Frederick Douglass* (New York: Atheneum, 1968), p. 135.

35. Elizabeth Cady Stanton, Susan B. Anthony, and Matilda Joslyn Gage (eds.), *History of Woman Suffrage* (2 vols.; New York, 1881-1882), II, p. 329.

36. Quarles, *Black Abolitionists,* p. 178.

37. Quarles, *Frederick Douglass,* p. 131.

38. Quarles, *Black Abolitionists,* p. 7.

39. *Ibid,* pp. 178-80.

40. Despite their long-time interest in anti-slavery work, however, Quakers tended to drop out of the new movement, unable to stomach its militancy and embarrassed by charges by blacks that Friends practiced racial discrimination in their meetings. See Quarles, *Black Abolitionists,* pp. 72-73.

41. Kraditor, *American Abolitionism,* p. 144.

42. Many abolitionists vociferously denounced the war against Mexico which they feared was aimed at spreading slavery. Frederick Douglass was not expressing atypical sentiments when he blasted the war against "unoffending Mexicans" as a war "against freedom, against the Negro, and against the interests of the workingmen of this country."

43. For a full discussion of this subject see Leon Litwack's authoritative book, *North of Slavery.*

44. Litwack, *North of Slavery,* pp. 48-50.

45. Wesley, "Negroes in Anti-Slavery Political Parties," p. 36.

46. Litwack, *North of Slavery,* pp. 216-18, 221.

47. Aptheker (ed.), *"One Continual Cry,"* p. 94; Aptheker (ed.), *Docu-*

mentary History, I, pp. 32-34, 52-53, 57-59, 61, 117, 171-72, 202; Foner (ed.), *Frederick Douglass,* I, pp. 98-100.

48. James M. McPherson, "A Brief for Equality: The Abolitionist Reply to the Racist Myth, 1860-1865," in Martin Duberman (ed.), *The Antislavery Vanguard* (Princeton, N.J.: Princeton University Press, 1965); William H. Pease & Jane H. Pease, "Antislavery Ambivalence: Immediatism, Expediency, Race," *American Quarterly,* Vol. XVII, No. 4 (Winter, 1965), pp. 683-84.

49. Kraditor, *American Abolitionism,* p. 237.

50. Nelson (ed.), *Documents of Upheaval,* p. xv.

51. Kraditor, *American Abolitionism,* p. 264n.

52. Frederick Douglass also employed the "white slaves" argument on at least one occasion, but it is notable that in his usage there is not the suggestion that white slavery was more shocking than black enslavement. See Foner (ed.), *Frederick Douglass,* III, pp. 218-22.

53. McPherson, "A Brief for Equality," pp. 164-69; Litwack, *North of Slavery,* pp. 224-26; Pease & Pease, "Antislavery Ambivalence," 685-86.

54. Litwack, *North of Slavery,* p. 216.

55. Quarles, *Black Abolitionists,* p. 39.

56. Pease & Pease, "Antislavery Ambivalence," p. 691.

57. Aptheker (ed.), *"One Continual Cry,"* p. 71.

58. Ruchames (ed.), *The Abolitionists,* pp. 83-86.

59. Quarles, *Black Abolitionists,* p. 169.

60. McPherson, "A Brief for Equality," p. 167. It fell to pioneer Negro historians to lead the way in calling attention to evidence of flourishing and highly advanced civilizations that existed in Africa at a time when Europeans were still roaming the forests as savages.

61. Quarles, *Black Abolitionists,* p. 48.

62. *Ibid,* p. 235.

63. Gerda Lerner, "The Grimké Sisters and the Struggle Against Race Prejudice," *Journal of Negro History,* Vol. XLVIII, No. 4 (October, 1963).

64. Leon F. Litwack, "The Emancipation of the Negro Abolitionist," in Duberman (ed.), *The Antislavery Vanguard,* pp. 140-41.

65. *Ibid,* p. 145.

66. Quarles, *Black Abolitionists,* p. 49.

67. Litwack, "Negro Abolitionist," pp. 141-42.

68. John L. Myers, "American Antislavery Society Agents and the Free

Negro," *Journal of Negro History* (July, 1967).

69. Kraditor, *American Abolitionism*, p. 244.

70. Foner (ed.), *Frederick Douglass*, II, p. 11.

71. John L. Thomas, *The Liberator, William Lloyd Garrison: A Biography* (Boston: Little, Brown and Company, 1963), p. 346.

72. Foner (ed.), *Frederick Douglass*, I, p. 78.

73. *Ibid*, p. 94.

74. *Ibid*, p. 82.

75. *Ibid*, II, pp. 52-53.

76. *Ibid*, I, pp. 398-99.

77. *Ibid*, II, pp. 58-59.

78. Taking a similar tack, white abolitionists also frequently exhorted free blacks to reform their personal lives and thereby demonstrate that they were "worthy" of freedom.

79. Williston H. Lofton, "Abolition and Labor," *The Journal of Negro History*, Vol. XXXIII, No. 3 (July, 1948).

80. Wesley, "Negroes in Anti-Slavery Political Parties," p. 45.

81. Eric Foner, "Politics and Prejudice: The Free Soil Party and the Negro, 1849-1852," *The Journal of Negro History*, Vol. L, No. 4 (October, 1965), p. 239.

82. James M. McPherson, *The Struggle for Equality: Abolitionists and the Negro in the Civil War and Reconstruction* (Princeton, N.J.: Princeton University Press, 1964), p. 3.

83. Eric Foner, "Politics and Prejudice," p. 240.

84. Litwack, *North of Slavery*, pp. 46-47; Patrick W. Riddleberger, "The Radicals' Abandonment of the Negro during Reconstruction," *The Journal of Negro History*, Vol. XLV, No. 2 (April, 1960), p. 89.

85. Paul M. Angle (ed.), *The Lincoln Reader* (New Brunswick, N.J.: Rutgers University Press, 1947), pp. 85-86.

86. *Ibid*, pp. 250-51, 403.

87. Additional discussion of these topics is found in Ch. III, pp. 8-10, and Ch. VI.

88. McPherson, "A Brief for Equality," p. 174.

89. Garrison supported universal suffrage without distinction as to race or sex. However, he also supported Lincoln in the campaign of 1864, defending Lincoln's reluctance to grant suffrage to the black men of the South. Garrison thought that emancipation was the most crucial issue and with the war not yet won, Lincoln should be supported. Further, he felt it hypocritical for the North to demand suffrage for

the freedmen in the South when many Northern states had limited or no black suffrage. It is because of his support of Lincoln that Garrison's defense of black suffrage is questioned. After Lincoln's death and with Southern persecution of freedmen becoming evident, Garrison belatedly demanded suffrage for black men as a means for their political self-defense. See Louis Ruchames, "William Lloyd Garrison and the Negro Franchise," *The Journal of Negro History*, Vol. L, No. 1 (January, 1965).

90. McPherson, *The Struggle for Equality*, p. 429.
91. James M. McPherson, "Abolitionists and the Civil Rights Act of 1875," *The Journal of American History*, Vol. LII, No. 3 (December, 1965).
92. McPherson, *The Struggle for Equality*, p. 430.
93. *Ibid*, pp. 234-35; William Z. Foster, *The Negro People in American History* (New York: International Publishers, 1954), pp. 267, 320.
94. McPherson, *The Struggle for Equality*, p. 123.
95. Riddleberger, "Radicals' Abandonment of the Negro."
96. McPherson, "Abolitionists and the Civil Rights Act of 1875."

Chapter III

1. Herbert Shapiro, "The Populists and the Negro: A Reconsideration," August Meir and Elliott Rudwick (eds.), *The Making of Black America* (2 Vols.; New York: Atheneum, 1969), II, pp. 28-29.
2. C. Vann Woodward, *The Strange Career of Jim Crow* (London and New York: Oxford University Press, 1966), p. 64.
3. Norman Pollack (ed.), *The Populist Mind* (Indianapolis and New York: Bobbs-Merrill Company, 1967), pp. 359-60.
4. *Ibid*, pp. 371-72.
5. *Ibid*, pp. 369-70.
6. *Ibid*, p. 365.
7. Francis M. Wilhoit, "An Interpretation of Populism's Impact on the Georgia Negro," *The Journal of Negro History* (April, 1967), p. 116; Paul Lewinson, *Race, Class and Party* (New York: Russell & Russell, 1963), pp. 70-71.
8. C. Vann Woodward, *Origins of the New South: 1877-1913* (Baton Rouge: Louisiana State University Press, 1951), pp. 252-53.
9. C. Vann Woodward, "Populism and the Intellectuals," in Raymond J.

Cunningham (ed.), *The Populists in Historical Perspective* (Boston: D.C. Heath & Company, 1968), p. 63.

10. Woodward, *Origins of the New South,* pp. 246-47, 254.

11. John D. Hicks, *The Populist Revolt* (Lincoln: University of Nebraska Press, 1961), pp. 40-42; Woodward, *Origins of the New South,* pp. 179-84.

12. Hicks, *The Populist Revolt,* p. 51.

13. *Ibid,* p. 37.

14. Herbert Aptheker (ed.), *A Documentary History of the Negro People in the United States* (2 vols.; New York: Citadel Press, 1951), II, pp. 747-48.

15. William Z. Foster, *The Negro People in American History* (New York: International Publishers, 1954), pp. 77-78.

16. Kenneth M. Stampp, *The Peculiar Institution: Slavery in the Ante-Bellum South* (New York: Vintage, 1956), pp. 38-44, 82-83, 175-83, 425-29.

17. W.E.B. Du Bois, *Black Reconstruction in America, 1860-1880* (Cleveland and New York: Meridian Books, 1962), Ch. XV; John Hope Franklin, *Reconstruction: After the Civil War* (Chicago and London: University of Chicago Press, 1961), pp. 107-09.

18. John Hope Franklin, *From Slavery to Freedom: A History of Negro Americans* (New York: Vintage, 1967), p. 304; Franklin, *Reconstruction,* p. 59. That the Republicans may have acted as much from principle as expediency is suggested in LaWanda and John H. Cox, "Negro Suffrage and Republican Politics: The Problem of Motivation in Reconstruction Historiography," *The Journal of Southern History,* Vol. 33, No. 3 (August, 1967).

19. For a discussion of the relative influence of political and economic considerations in the abandonment of Reconstruction, see William B. Hesseltine, "Economic Factors in the Abandonment of Reconstruction," *Mississippi Valley Historical Review,* Vol. XXII, No. 2 (September, 1935).

20. Kenneth M. Stampp, *The Era of Reconstruction, 1865-1877* (New York: Vintage, 1965), pp. 124-31; Martin Abbott, "Free Land, Free Labor, and the Freedmen's Bureau," *Agricultural History,* Vol. XXX, No. 4 (October, 1956); LaWanda Cox, "The Promise of Land for the Freedmen," *Mississippi Valley Historical Review,* Vol. XLV, No. 3 (December, 1958).

21. Hicks, *The Populist Revolt,* p. 52.

22. *Ibid,* p. 105.
23. *Ibid,* pp. 112-13.
24. *Ibid,* pp. 119-21.
25. *Ibid,* p. 115; Jack Abramowitz, "The Negro in the Populist Movement," *The Journal of Negro History,* Vol. XXXVIII, No. 3 (July, 1953), p. 257.
26. William W. Rogers, "The Negro Alliance in Alabama," *The Journal of Negro History* (January, 1960), p. 40.
27. Aptheker (ed.), *Documentary History,* II, p. 810.
28. C. Vann Woodward, *Tom Watson: Agrarian Rebel* (London and New York: Oxford University Press, 1963), p. 219.
29. *Ibid,* p. 218; Woodward, *Origins of the New South,* pp. 193, 245-46.
30. Woodward, *Origins of the New South,* pp. 205-06.
31. Norman Pollack, *The Populist Response to Industrial America* (New York: Norton, 1962), pp. 43-44; Pollack, *The Populist Mind,* pp. 403-66.
32. Hicks, *The Populist Revolt,* p. 115; George B. Tindall, *A Populist Reader* (New York: Harper Torchbooks, 1966), pp. 75-77.
33. Richard Hofstadter, *The Age of Reform: From Bryan to F.D.R.* (New York: Vintage, 1955), pp. 121-23.
34. Charles Crowe, "Tom Watson, Populists, and Blacks Reconsidered," *The Journal of Negro History,* Vol. LV, No. 2 (April, 1970), p. 109.
35. Clarence A. Bacote, "Negro Proscriptions, Protests, and Proposed Solutions in Georgia, 1880-1908," in Charles E. Wynes (ed.), *The Negro in the South Since 1865* (New York: Harper Colophon Books, 1968), p. 152.
36. Hicks, *The Populist Revolt,* p. 145.
37. *Ibid,* Ch. VI.
38. *Ibid,* p. 243.
39. Pollack (ed.), *The Populist Mind,* pp. 390-91. The so-called distinction between political equality and social equality presented a neat racist trap into which Southern reformers, under the influence of white supremacist thinking, consistently stumbled. By identifying social equality both with civil rights (equal access to public facilities) and social relations between the races, Southern Democrats were able to play upon white fears of racial amalgamation to deny civil rights to black people. Political equality usually was restricted in meaning to merely black suffrage. Accepting these views, white reformers hesitat-

ed to advocate black office-holding because this went beyond political equality to "black domination," and they opposed civil rights because this was equated with "defiling" the white race. The propagation of such deliberately misleading verbal devices amply demonstrated how the ideology of white supremacy, forced to give ground in one area, shored up its defenses by quarantining the area of retreat with a restrictive understanding that implied all else would remain as under the status quo antebellum. To challenge such insidious definitions and distinctions would have been to attack white supremacy. This the Populist reformers could not do. Their failure made it all the easier for Democrats later to check the limited retreat of white supremacy by disfranchising black voters.

40. C. Vann Woodward, "Tom Watson and the Negro in Agrarian Politics," in Wynes (ed.), *Negro in the South,* pp. 40-41.
41. Bacote, "Negro Proscriptions, etc.," p. 158.
42. Pollack (ed.), *The Populist Mind,* pp. 394-96.
43. Abramowitz, "The Negro in the Populist Movement," pp. 261, 263.
44. Woodward, *Origins of the New South,* pp. 212-15.
45. Aptheker (ed.), *Documentary History,* II, pp. 697-703.
46. Robert Saunders, "Southern Populists and the Negro, 1893-1895," *The Journal of Negro History,* Vol. LIV, No. 3 (July, 1969), pp. 248-49.
47. Woodward, *Origins of the New South,* pp. 211-12.
48. Saunders, "Southern Populists and the Negro," p. 247.
49. Rogers, "The Negro Alliance in Alabama," p. 41.
50. Pollack (ed.), *The Populist Mind,* pp. 392-93.
51. Joseph H. Taylor, "Populism and Disfranchisement in Alabama," *The Journal of Negro History,* Vol. XXXIV, No. 4 (October, 1949), pp. 415-16.
52. Woodward, *Origins of the New South,* p. 262.
53. Abramowitz, "The Negro in the Populist Movement," p. 280.
54. Taylor, "Populism and Disfranchisement in Alabama," p. 417n.
55. Pollack (ed.), *The Populist Mind,* pp. 391-92.
56. Taylor, "Populism and Disfranchisement in Alabama," pp. 423-24.
57. *Ibid,* pp. 422-23.
58. Woodward, *Origins of the New South,* p. 258.
59. Charles E. Wynes, *Race Relations in Virginia, 1870-1902* (Charlottesville: University of Virginia Press, 1961), p. 146.
60. *Ibid,* p. 47.

61. *Ibid,* pp. 49-50.
62. Woodward, *Origins of the New South,* p. 327.
63. Wynes, *Race Relations in Virginia,* pp. 48, 60, 149.
64. Helen G. Edmonds, *The Negro and Fusion Politics in North Carolina, 1894-1901* (Chapel Hill: University of North Carolina Press, 1951), pp. 36-37, 136, 218.
65. *Ibid,* p. 137.
66. *Ibid,* p. 145.
67. *Ibid,* p. 158; Abramowitz, "The Negro in the Populist Movement," p. 284.
68. Saunders, "Southern Populists and the Negro," p. 241; Alex Mathews Arnett, *The Populist Movement in Georgia* (New York: Columbia University, 1922), pp. 153-54.
69. Crowe, "Tom Watson, Populists, and Blacks Reconsidered," p. 102.
70. Wilhoit, "Populism's Impact on the Georgia Negro," p. 118.
71. Abramowitz, "The Negro in the Populist Movement," pp. 275-76.
72. Wilhoit, "Populism's Impact on the Georgia Negro," pp. 119-22.
73. Woodward, "Tom Watson and the Negro in Agrarian Politics," p. 55.
74. Hicks, *The Populist Revolt,* p. 343.
75. *Ibid,* p. 345; Pollack, *Populist Response to Industrial America,* pp. 105, 130-36.
76. For the details of this debate see the articles by Hofstadter and Pollack in Cunningham (ed.), *The Populists in Historical Perspective;* also, Pollack, *Populist Response to Industrial America,* pp. 103-43.
77. Abramowitz, "The Negro in the Populist Movement," pp. 287-88.
78. August Meier, *Negro Thought in America, 1880-1815* (Ann Arbor: University of Michigan Press, 1963), pp. 110-14.
79. Jack Abramowitz, "John B. Rayner—A Grass-Roots Leader," *The Journal of Negro History,* Vol. XXXVI, No. 2 (April, 1951), p. 193.
80. Aptheker (ed.), *Documentary History,* II, pp. 757-58.
81. Bacote, "Negro Proscriptions, etc.," pp. 171-79.

Chapter IV

1. Charles H. Hession and Hyman Sardy, *Ascent to Affluence: A History of American Economic Development* (Boston: Allyn and Bacon, Inc., 1969), p. 424.
2. *Ibid,* p. 422; Paul A. Baran and Paul M. Sweezy, *Monopoly Capital:*

An Essay on the American Economic and Social Order (New York and London: Monthly Review Press, 1966), pp. 220-21.

3. Hession and Sardy, *Ascent to Affluence*, pp. 463-70.

4. Quoted in Richard Hofstadter, *Social Darwinism in American Thought, 1860-1915* (Philadelphia: University of Pennsylvania Press, 1945), p. 156.

5. *Ibid*, p. 147.

6. Thomas F. Gossett, *Race: The History of an Idea in America* (New York: Schocken Books, 1965), pp. 160-75; Fred H. Matthews, "White Community and 'Yellow Peril,'" *The Mississippi Valley Historical Review*, Vol. L, No. 4 (March, 1964).

7. Gossett, *Race*, pp. 418-24.

8. *Ibid*, pp. 311-12.

9. Hofstadter, *Social Darwinism*, p. 148.

10. *Ibid*, p. 166.

11. Vernon L. Parrington, "The Progressive Era: A Liberal Renaissance," in Arthur Mann (ed.), *The Progressive Era: Liberal Renaissance or Liberal Failure?* (New York: Holt, Rinehart and Winston, 1963), p. 7.

12. James Weinstein, *The Corporate Ideal in the Liberal State: 1900-1918* (Boston: Beacon Press, 1968).

13. Richard Hofstadter (ed.), *The Progressive Movement, 1900-1915* (Englewood Cliffs, N.J.: Prentice-Hall, Inc., 1963), p. 131.

14. Richard Hofstadter, *The American Political Tradition* (New York: Vintage Books, 1948), p. 209.

15. *Ibid*, p. 212.

16. George E. Mowry, *The Era of Theodore Roosevelt, 1900-1912* (New York: Harper Torchbooks, 1962), p. 107.

17. Hofstadter, *American Political Tradition*, p. 222.

18. Mowry, *The Era of Theodore Roosevelt*, p. 55.

19. Hofstadter, *American Political Tradition*, pp. 223-24.

20. Mowry, *The Era of Theodore Roosevelt*, p. 89; Hession and Sardy, *Ascent to Affluence*, p. 580. Years later the economic crisis provoked by the Great Depression impelled Franklin Delano Roosevelt to adopt a similar strategy of reform-to-avoid-revolution.

21. Hofstadter, *American Political Tradition*, p. 226.

22. *Ibid*, p. 232.

23. Mowry, *The Era of Theodore Roosevelt*, p. 142.

24. John Hope Franklin, *From Slavery to Freedom: A History of Negro Americans* (New York: Vintage, 1969), p. 439.

25. *Ibid,* p. 443.

26. Thomas R. Cripps, "The Reaction of the Negro to the Motion Picture Birth of a Nation," *The Historian,* Vol. XXV, No. 3 (May, 1963).

27. Rayford W. Logan, *The Betrayal of the Negro* (London: Collier Books, 1965), pp. 85-86. Black people were especially disturbed by the widespread and almost daily occurrences of lynchings. A remarkable black woman, Ida Wells, took the lead in organizing the early anti-lynching campaign. A tireless organizer, writer and orator, she later married Ferdinand Lee Barnett and became a leader in the militant Afro-American Council during the period when this group opposed the submissive policies of Booker T. Washington.

28. Franklin, *From Slavery to Freedom,* pp. 434-35.

29. One historian contends that in fact Roosevelt found it politically expedient to adopt anti-black policies even earlier, in 1903. See Seth M. Scheiner, "President Theodore Roosevelt and the Negro, 1901-1908," *The Journal of Negro History,* Vol. XLVII, No. 3 (July, 1962).

30. Anti-imperialist black leaders such as W.E.B. Du Bois, Charles Baylor, Clifford Plummer and Lewis Douglass repeatedly argued that imperialism and racism were linked indissolubly, and that therefore "the American Negro cannot become the ally of imperialism without enslaving his own race."

31. Franklin, *From Slavery to Freedom,* pp. 421-23.

32. August Meier, *Negro Thought in America, 1880-1915* (Ann Arbor: The University of Michigan Press, 1966), p. 112.

33. Hanes Walton, Jr., *The Negro in Third Party Politics* (Philadelphia: Dorrance & Company, 1969), p. 49.

34. Logan, *The Betrayal of the Negro,* pp. 347-48.

35. Meier, *Negro Thought in America,* p. 165.

36. Walton, *The Negro in Third Party Politics,* p. 51.

37. Henry Blumenthal, "Woodrow Wilson and the Race Question," *The Journal of Negro History,* Vol. XLVIII, No. 1 (January, 1963).

38. Arthur S. Link, *Woodrow Wilson and the Progressive Era, 1910-1917* (New York: Harper Torchbooks, 1963), pp. 65-66.

39. Blumenthal, "Woodrow Wilson and the Race Question," pp. 11-12.

40. Wilson's old critic, William Trotter, had also journeyed to France to lobby without success for recognition of racial equality by the Ver-

sailles conference.

41. Walton, *The Negro in Third Party Politics,* p. 54.

42. C. Vann Woodward, *Origins of the New South, 1877-1913* (Baton Rouge: Louisiana State University Press, 1951), Ch. XIV.

43. George E. Mowry, *The California Progressives* (Chicago: Quadrangle Books, 1963), p. 154.

44. Roger Daniels, *The Politics of Prejudice: The Anti-Japanese Movement in California and the Struggle for Japanese Exclusion* (New York: Atheneum, 1969), p. 55.

45. Mowry, *The California Progressives,* p. 155.

46. Daniels, *The Politics of Prejudice,* p. 63.

47. Gilbert Osofsky, "Progressivism and the Negro: New York, 1900-1915," *American Quarterly,* Vol. 16, No. 2, Part 1 (Summer, 1964).

48. Meier, *Negro Thought in America,* pp. 134-35.

49. William L. O'Neill, *Everyone was Brave: The Rise and Fall of Feminism in America* (Chicago: Quadrangle Books, 1969), pp. 94-95.

50. *Ibid,* pp. 138-39, 153-62.

51. Osofsky, "Progressivism and the Negro," p. 156.

52. Horace R. Cayton and George S. Mitchell, *Black Workers and the New Unions* (Chapel Hill: University of North Carolina Press, 1939), pp. 398-412.

53. Dewey W. Grantham, Jr., "The Progressive Movement and the Negro," in Charles E. Wynes (ed.), *The Negro in the South Since 1865* (New York and Evanston: Harper Colophon, 1968), p. 67.

54. Meier, *Negro Thought in America,* pp. 88-89.

55. Harvey Wish, "Negro Education and the Progressive Movement," *The Journal of Negro History,* Vol. XLIX, No. 3 (July, 1964).

56. Herbert Aptheker (ed.), *A Documentary History of the Negro People in the United States* (2 vols.; New York: The Citadel Press, 1951), II, pp. 704-5.

57. Emma Lou Thornbrough, "The National Afro-American League, 1887-1908," *Journal of Southern History,* Vol. XXVII, No. 4 (November, 1961), p. 498.

58. Fortune had been warned by some Southern blacks about the problems of organizing a militant protest group in the South. Economic dependency and lack of power made any protest of white rule dangerous. Yet Southern blacks were not entirely passive during this period. All the states and many of the cities that passed Jim Crow laws for

streetcars at the turn of the century witnessed boycotts that lasted anywhere from a few weeks to two or three years. Although a few boycotts were temporarily successful, all failed in the end. Perhaps the
reason for the willingness of the Southern black population to support
boycotts, but not more militant protest, lies in the fact that boycotts
were a way of protesting discrimination while accommodating to it—
what has been described as "conservative protest." Jim Crow laws
were created to keep blacks from riding with whites; blacks boycotting
the streetcars hurt the transportation companies financially but did
not challenge the right of whites to ride alone. For a discussion of
the streetcar boycotts, see August Meier and Elliott Rudwick, "The
Boycott Movement Against Jim Crow Streetcars in the South, 1900-
1906," *Journal of American History*, Vol. 55, No. 4 (March, 1969).

59. After 1900 Fortune veered increasingly toward the conservatives of
the Tuskegee camp.

60. Much of the following summary of Trotter's life is based upon the
recent biography by Stephen R. Fox, *The Guardian of Boston: William Monroe Trotter* (New York: Atheneum, 1970).

61. *Ibid*, p. 25.

62. *Ibid*, p. 27.

63. *Ibid*, p. 33.

64. *The Autobiography of W.E.B. Du Bois* (New York: International
Publishers, 1968), p. 248.

65. Aptheker, *Documentary History*, II, pp. 901-10.

66. In fact, Fortune accused Du Bois of stealing the statement of principles
he had framed for the League in 1890.

67. Elliott M. Rudwick, "The Niagara Movement," *The Journal of
Negro History*, Vol. XLII, No. 3 (July, 1957).

68. Although the Niagara Movement called only for black manhood suffrage—as guaranteed by the Constitution—Du Bois supported the
woman suffrage movement in later years while editing the NAACP
journal, *Crisis*. Woman suffrage meant votes for black women who,
Du Bois said, "are moving quietly but forceably toward the intellectual leadership of the race."

69. Fox, *The Guardian of Boston*, p. 113.

70. Rudwick, "The Niagara Movement," p. 199.

71. Meier, *Negro Thought in America*, p. 180.

72. Fox, *The Guardian of Boston*, pp. 127-29; Aptheker, *Documentary
History*, II, pp. 915-27.

73. Fox, *The Guardian of Boston,* p. 135.

74. W.E.B. Du Bois, *Dusk of Dawn,* (New York: Schocken Books, 1968), p. 95.

75. Fox, *The Guardian of Boston,* pp. 19, 35, 255.

76. Du Bois, *Dusk of Dawn,* p. 94.

77. *Ibid,* pp. 72-73.

78. Meier, *Negro Thought in America,* pp. 207-47.

79. Du Bois, *Dusk of Dawn,* p. 70.

80. Francis L. Broderick, *W.E.B. Du Bois: Negro Leader in a Time of Crisis* (Stanford: Stanford University Press, 1959), pp. 100-01, 106. By 1930 Du Bois had come to realize that radicalism and liberalism (whether white or black) were inconsistent, and in 1934 he resigned from the NAACP. He returned to the group briefly in the 1940s, but this only confirmed his alienation from the organization.

Chapter V

1. Helen L. Summer, "The Historical Development of Women's Work in the United States," *The Economic Position of Women: Proceedings of the Academy of Political Science in the City of New York,* Vol. I, No. 1 (1910), p. 19.

2. *Ibid,* p. 17 (note 1).

3. Charlotte Perkins Gilman was one of the very few women to analyze and suggest alternatives to woman's role in the home.

4. William L. O'Neill, *Everyone Was Brave: The Rise and Fall of Feminism in America* (Chicago: Quadrangle Books, 1969), pp. 159-160.

5. Aileen S. Kraditor, *The Ideas of the Woman Suffrage Movement: 1890-1920* (New York and London: Columbia University Press, 1965), pp. 110-111.

6. Senator George Vest, a Democrat, appealed to the subjective prejudices and desires of his compatriots when he spoke against woman suffrage in the 49th Congress in 1887. "For my part," he said, "I want when I go to my home. . . not to be received in the masculine embrace of some female ward politician, but to the ernest, loving look and touch of a true woman. . . . I want those blessed, loving details of domestic life and domestic love." Aileen S. Kraditor, *Up From the Pedestal* (Chicago: Quadrangle Books, 1968), p. 195. For a full discussion of the arguments developed for and against suffrage see Aileen S. Kraditor, *Ideas,* Chapters II and III.

7. Kraditor, *Ideas,* p. 31.

8. Alan P. Grimes, *The Puritan Ethic and Woman Suffrage* (New York: Oxford University Press, 1967), pp. 102, 111, 131. One slogan of the anti-Chinese movement was "Women's Rights and No More Chinese Chambermaids."

9. Unfortunately there have been few attempts to study the relationship of white suffragists to black women and the suffrage movement's response to racism. Among the standard studies of the woman's rights movement Eleanor Flexner's *Century of Struggle* offers information on the activities of black women. She, however, avoids dealing with the racism in the white movement. Aileen Kraditor's *Ideas of the Woman Suffrage Movement* does offer an in-depth analysis of the alliance between white supremacy and the women suffrage movement. But her study is confined to the years 1890-1920 and thereby contributes to a false impression that the origins of racism in the woman suffrage movement were limited to the influences on the movement at the turn of the century. William O'Neill in his books, *Everyone Was Brave* and *The Woman Movement,* dutifully notes the racism among white women but he is neither interested in analyzing this nor in discussing the independent activities of black women. Andrew Sinclair's *The Emancipation of the American Woman* exhibits the most serious failure in dealing with racism because the author adheres to many of the same racist assumptions that typified the white feminists. The contemporary resurgence of feminism may be stirring a new interest in the relationship between the struggles for racial equality and women's rights. See for example, Catherine Stimpson, "Thy Neighbor's Wife, Thy Neighbor's Servants: Women's Liberation and Black Civil Rights," in Vivian Gornick and Barbara K. Moran (eds.), *Woman in Sexist Society: Studies in Power and Powerlessness* (New York and London: Basic Books, Inc., 1971).

10. See Aileen S. Kraditor, *Means and Ends in American Abolitionism* (New York: Pantheon Books, 1969), Chapter 3.

11. *The Letters of Theodore Weld, Angelina Grimké Weld and Sarah Grimké,* 1822-1844 (2 vols.; New York, 1934), pp. 428-429.

12. Eleanor Flexner, *Century of Struggle: The Woman's Rights Movement in the United States* (New York: Atheneum, 1968), pp. 47, 344 (note 19).

13. *Ibid,* pp. 74-76.

14. Elizabeth Cady Stanton, Susan B. Anthony, and Matilda Joslyn Gage (eds.), *History of Woman Suffrage* (2 vols.: New York: Fowler and

Wells, 1881-1882), I, pp. 108, 137.

15. Flexner, *Century of Struggle,* p. 70.

16. Gunnar Myrdal, *An American Dilemma* (2 vols.; New York and London: Harper and Brothers, 1944), II, pp. 1073-1078: quoted in Chilton Williamson, *American Suffrage: From Property to Democracy, 1760-1860* (Princeton: Princeton University Press, 1960), p. 279.

17. Lucretia Mott wrote to Elizabeth Cady Stanton: "We are now in the midst of a convention of the colored people of this city. Douglass & Delany—Remond & Garnet are here—all taking an active part— and as they include women & white women too, I can do no less, with the interest I feel in the cause of the slave, as well as of women, than be present & take a little part—So yesterday, in a pouring rain, Sarah Pugh & self, walked down there & expect to do the same to-day." Philip S. Foner, *The Life and Writings of Frederick Douglass* (4 vols.; New York: International Publishers, 1950), II, pp. 18-19.

18. *Ibid,* p. 19; Benjamin Quarles, *Frederick Douglass* (New York: Atheneum, 1968), pp. 133-136. See also Benjamin Quarles, "Frederick Douglass and the Woman's Rights Movement," *Journal of Negro History,* Vol. XXV, No. 1 (1940).

19. Stanton, Anthony and Gage (eds.), *History of Woman Suffrage,* I, p. 103.

20. *Ibid,* pp. 115-117.

21. Hertha Pauli, *Her Name Was Sojourner Truth* (New York: Appleton-Century-Crofts, 1962), pp. 189-190.

22. Earl Conrad, "I Bring You General Tubman," *The Black Scholar,* Vol. I, No. 3-4 (1970), pp. 3-7; Sue Davis, "Harriet Tubman: The Moses of Her People," *Women: A Journal of Liberation,* Vol. I, No. 3 (1970), pp. 12-45; John Hope Franklin, *From Slavery to Freedom* (New York: Vintage Books, 1969), p. 259.

23. Angela Davis, "Reflections on the Black Woman's Role in the Community of Slaves," *The Black Scholar,* Vol. III, No. 4 (1971), pp. 9-11.

24. Stanton, Anthony and Gage (eds.), *History of Woman Suffrage,* I, pp. 814-815.

25. *Ibid,* p. 811.

26. Davis, "Reflections on the Black Woman's Role," *The Black Scholar,* Vol. III, No. 4 (1971), pp. 3-15.

27. James S. Allen, *Reconstruction: The Battle for Democracy* (New York: International Publishers, 1937), p. 85.

28. For example, Frances Dana Gage sent a letter to Congress saying that when she had worked with the Freedmen's Aid Society black women had come to her saying they did not want to marry the men they lived with because then their husbands would have power over them. A Democrat cited her letter during a debate whether to grant black male suffrage in the District of Columbia. The senator argued that black men who abused their wives were unfit to vote. Stanton, Anthony and Gage (eds.), *History of Woman Suffrage,* II, pp. 94-97, 103; Foner, *Frederick Douglass,* IV, p. 42.

29. Ida Husted Harper, *The Life and Work of Susan B. Anthony* (2 vols.: Indianapolis and Kansas City: Bowen Merrill Co., 1899), I, pp. 256-59.

30. *Ibid,* p. 297. Train's association with the paper was short-lived. He was soon off to Ireland.

31. Stanton, Anthony and Gage (eds.), *History of Woman Suffrage,* II, p. 382; Foner, *Frederick Douglass,* IV, pp. 41-44, 212-213.

32. Harper, *Susan B. Anthony,* Vol. I, pp. 258, 269, 314; Stanton, Anthony and Gage (eds.), *History of Woman Suffrage,* II, pp. 214-215, 265.

33. Stanton, Anthony and Gage (eds.), *History of Woman Suffrage,* II, p. 215.

34. Stanton, Anthony and Gage (eds.), *History of Woman Suffrage,* II, pp. 94-95.

35. Harper, *Susan B. Anthony,* I, pp. 323-324.

36. Stanton, Anthony and Gage (eds.), *History of Woman Suffrage,* II, pp. 391-392.

37. *Ibid,* pp. 193-194, 928. Elizabeth Cady Stanton reported that Sojourner Truth commented on her call for universal suffrage, "If you bait the suffrage-hook with a woman you will certainly catch a black man." This would imply that she did not oppose black male suffrage but looked upon it as a partial victory.

38. Foner, *Frederick Douglass,* IV, p. 44.

39. Henry Blackwell opposed "black rule" in the South and in 1867 wrote an open letter to Southern legislatures showing how woman suffrage would guarantee white supremacy in the South even with black suffrage. His arguments were based on statistics that showed the estimated number of white women in the South equaled the total number of blacks, male and female. Stanton, Anthony and Gage (eds.), *History of Woman Suffrage,* II, pp. 397, 929-931.

40. Personal animosities also played a part. Robert Riegel notes that the participants, their biographers and historians vary in their emphasis

on what caused the original break, some thinking that other considerations were more important than the disagreement over the Fifteenth Amendment. Robert E. Riegel, "The Split of the Feminist Movement in 1869," *Mississippi Valley Historical Review,* Vol. XLIX, No. 3 (1962),

41. Andrew Sinclair, *The Emancipation of the American Woman* (New York: Harper and Row, 1966), p. 191.

42. O'Neill, *Everyone Was Brave,* pp. 19-20.

43. William L. O'Neill (ed.), *The Woman Movement: Feminism in the United States and England* (Chicago: Quadrangle Books, 1971), pp. 119-121.

44. Kraditor, *Ideas,* pp. 30, 164, 216.

45. Ida Husted Harper (ed.), *History of Woman Suffrage* (New York: The National American Woman Suffrage Association, 1922), V, p. 106.

46. Kraditor, *Ideas,* p. 131.

47. *Ibid,* pp. 132-136.

48. Alfreda M. Duster (ed.), *Crusade For Justice: The Autobiography of Ida B. Wells* (Chicago and London: University of Chicago Press, 1970), pp. 229-30.

49. Kraditor, *Ideas,* pp. 169-172.

50. *Ibid,* p. 166. For an illustration of the type of speeches Southern women could make from the NAWSA platform see Kraditor, *Up From the Pedestal,* pp. 262-265.

51. Duster (ed.), *Ida B. Wells,* pp. 72-75; Foner, *Frederick Douglass,* IV, pp. 410-411.

52. Harper, *Susan B. Anthony,* II, pp. 853-854.

53. Duster (ed.), *Ida B. Wells,* p. 64.

54. Gerda Lerner, *Black Women in White America: A Documentary History* (New York: Pantheon Books, 1972), p. 437.

55. August Meier, *Negro Thought in America: 1880-1915* (Ann Arbor: University of Michigan Press, 1966), pp. 134-135.

56. Lerner, *Black Women in White America,* pp. 441-443. For an account of the General Federation of Women's Clubs' refusal to accept black clubs for membership see Rayford W. Logan, *The Betrayal of the Negro: From Rutherford B. Hayes to Woodrow Wilson* (London: Collier-Macmillian Ltd., 1965), pp. 238-241.

57. Carrie Chapman Catt and Nettie Rogers Shuler, *Woman Suffrage and Politics: The Inner Story of the Suffrage Movement* (Seattle and Lon-

don: University of Washington Press, 1969), p. 107.

58. O'Neill, *Everyone Was Brave,* p. 275.

59. Lerner, *Black Women in White America,* pp. 472-477.

Chapter VI

1. Joseph G. Rayback, *A History of American Labor* (New York: The Free Press, 1966), p. 24.

2. William M. Tuttle, Jr., "Labor Conflict and Racial Violence: The Black Worker in Chicago, 1894-1919," *Labor History,* Vol. 10 (Summer, 1969), p. 429.

3. Julius Jacobson (ed.), *The Negro and the American Labor Movement* (Garden City, N.Y.: Doubleday-Anchor, 1968), p. 19.

4. Sterling D. Spero & Abram L. Harris, *The Black Worker* (New York: Atheneum, 1968), pp. 5-6.

5. Robert Starobin, "Disciplining Industrial Slaves in the Old South," *The Journal of Negro History,* Vol. LIII, No. 2 (April, 1968); Sydney Bradford, "The Negro Ironworker in Ante Bellum Virginia," *The Journal of Southern History,* Vol. XXV, No. 2 (May, 1959); Charles S. Johnson, "The Conflict of Caste and Class in an American Industry," *American Journal of Sociology,* Vol. XLII, No. 1 (July, 1936).

6. Spero & Harris, *The Black Worker,* pp. 6-7.

7. Ray Marshall, *The Negro Worker* (New York: Random House, 1967), p. 7.

8. Spero & Harris, *The Black Worker,* p. 10.

9. Charles H. Wesley, *Negro Labor in the United States, 1850-1925* (New York: Vanguard Press, 1927), pp. 71-72, 80-83.

10. Rayback, *American Labor,* p. 100.

11. *Ibid,* p. 101.

12. W.E.B. Du Bois, *Black Reconstruction in America, 1860-1880* (Cleveland and New York: Meridian Books, 1964), p. 57.

13. *Ibid,* p. 58.

14. *Ibid,* p. 67.

15. Williston H. Lofton, "Northern Labor and the Negro During the Civil War," *The Journal of Negro History,* Vol. XXXIV, No. 3 (July, 1949).

16. Marshall, *The Negro Worker,* p. 57.

17. *Ibid,* p. 63.

18. Spero & Harris, *The Black Worker,* p. 75.
19. Quoted by Marc Karson and Ronald Radosh, "The American Federation of Labor and the Negro Worker, 1894-1949," in Jacobson (ed.), *The Negro and the American Labor Movement,* p. 181.
20. Herman D. Bloch, "Craft Unions and the Negro in Historical Perspective," *The Journal of Negro History,* Vol. XLII, No. 1 (January, 1958).
21. Bernard Mandel, "Samuel Gompers and the Negro Workers, 1886-1914," *The Journal of Negro History,* Vol. XL, No. 1 (January, 1955), pp. 52-53.
22. Ray Marshall, *The Negro and Organized Labor* (New York: John Wiley & Sons, 1965), p. 22.
23. Roger Daniels, *The Politics of Prejudice* (New York: Atheneum, 1969), pp. 16-30; Alexander Saxton, "Race and the House of Labor," in Gary B. Nash and Richard Weiss (eds.), *The Great Fear: Race in the Mind of America* (New York: Holt, Rinehart and Winston, 1970), pp. 107-114.
24. For example, in 1911 AFL organizers near Fresno, Calif., tried to convince employers to accept the white union affiliate, the United Laborers of America, because this could eliminate the Japanese from harvesting grapes. See Philip S. Foner, *History of the Labor Movement in the United States* (4 vols.; New York: International Publishers, 1947-1965), IV, p. 260.
25. Carey McWilliams, *North From Mexico* (New York: Greenwood Press, 1968), pp. 193-95.
26. Wesley, *Negro Labor in the U.S.,* p. 142.
27. Tuttle, "Labor Conflict and Racial Violence."
28. Spero & Harris, *The Black Worker,* pp. 65-66.
29. *Ibid,* p. 132.
30. *Ibid,* pp. 131-132.
31. Wesley, *Negro Labor in the U.S.,* p. 262.
32. Mandel, "Samuel Gompers and the Negro Workers," p. 46.
33. John R. Commons and Associates (eds.) *A Documentary History of American Industrial Society,* Vol. IX (Cleveland: Arthur H. Clark Co., 1910), pp. 185-88; Sumner Eliot Matison, "The Labor Movement and the Negro During Reconstruction," *The Journal of Negro History,* Vol. XXXIII, No. 4 (October, 1948).
34. For a discussion of the ideological differences between black and white labor see Preston Valien, "The 'Mentalities' of Negro and White

Workers: An 'Experimental School' Interpretation of Negro Trade Unionism," *Social Forces,* Vol. 27 (May, 1949).

35. A similar altercation with roles reversed had occurred at the 1869 meeting of the black national labor convention when two white delegates were accused of being secret emissaries of the Democratic Party.

36. Wesley, *Negro Labor in the U.S.,* pp. 187-89.

37. Like most of the rest of the labor movement (including black labor groups), however, the Knights were hostile to Chinese contract labor. A black leader of the Knights, Frank J. Ferrell, was prominent in the unsuccessful fight to include Chinese workers in the organization.

38. Sidney H. Kessler, "The Organization of Negroes in the Knights of Labor," *The Journal of Negro History,* Vol. XXXVII, No. 3 (July, 1952), pp. 272-73.

39. *Ibid,* p. 265.

40. Foner, *Labor Movement in the U.S.,* IV, pp. 37, 70, 114, 123, 129; Rayback, *American Labor,* pp. 238, 282.

41. Foner, *Labor Movement in the U.S.,* IV, pp. 65, 88-95, 239.

42. *Ibid,* pp. 123-25, 127, 168.

43. Spero & Harris, *The Black Worker,* p. 331. There is some disagreement about the reliability of this figure since the IWW never published any official statistics on black membership.

44. *Ibid,* pp. 333-36.

45. Foner, *Labor Movement in the U.S.,* IV, pp. 252-54.

46. *Ibid,* pp. 120, 549.

47. *Ibid,* pp. 114, 145, 159, 167.

48. Philip S. Foner, "The IWW and the Black Worker," *The Journal of Negro History,* Vol. LV, No. 1 (January, 1970), p. 50.

49. Spero & Harris, *The Black Worker,* p. 228.

50. Marshall, *The Negro Worker,* pp. 43-44; Paul B. Worthman, "Black Workers and Labor Unions in Birmingham, Alabama, 1897-1904," *Labor History,* Vol. 10 (Summer, 1969).

51. Spero & Harris, *The Black Worker,* pp. 379-81.

52. Kenneth B. Clark, *Dark Ghetto: Dilemmas of Social Power* (New York: Harper Torchbooks, 1967), pp. 43-45.

53. Marshall, *The Negro Worker,* pp. 28-29.

54. Marshall, *The Negro and Organized Labor,* pp. 43-44.

55. Marshall, *The Negro Worker,* pp. 32-33.

56. Amy Jacques-Garvey (ed.), *Philosophy and Opinions of Marcus Garvey,* Vol. II (New York Atheneum, 1970), pp. 69-70.

57. This utopian reasoning ignored the fact that the black capitalist, like his white counterpart, would still seek to minimize his labor costs, and from an economic standpoint would not necessarily be more favorable to the black worker than a white employer similarly seeking cheap labor.

58. Horace R. Cayton and George S. Mitchell, *Black Workers and the New Unions* (Chapel Hill: University of North Carolina Press, 1939), pp. 384-87.

59. Brailsford R. Brazeal, *The Brotherhood of Sleeping Car Porters* (New York: Harper & Brothers, 1946), pp. 50-56.

60. Cayton and Mitchell, *Black Workers and the New Unions*, pp. 376-77.

61. Marshall, *The Negro Worker*, pp. 84-85; William Kornhauser, "The Negro Union Official: A Study of Sponsorship and Control," *The American Journal of Sociology*, Vol. LVII (March, 1952).

62. Spero & Harris, *The Black Worker*, pp. 79, 448, 457.

63. McWilliams, *North From Mexico*, pp. 190-91.

Chapter VII

1. David A. Shannon, *The Socialist Party of America* (Chicago: Quadrangle Books, 1967), pp. 53f.

2. Giles Radice, *Democratic Socialism: A Short Survey* (New York: Praeger, 1966), pp. 1-15.

3. Wilson Record, "The Development of the Communist Position on the Negro Question in the United States," *Phylon*, Vol. XIX, No. 3 (1958), p. 313.

4. V.I. Lenin, *The Right of Nations to Self-Determination* (New York: International Publishers, 1951), pp. 76-78.

5. *Ibid*, see Lenin's discussions of Poland and Norway.

6. Lenin, *Imperialism, the Highest Stage of Capitalism* (Moscow: Foreign Languages Publishing House n.d.), p. 183.

7. Eric Hobsbawm, "Lenin and the 'Aristocracy of Labor,'" *Monthly Review*, Vol. 21, No. 11 (April, 1970), p. 54.

8. Lenin, *Imperialism*, p. 218.

9. William Z. Foster, *The Negro People in American History* (New York: International Publishers, 1954), p. 403.

10. Hanes Walton, Jr., *The Negro in Third Party Politics* (Philadelphia:

Dorrance & Company, 1969), p. 61.

11. Sally M. Miller, "The Socialist Party and the Negro, 1901-1920," *The Journal of Negro History,* Vol. LVI, No. 3 (July, 1971), p. 226.

12. Shannon, *The Socialist Party of America,* pp. 50, 51-52.

13. James Weinstein, *The Decline of Socialism in America, 1912-1925* (New York: Vintage, 1969), p. 69.

14. Miller, "The Socialist Party and the Negro," p. 221.

15. Sterling D. Spero and Abram L. Harris, *The Black Worker* (New York: Atheneum, 1968), p. 408.

16. Shannon, *The Socialist Party of America,* pp. 49-50.

17. Weinstein, *Decline of Socialism,* p. 70.

18. Shannon, *The Socialist Party of America,* p. 52.

19. Kenneth McNaught, "Socialism and the Progressives: Was Failure Inevitable?" in Alfred F. Young (ed.) *Dissent: Explorations in the History of American Radicalism* (Dekalb, Ill.: Northern Illinois University Press, 1968), pp. 253-71.

20. Jerold S. Auerbach, "Southern Tenant Farmers: Socialist Critics of the New Deal," *Labor History,* Vol. 7, No. 1 (1966).

21. Wilson Record, *The Negro and the Communist Party* (Chapel Hill: University of North Carolina Press, 1951), pp. 29-32, 75-77, 143-46; Foster, *The Negro People in American History,* pp. 501-04; William A. Nolan, *Communism versus the Negro* (Chicago: Henry Regnery Company, 1951), pp. 116-18.

22. Foster, *The Negro People in American History,* p. 480.

23. Benjamin J. Davis, *Communist Councilman from Harlem* (New York: International Publishers, 1969).

24. Foster, *The Negro People in American History,* pp. 489-91, 499-501.

25. Nolan, *Communism versus the Negro,* pp. 118-22.

26. Record, *Negro and the CP,* pp. 72-73.

27. John Beecher, "The Share Croppers' Union in Alabama," *Social Forces,* Vol. 13 (1934-35), p. 132.

28. Record, *Negro and the CP,* pp. 86-90.

29. The CP was accused of virtually sacrificing the Scottsboro boys to martyrdom for propaganda purposes. For a recent re-evaluation of the evidence that questions this interpretation, see Hugh T. Murray, Jr., "The NAACP Versus the Communist Party: The Scottsboro Rape Cases, 1931-1932," *Phylon,* Vol. XXVIII, No. 3 (1967).

30. Record, *Negro and the CP,* p. 306.

31. Nathan Glazer, *The Social Basis of American Communism* (New York: Harcourt, Brace & World, Inc., 1961), pp. 174-75.

32. St. Clair Drake and Horace R. Cayton, *Black Metropolis: A Study of Negro Life in a Northern City* (2 vols.; New York: Harbinger, 1970), II, p. 736.

33. Glazer, *The Social Basis of American Communism,* p. 176.

34. A classic illustration of these shifting tactics is evidenced in the history of the party's relations with the NAACP, amply described in Wilson Record, *Race and Radicalism: The NAACP and the Communist Party in Conflict* (Ithaca, N.Y.: Cornell University Press, 1964).

35. Record, *Negro and the CP,* p. 153.

36. *Ibid,* pp. 184-85, 198-99.

37. *Ibid,* pp. 219-20.

38. Theodore Draper, *American Communism and Soviet Russia* (New York: Viking-Compass, 1963), pp. 345-53.

39. Lenin, *The Right of Nations to Self-Determination,* pp. 11, 65, 73.

40. J. Stalin, *Marxism and the National Question* (Moscow: Foreign Languages Publishing House, 1954), p. 16.

41. Harold W. Cruse, "Revolutionary Nationalism and the Afro-American," *Studies on the Left,* Vol. II, No. 3 (1962).

42. Harry Haywood, *Negro Liberation* (New York: International Publishers, 1948).

43. Joseph C. Mouledous, "From Browderism to Peaceful Co-Existence: An Analysis of Developments in the Communist Position on the American Negro," *Phylon,* Vol. XXV, No. 1 (1964).

44. Ernest Kaiser, "Racial Dialectics: The Aptheker-Myrdal School Controversy," *Phylon,* Vol. IX, No. 4 (1948).

45. Genovese, for example, accuses "official" Marxist historical writers—including Marx and Engels—of failing to investigate the independent role played by ideology in unifying and strengthening the slavery-based society of the antebellum South. Eugene D. Genovese, *In Red and Black: Marxian Explorations in Southern and Afro-American History* (New York: Pantheon, 1971), pp. 315-53.

46. Glazer, *The Social Basis of American Communism,* p. 172; Irving Howe and Lewis Coser, *The American Communist Party: A Critical History* (New York: Praeger, 1962), pp. 208-11.

47. Claudia Jones, "An End to the Neglect of the Problems of the Negro Woman!" *Political Affairs* (June, 1949).

48. Nolan, *Communism versus the Negro,* pp. 177-78; Drake and Cayton, *Black Metropolis,* I, pp. 137-38n.

49. See articles by Pettis Perry in *Political Affairs,* October, 1949; May, 1950; December, 1950; October, 1951.

50. Draper, *American Communism and Soviet Russia,* p. 320; Record, *Negro and the CP,* pp. 26, 52, 62, 115-17.

51. Draper, *American Communism and Soviet Russia,* p. 321.

52. Glazer, *The Social Basis of American Communism,* pp. 130-68; Harold Cruse, *The Crisis of the Negro Intellectual* (New York: William Morrow, 1967), pp. 147-70; Pettis Perry, "Press Forward the Struggle Against White Chauvinism," *Political Affairs* (May, 1950), p. 144.

53. David A. Shannon, *The Decline of American Communism* (New York: Harcourt, Brace & Company, 1959), pp. 246-47.

54. Draper, *American Communism and Soviet Russia,* pp. 357-76.

55. James P. Cannon, *The History of American Trotskyism* (New York: Pioneer Publishers, 1944).

56. George Breitman (ed.), *Leon Trotsky on Black Nationalism and Self-Determination* (New York: Merit Publishers, 1967), p. 8.

57. "Documents on the Negro Struggle," *Bulletin of Marxist Studies, No. 4* (New York: Pioneer Publishers, n.d.), p. 4.

58. Breitman (ed.), *Trotsky on Black Nationalism,* p. 16.

59. *Ibid,* pp. 10-19.

60. Cannon, *History of American Trotskyism,* pp. 252-53.

61. Breitman (ed.), *Trotsky on Black Nationalism,* pp. 29,31.

62. *Ibid,* pp. 33-45, *passim.*

63. *Ibid,* pp. 51-52.

64. Daniel Guerin, *Negroes on the March* (New York: Distributed by George L. Weissman, 1956), pp. 131-32.

65. "Documents on the Negro Struggle," p. 8.

66. *Ibid,* pp. 35-41.

67. See Harold Cruse, George Breitman, Clifton DeBarry, *Marxism and the Negro Struggle* (New York: Pioneer Publishers, 1965).

68. Herbert G. Gutman, "Peter H. Clark: Pioneer Negro Socialist, 1877," *The Journal of Negro Education,* Vol. XXXIV, No. 4 (Fall, 1965).

69. August Meier, *Negro Thought in America, 1880-1915* (Ann Arbor: University of Michigan Press, 1966), pp. 46-48.

70. *Ibid,* pp. 203-4.

71. Francis L. Broderick, *W.E.B. Du Bois: Negro Leader in a Time of*

Crisis (Stanford, Calif.: Stanford University Press, 1959), pp. 137-49.

72. Draper, *American Communism and Soviet Russia,* pp. 322-26.

73. Theodore G. Vincent, *Black Power and the Garvey Movement* (Berkeley, Calif.: Ramparts Press, [1971]), p. 76.

74. *Ibid,* p. 79.

75. Draper, *American Communism and Soviet Russia,* p. 324.

76. Vincent, *Black Power and the Garvey Movement,* pp. 78-85.

77. Spero and Harris, *The Black Worker,* p. 390.

78. Richard Wright, "Blueprint for Negro Literature," in John A. Williams and Charles F. Harris (eds.), *Amistad 2: Writings on Black History and Culture* (New York: Vintage, 1971), pp. 5-9.

79. Richard Wright, "How Bigger was Born," in Richard Wright, *Native Son* (New York: Grosset & Dunlap, 1940), pp. xxiv-xxvii.

80. *Ibid,* pp. xxvii, xxix-xxxii.

81. *Ibid,* p. xxiv; "Richard Wright," in Richard Crossman (ed.), *The God that Failed* (New York: Bantam Matrix, 1965), pp. 105-6.

82. Crossman (ed.), *The God that Failed,* p. 117.

83. See articles by Samuel Sillen in *New Masses,* March 5, 1940; April 23, 1940; April 30, 1940; May 21, 1940.

84. Edward Margolies, *Native Sons: A Critical Study of 20th Century Negro American Authors* (Philadelphia and New York: J.B. Lippincott Company, 1969), p. 70.

85. *New Masses,* August 29, 1944, pp. 25-26.

86. William Z. Foster, *History of the Communist Party of the United States* (New York: International Publishers, 1952), p. 424.

87. Richard Wright claimed that at one time blacks had to fight for the right to set up an all-black committee within the CP. See Guerin, *Negroes on the March,* p. 186n.

88. Colin Legum, *Pan-Africanism: A Short Political Guide* (New York: Frederick A. Praeger, 1965), p. 24.

89. George Shepperson, "Notes on Negro American Influences on the Emergence of African Nationalism," *Journal of African History,* Vol. I, No. 2 (1960).

90. *Ibid;* see also George Shepperson, "Pan-Africanism and 'Pan-Africanism': Some Historical Notes," *Phylon,* Vol. 23, No. 4 (1962).

91. Legum, *Pan-Africanism,* pp. 28-30.

92. Elliott M. Rudwick, "Du Bois versus Garvey: Race Propagandists

at War," *The Journal of Negro Education,* Vol. 28, No. 4 (1959), pp. 423, 426.

93. *Ibid,* p. 424.

94. E. David Cronon, *Black Moses: The Story of Marcus Garvey* (Madison: University of Wisconsin Press, 1969), p. 152.

95. *Ibid,* p. 196.

96. *Ibid,* p. 198.

97. Record, *Negro and the CP,* pp. 40-41.

98. For a discussion of Garvey's contact with the KKK, see Cronon, *Black Moses,* pp. 188-90; Vincent, *Black Power and the Garvey Movement,* pp. 190-91, 205-06.

99. Draper, *American Communism and Soviet Russia,* p. 330.

100. C.L.R. James, *A History of Pan-African Revolt* (Washington: Drum and Spear Press, 1969), pp. 81-82.

101. James R. Hooker, *Black Revolutionary: George Padmore's Path from Communism to Pan-Africanism* (New York: Praeger, 1967), pp. 93-95.

102. Legum, *Pan-Africanism,* p. 32.

103. Hooker, *Black Revolutionary,* p. 31.

104. *Ibid,* pp. 33, 48, 56.

105. Legum, *Pan-Africanism,* pp. 38-39.

106. Hooker, *Black Revolutionary,* pp. 128-29.

107. Kwame Nkrumah, *Dark Days in Ghana* (New York: International Publishers, 1968); *Handbook of Revolutionary Warfare* (New York: International Publishers, 1969); *Class Struggle in Africa* (New York: International Publishers, 1970).

108. Robert L. Allen, *Black Awakening in Capitalist America,* pp. 247-53.

109. Stokely Carmichael, *Stokely Speaks: Black Power to Pan-Africanism* (New York: Random House, 1971), pp. xvi, 221, 226.

110. Kwame Nkrumah, *Class Struggle in Africa,* p. 26.

111. *Ibid,* p. 25.

Chapter VIII

1. Thomas F. Gossett, *Race: The History of an Idea in America* (New York: Schocken Books, 1965), pp. 3-16; Frank M. Snowden, Jr.,

Blacks in Antiquity: Ethiopians in the Greco-Roman Experience (Cambridge, Mass.: The Belknap Press of Harvard University Press, 1970), pp. 216-18.

2. Paul A. Baran, *The Political Economy of Growth* (New York and London: Modern Reader, 1968), pp. 136-39.

3. Oliver C. Cox, *Capitalism as a System* (New York: Monthly Review, 1964).

4. Stanley M. Elkins, *Slavery: A Problem in American Institutional and Intellectual Life* (Chicago and London: The University of Chicago Press, 1968), pp. 52-80; Max Weber, *The Protestant Ethic and the Spirit of Capitalism* (New York: Charles Scribner's Sons, 1958).

5. Eugene D. Genovese, *The World the Slaveholders Made* (New York: Vintage, 1971), pp. 21-113, *passim;* Genovese, *In Red and Black: Marxian Explorations in Southern and Afro-American History* (New York: Pantheon, 1971), pp. 23-52, 158-72.

6. Oliver C. Cox, *Caste, Class and Race* (Garden City, N.Y.: Doubleday, 1948), Chapter 16. Some contemporary scholars have denied that there was any causal link between capitalist slavery and racism. These writers place greater stress on psychological variables or pre-existing attitudes in accounting for the development of racism, yet their own evidence reveals the crucial role played by the institutionalization of slavery in the English colonies (and English contact with other slave-trading nations) in fostering and shaping the ideology of racism. See Oscar Handlin, *Race and Nationality in American Life* (Garden City, N.Y.: Doubleday-Anchor, 1957); Carl Degler, "Slavery and the Genesis of American Race Prejudice," in Melvin Drimmer (ed.), *Black History: A Reappraisal* (Garden City, N.Y.: Doubleday, 1968). A critique of Degler's thesis that black slavery was molded by preexisting prejudices and discrimination can be found in Louis Ruchames (ed.), *Racial Thought in America*, Vol. I (New York: Grosset & Dunlap, 1970), pp. 13-15. A similar argument is found in George M. Frederickson, "Toward a Social Interpretation of the Development of American Racism," in Nathan I. Huggins, Martin Kilson and Daniel M. Fox (eds.), *Key Issues in the Afro-American Experience*, Vol. I (New York: Harcourt, Brace, Jovanovich, 1971). For a detailed examination of this subject see Winthrop D. Jordan, *White over Black: American Attitudes Toward the Negro, 1550-1812* (Baltimore, Md.: Penguin Books, 1969).

7. James Boggs, *Racism and the Class Struggle* (New York and London: Monthly Review Press, 1970), pp. 150-52.

8. Eric Williams, *Capitalism and Slavery* (New York: Capricorn Books, 1966). Even those whites in Europe who were severely exploited had no reason to oppose racism since colonialism and slavery offered them an unprecedented opportunity to emigrate and acquire land and labor resources relatively cheaply.

9. Some of the complexities of this debate are traced in George M. Frederickson, *The Black Image in the White Mind: The Debate on Afro-American Character and Destiny, 1817-1914* (New York: Harper & Row, 1971).

10. Paul A. Baran and Paul M. Sweezy, *Monopoly Capital: An Essay on the American Economic and Social Order* (New York and London: Monthly Review Press, 1966), Chapter 3.

11. Here we see a modern bourgeois counterpart of the older mercantilist interest in religious education and conversion. The bourgeois evangelism at the turn of the century can also be considered an anticipation of the full-blown cultural chauvinism that would emerge after World War I.

12. Frederickson, *The Black Image in the White Mind,* Chapter 8; Gossett, *Race,* pp. 66-68, Chapters VII, VIII, XIII.

13. Frederickson, *The Black Image in the White Mind,* Chapter 10.

14. Martin Nicolaus, "The Theory of the Labor Aristocracy," *Monthly Review,* Volume 21, No. 11 (April, 1970).

15. The structural limits of integrationism are discussed in Robert L. Allen, *Black Awakening in Capitalist America* (Garden City, N.Y.: Doubleday-Anchor, 1970).

16. Eric R. Wolf, *Peasant Wars of the Twentieth Century* (New York: Harper & Row, 1969).

17. Gossett, *Race,* p. 341.

18. Allen, *Black Awakening in Capitalist America,* pp. 17–20.

Recent Social Reform Movements

As the struggle against racial slavery catalyzed social change in the mid-nineteenth century, so did the struggle against racial discrimination midwife social change movements in the 1960s and 1970s. The black freedom movement shaped the political consciousness of an entire generation of young Americans of all races, women as well as men. In subsequent years many of those whose first political experience was in the civil rights movement in the sixties emerged as leaders of the New Left, the anti-Vietnam War movement, the women's liberation movement and other struggles. The black freedom movement prompted untold numbers of people to reexamine their own life situations, to reexamine the society in which they live and to ask the question: Why should anyone be allowed to treat me as less than a full human being? It is no exaggeration to suggest that the black freedom movement was the wellspring, the source of new consciousness and social activism during this recent period. Indeed, the social and ideological impact of the modern black freedom movement has been profound and reverberates throughout American society to this day.

This postscript describes the development of the modern black freedom movement and discusses the central role it has played ideologically in the emergence of other social change movements.

Civil Rights Movement

The South

Several factors are important to understanding the origins of the southern civil rights movement. First, the labor demands created by World War II and the Korean War opened up new jobs for black workers in the defense plants. Moreover, the war in Europe was partly a struggle against Nazi racism and implicitly challenged segregation at home. Many black people came to believe that if the Jim Crow system of segregation were permanently eliminated they would have access to jobs and educational opportunities that had been denied them in the past.

Second, the postwar years saw the emergence of independence movements in Asia and Africa. Many black people, including the young Martin Luther King, Jr., were impressed by the nonviolent resistance struggle organized by Mahatma Gandhi in India to gain that country's independence from Britain. Other self-government struggles were taking place in several countries in Africa, including the Gold Coast (later to become the first African colony to gain its independence as Ghana in 1957), and Kenya, through the so-called Mau Mau movement. Moreover, in 1945 black Americans, West Indians and Africans attended the fifth Pan-African Congress, which called for an end to colonialism and racial discrimination. The Bandung Conference on Asian-African problems in 1955 further heightened black awareness of the changing international situation. As independence movements gained strength in Asia and Africa, the question of black people's status in the United States became more urgent. Black Americans' awareness of freedom movements in other parts of the world made them even less patient with segregation and discrimination at home.

Third, the changing international situation also affected U.S. domestic racial policy. As the United States emerged as a world power in the postwar years it was confronted, on the one hand, with the birth of the United Nations and the anti-racist, human rights stance of that world body, and, on the other hand, with the developing Cold War confrontation with the Soviet Union in which the U.S. found its domestic racial policies sharply denounced before the world. Sensitive to the credibility problems posed by the existence of legally sanctioned racial segregation, the Truman Administration took steps to integrate the armed forces and to encourage the lowering of racial barriers in other areas of American life. The stage was set for an important breakthrough.

For many years the NAACP had been waging a legal battle in the courts to outlaw segregation. In *Brown* v. *The Board of Education*, 1954, the U.S. Supreme Court ruled that the so-called doctrine of "separate but equal"—segregation—was unconstitutional, at least as far as the public schools were concerned. This decision was a cause for jubilation, and many black people throughout the South felt that if segregation could be outlawed in the schools then it could be outlawed on the job, in buses, in public parks—in short, everywhere.

But the struggle to end segregation was not to be easy. By 1955 it was apparent that the white South intended to defy the Court ruling and maintain segregation. The first of the racist white citizens councils was organized just two months after the Supreme Court decision. Southern school boards announced that they would never accept or implement desegregation of the public schools. White politicians vowed that the South would always remain segregated.

Black people were angered by this racist reaction, but no one was quite sure what should be the next step in the fight against segregation. It was in this context that Mrs. Rosa Parks, a black woman weary from work, refused to give up her seat on a city bus to a white man in Montgomery, Alabama. Mrs. Parks was arrested and fined, but her arrest galvanized the black community, which began organizing a massive boycott of the city buses. They realized that progressive change would require massive direct action on the part of thousands of people.

Martin Luther King, Jr. A young Baptist minister, Martin Luther King, Jr., was named to head up the boycott committee. The choice of King was fortunate. Although inexperienced, King was open-minded and he quickly grasped the importance of what the black community of Montgomery was doing. Martin Luther King understood—and perhaps this was his major insight—that if ordinary people did not themselves actively work for change, then little change could be expected. The judicial struggle pursued by the NAACP might result in favorable rulings, but what was the value of court decisions if their implementation was blocked?

Ironically, the segregation of black people in southern towns and cities was turned to advantage in the struggle against discrimination. Segregation had helped foster the development of independent black institutions—churches and community groups—which served as bases for organizing campaigns. Moreover, the substantial growth of black populations in many urban areas during and after the war years gave the black community potentially powerful economic leverage. It became apparent that business and political elites could be compelled through massive direct action—in the form of boycotts, demonstrations and marches—to accept and implement social change. King learned from his study of the Gandhian movement and his experience in Montgomery that masses of people in motion could change the course of history.

It took more than a year for the bus boycott to force the desegregation of public transportation facilities in Montgomery, but this struggle represented a clear victory for the new tactics of nonviolent direct action and provided an example that was soon to be emulated in dozens of other cities throughout the South.

Martin Luther King assumed the leadership of many of these battles. In 1957, he organized the Southern Christian Leadership Conference, a group of black church leaders from ten states. Using this organization as a base, King led desegregation campaigns in cities such as Albany, Georgia, Birmingham, Alabama, St. Augustine, Florida, and Selma, Alabama. In 1963 he played a major role in mobilizing the March on Washington, a huge demonstration by more than a quarter of a million people that helped bring about passage of the Civil Rights Act.

Meanwhile, skirmishes were taking place all over the South. In 1957 black high school students in Little Rock, Arkansas, and other cities bravely walked through racist white mobs to attend high schools previously restricted to white students.

In February 1960, the black student movement began with a sit-in at a Woolworths lunch counter in Greensboro, North Carolina. Four black college students walked into the store, made several purchases and then sat at the lunch counter and ordered coffee. They were refused service, but this was the inception of a new tactic in the movement against discrimination. The students and others came back to sit in time and again until Woolworths changed its policies and began serving black people at the lunch counter. The sit-in tactic spread rapidly, and within a few years many restaurants, hotels, movie theaters, libraries, supermarkets and amusement parks had been compelled to allow anyone to use their facilities, regardless of race.

Many of the sit-ins were organized by a newly formed black student group called the Student Nonviolent Coordinating Committee (SNCC). SNCC became the heart of the black student movement in the South. SNCC organizers were sent into every southern state, often with no money and surviving on the generosity of the local black community. The organizers would pull together a committee to build a local campaign against racial discrimination. Student movement leaders such as Stokely Carmichael and H. "Rap" Brown, who later became internationally famous, began their careers as SNCC organizers in small black communities in the South.

In the North, many liberal whites, including white college students, were sympathetic toward the civil rights movement in the South. They showed their concern by providing moral and financial support to the black freedom movement and by themselves going South to take part in the struggle. Some whites joined the freedom rides organized by the Congress of Racial Equality (CORE), which had been founded in 1942. The purpose of the freedom rides was to desegregate interstate transportation facilities. Very often the freedom riders were brutally attacked by racist white mobs, and more than once the bus on which they were riding was burned. By taking part in sit-ins, freedom rides, marches and demonstrations, literally thousands of white people were politicized and brought into the movement for social change.

By 1963 conditions were indeed changing in the South. In many cities Jim Crow segregation was slowly giving way to racial integration. However, the struggle was far from over and there was still much violence. In April 1963 fire hoses and police dogs were used to attack a peaceful civil rights demonstration in Birmingham, Alabama. Later that year civil rights activist Medgar Evers was shot to death in Jackson, Mississippi and four young black girls were killed in Birmingham, Alabama, when a bomb exploded in the church they were attending. The next year three civil rights workers, two whites and one black, were brutally murdered near Philadelphia, Mississippi, where they had gone to participate in a summer voter registration project.

Despite these murders it was clear that the mass struggles by black people were having an impact. In 1964 President Lyndon Johnson signed the Civil Rights Act, the most far-reaching civil rights legislation since Reconstruction. This was followed in 1965 by the Voting Rights Act. For the first time in this century black people in many parts of the South had the right to vote and the right of access to public and private facilities.

As conditions in the South began to change it became more obvious that racial oppression was not a problem restricted to the South. Black people were at the bottom of the ladder in the North and West just as they were in the South. Many civil rights leaders, including Martin Luther King, felt the time was ripe for the black freedom movement to spread, especially into the North. Conditions in the North, however, were different from those in the South and the movement soon ran into serious problems. These problems can be understood in the light of the goals, methods and leadership of the southern civil rights movement in contrast to those of the northern black movement.

The North

The goals of the civil rights movement were to remove laws upholding racial segregation and to achieve integration. Many black activists in the South regarded legalized segregation as the chief enemy, the main source of racial oppression and exploitation. But in the North there was little official (*de jure*) segregation of the races; that is, there were few formal laws prohibiting black people from going certain places or doing certain things. However, in the North there was considerable informal (*de facto*) discrimination practiced by businesses, realtors, colleges and private associations. Black people in the North were not angry because they were forced by law to ride at the back of the bus—they were not. They were angry because they did not have access to good jobs, decent housing or an adequate education for their children. But since there were few laws in the North that denied black people access to services and facilities, it was less clear what the objective of the movement should be—although some activists were beginning to think that it was "the system," the capitalist system, that needed changing.

Martin Luther King and many leaders of the southern movement were firmly committed to nonviolent, passive resistance as the best method for bringing about change, and also as a moral principle. Black activists in the North, however, while approving of direct action, thought it was insane to turn the other cheek to violent racists who were bent on maiming and killing. Self-defense was the intelligent response, they contended. This was certainly the position taken by Malcolm X, who frequently criticized the nonviolent tactics of the southern movement.

Many of the leaders of the southern movement were ministers and college students with middle-class backgrounds and aspirations. They were fairly secure economically and they tended to think less in terms of access to jobs and more in terms of access to social amenities such as restaurants, theaters and hotels. Essentially, what many of the middle-class black leaders wanted was access to the same privileges and services as middle-class whites. But for working-class and poor blacks, especially in the North, the problem wasn't getting into a restaurant but getting money to buy food.

Many of the southern leaders who were rooted in the Christian church approached the struggle for social change with a moralistic perspective. They tended to think of racism as a kind of moral defect in the conscience of white America. They espoused the moral power of suffering and of loving one's enemies. For them America needed a cleansing of its conscience, a moral reform; they seldom thought in terms of political transformation. But street-wise militants in the North were much more cynical about the state of the nation's conscience. As far as they were concerned, white America had no conscience. They believed it was pointless to talk about moral reform; what was needed, they said, was a redistribution of political power.

Power is the name of the game in America, the militants argued, and those without power are bound to be oppressed no matter how morally pure they may be.

Malcolm X. Perhaps the person who most exemplified the attitudes of black militants in the North was Malcolm X. He was born Malcolm Little in Omaha, Nebraska, in 1925. His father, who was a follower of Marcus Garvey, was brutally murdered by the Ku Klux Klan. After his father's death Malcolm's mother was barely able to feed the family and keep it together. Eventually the pressure became too great. His mother lost her mind and Malcolm was sent to live with various foster families. Finally, he moved to Boston to live with an elder sister. As a young man Malcolm became involved in the petty criminal underworlds of Boston's Roxbury district and Harlem in New York City. Eventually he was arrested for armed robbery and sentenced to ten years in prison.

It was while in prison that Malcolm came in contact with the teachings of Elijah Muhammad, who was the leader of the Nation of Islam, a nationalistic, religious sect also known as the Black Muslims. Malcolm was probably attracted to the Muslims by their open denunciation of the "white devils" who oppressed the black race, and by the Muslims' campaigns for self-help and uplift among converts. He joined the Muslims and changed his last name to "X" to signify his new status, thus abandoning the "slave" name. When Malcolm was released from prison in 1952, he worked hard for the Muslims. He was a powerful orator and his speeches gained him a national reputation. By 1963 he had become the leading public spokesman for the Black Muslims.

Malcolm X gradually became disillusioned with the Muslims because they were not activists. They believed that their members should abstain from social protest or any involvement in the political process and that Allah would eventually solve all problems. But Malcolm was impatient. In 1964 he broke with the Muslims and formed his own organization in Harlem. Malcolm X called himself a disciple of black nationalism, which he defined as the effort of black people to organize a movement of their own to fight for freedom, justice and equality. He denounced the civil rights movement as a bastion of white liberals who were only superficially committed to black interests. The essence of black nationalism, he said, was the idea that blacks, rather than whites, should control the economy, politics, institutions and organizations of their own communities. He thus identified black nationalism with the concept of self-determination, which had developed out of the socialist and nationalist liberation movements in other parts of the world.

Malcolm also began to think that the political economy of American society was the main enemy of black freedom. He began to argue that the capitalist system was the cause of racism and exploitation. Moreoever, he suggested that socialism was the solution. In one of Malcolm's last speeches before his assassination he urged his listeners to look at Africa:

> Almost every one of the countries that has gotten independence has devised some kind of socialistic system, and this is no accident. This is another reason why I say that you and I here in America—who are looking for a job, who are looking for better housing, looking for a better education—before you start trying to be incorporated, or integrated, or disintegrated into this capitalistic system, you should look over there and find out what the people who have gotten their freedom are adopting to provide themselves with better housing and better education and better food and clothing. None of them are adopting the capitalistic system because they realize they can't. You can't operate a capitalistic system unless you are vulturistic; you have to suck someone else's blood to be a capitalist. You show me a capitalist and I'll show you a bloodsucker. [1]

Although attacked by conservatives and moderates of both races, Malcolm's political perspective captured the attention of many young black activists in the North.

Equally important, Malcolm X called on black activists to internationalize their freedom fight. He called for solidarity among all oppressed peoples in the world. He spoke of "linking the problem of racism in Mississippi with the problem of racism in the Congo, or the problem of racism in South Vietnam." "It's all racism," he said. "It's all part of the vicious racist system that the Western powers have used to continue to degrade and exploit and oppress the people in Africa, Asia and Latin America." He said that "when these people in these different areas begin to see that the problem is

the same problem, and when 22 million black Americans see that
our problem is the same problem of the people who are being oppressed in South Vietnam and the Congo and Latin America—[and
when we realize that] the oppressed people of this earth make up a
majority, not a minority—then we approach our problem as a majority that can *demand*, not as a minority that has to beg.''[2]

Two Men, One Goal

Martin Luther King and Malcolm X were both assassinated at
precisely the point at which they began working actively and con-
sciously against the racism and exploitation generated by the American capitalist system, both at home and abroad. Was this just a co-
incidence, an accident of history, that both of these black leaders
were gunned down at similar points in their political development?

It is instructive to compare these two men. All too often they are
thought of as diametric opposites, but this is an oversimplification;
it does not allow for the fact that both men changed and developed.
Their political vision matured as they gained more experience. For
example, Malcolm had begun working on a plan to go before the
United Nations and formally charge the United States government
with violating the human rights of black people. He drew an analogy to support his position: ''If South Africa is guilty of violating the
human rights of Africans then America is guilty of worse violations
of the rights of Africans on the American continent. And if South
African racism is not a domestic issue only, then American racism is
not just a domestic but an international issue.''[3]

Malcolm traveled to Africa to build international support for his
plan but did not live long enough to put it into action. In less than a
year he was murdered, shot down by assassins at a public meeting in
New York in 1965.

By the mid-1960s Martin Luther King realized that civil rights
could not be meaningful so long as black people were denied jobs,
education and decent housing. This realization led him to criticize
the Vietnam War on the grounds that it drained funds from social
welfare programs and was immoral. As early as 1965 he urged President Johnson to initiate peace talks to end the war, and by 1967 King,

like Malcolm before him, had taken a position squarely in opposition to American intervention in Vietnam.

King also recognized the need to expand the scope of the movement, as in his unsuccessful open-housing campaign in Chicago and in the Poor People's Campaign, the purpose of which was to unify poor people in America, regardless of race, to struggle against their common oppression. Finally, in 1968 King's broadening vision led him to make the fateful journey to Memphis, Tennesse, where he offered his support to striking black sanitation workers in that city. Norman Pearlstine, writing in the March 8, 1968 issue of the *Wall Street Journal*, noted the potentially revolutionary significance of this move by King. The reporter pointed out that an alliance of black workers and civil rights groups could create a powerful coalition that could shake the South and indeed the nation. Martin Luther King was assassinated before such an alliance was made.

In the mid-1970s considerable evidence revealed that during the 1960s and early 1970s the U.S. government conspired to disrupt and destroy the black freedom movement. In particular, under the Freedom of Information Act a number of government documents were obtained by the press which revealed that the FBI had organized a secret nationwide conspiracy, known as COINTELPRO (Counter Intelligence Program), to "expose, disrupt, misdirect, discredit or otherwise neutralize" black freedom organizations and their leaders. The tactics employed in this illegal FBI program included everything from sending "anonymous" poison-pen letters, to red-baiting, planting agents and provocateurs in organizations, using illegal telephone taps and burglarizing files, provoking violent confrontations between different groups, and assassinating militant leaders. It is known, for example, that the FBI was directly involved in coordinating local police attacks on the Black Panthers, a militant black group founded in 1966 in Oakland, California, including the murder of Panther leaders Fred Hampton and Mark Clark in Chicago in 1969. It is also known that both Malcolm X and Martin Luther King were marked as targets of this FBI COINTELPRO operation, although the government has refused to release any documents that might show direct FBI involvement in their deaths.[4] When the whole truth is known it may be discovered that many movement activists who disappeared or died in the 1960s and 1970s were not killed by the Ku Klux Klan or right-wing fanatics but by hired government assassins.

Black Power

Malcolm X and Martin Luther King died but the movement continued. In fact, in 1966 the movement took a new turn when SNCC leaders coined the phrase "Black Power." The news media immediately sensationalized this new phrase and used it to conjure up racist hatreds and fears among the white population. White America seemed horrified at the thought that blackness and power could be combined. The rulers of white America, for their part, wanted black people to remain powerless.

Ostensibly black power meant that black people should control the institutions, labor and resources of their own communities. This control was to be exercised through economic cooperatives, election of black politicians, community control of schools and greater black involvement in local businesses. In a sense, black power was simply a reformulation of Malcolm X's conception of black nationalism. But matters were not to remain simple.

In 1967 the first of a series of black power conferences was held in Newark, New Jersey, bringing together black activists from all over the country. At that conference it became apparent that black power was such a broad and vague concept that it could be exploited by anybody black to justify almost anything they were doing. To some, black power meant more black politicians, so they used it to justify running for office. To others the slogan meant more black businesses, so they used it to justify becoming black capitalists. For still others black power meant that black people as a group should integrate into American society, while yet others thought it meant that black people should separate from American society. To the Black Panthers black power meant picking up the gun. Even Richard Nixon became an advocate of black power, which he defined as black capitalism. According to Nixon, what black people needed was a "piece of the action" of the capitalist system. He devised a minority business program that would "promote" the development of black capitalism, but the program was undermined by economic recession and cuts in the federal budget.

While black leaders debated what they meant by black power, black communities were finding living conditions more unbearable. In the late 1960s a series of urban rebellions broke out in many of the major cities of the United States. Spectacular rebellions occurred in New York, Newark, Detroit, Los Angeles and many other cities. Hundreds of black people were killed by police and National Guardsmen, and millions of dollars of property went up in flames. These rebellions reflected the anger and disillusionment of the black communities and reached their peak in April 1968, following the assassination of Martin Luther King. The death of King killed the dream that genuine freedom and equality were just around the corner. King was no radical, but as long as he was alive black militants and moderates alike could cling to the hope that nonviolent struggle would assure evolutionary change. In the eyes of many, his murder undermined that hope. Many former activists became disillusioned cynics while others talked ominously of guerrilla warfare and revolution.

The government employed every means at its disposal to repress and destroy the militant movements. One method of repression was the wholesale imprisonment of civil rights and anti-war activists, which had an important repercussion that the government certainly did not anticipate. It politicized the prisons and helped to launch the prison reform movement. The cases of prisoners such as the Soledad Brothers and George Jackson gave a focal point to this new movement, and the shooting of a judge in California's Marin County in 1970 brought national attention to a young woman named Angela Davis who was charged (but later acquitted) with supplying the guns used in that fatal escape attempt. The killing of George Jackson by prison guards in California in 1971 was a factor in the outbreak later that year of the Attica prison uprising, which was put down in a bloody assault by National Guardsmen and police.

SNCC activists were arrested so many times that the organization finally could no longer raise bail to get its people out of jail. The Black Panthers became targets of dozens of police attacks which resulted in the deaths of more than a score of Panthers, the imprisonment of many others, including Huey Newton and Bobby Seale, and caused others such as Eldridge Cleaver to flee into exile. As a consequence of this government repression many individuals left the Panthers out of fear for their lives. Those who remained split into two groups. One group sought respectability by allying itself with the Democratic party and running in elections for local offices in Oakland, California. The other group became increasingly involved in the criminal underworld of drugs and prostitution. As an effective organization, the Panthers, like SNCC, was virtually destroyed.

Violent repression was not the only tactic used by the government against the movements. The power elite also sought to co-opt some organizations and leaders by offering them foundation grants, money to set up businesses and jobs in the government's anti-poverty bureaucracy. In addition, the Democratic party opened its ranks to black politicians in an effort to head off the movement to develop an independent black political party, which had begun at the black political convention held in Gary, Indiana, in 1972.

The 1970s

In the 1970s the character of the situation facing the black freedom movement changed. The defeat of the United States in Vietnam, the growth of a strong organization among the oil-producing nations (Organization of Petroleum Exporting Countries), the success of national liberation movements in the former African colonies of Guinea-Bissau, Angola and Mozambique—together these forces brought an end to American hegemony in the Third World. The United States could no longer control and dominate the Third World, nor continue unlimited access at cheap prices to the resources of Third World countries. This situation produced a major economic crisis in America which resulted in recession and stagnation of the national economy. Unemployment skyrocketed along with inflation, and the government's fledgling black capitalism program was obliterated by the contractions of the economy.

Black people, and racial minorities generally, were the chief victims of this crisis, both materially and ideologically. The limited gains of the 1960s came under heavy attack as black people were made scapegoats for the economic crisis. This was true especially in the public sector. Reactionary forces in the mass media and academia launched a propaganda campaign to convince middle-class and working-class whites that their economic troubles were being caused by the alleged massive gains that black people had made in the public sector, such as in government employment, public educational institutions and social welfare programs. This ideological campaign was used to justify a wave of cutbacks and attacks in the public sector, including cutbacks in social services and educational programs, attacks on public school desegregation, black and ethnic studies programs, special college admissions programs for racial minorities and on affirmative action programs in employment.

These cutbacks and attacks were justified ideologically by what Joel Dreyfuss has called "the new racism" (and what I have termed cultural chauvinism). The new racism asserts that racial discrimination is no longer a serious problem in America society. That is, those blacks who are "qualified" are succeeding in climbing the economic ladder and making it into the middle class; and it is only those blacks who are "unqualified" who are falling behind. The purpose of this ideology was to convince whites (and middle-class blacks) that the black masses were being held down, not by racism and capitalist exploitation, but by their own individual cultural deficiencies: lack of thriftiness, lack of a work ethic, lack of respect for education, and broken families. This ideology was merely another version of the belief that victims are to blame for their own victimization.

The reality was quite different. The notion of an expanding middle class of "qualified" blacks was an illusion. A special report published by the National Urban League in 1978 pointed out that "there is no evidence of a significant increase in the proportion of middle-class blacks in recent years. If anything, the data suggest that economic gains of middle- and upper-income blacks have been eroded under the twin evils of record inflation and recession. Between 1972 and 1975 the proportion of black families with incomes of $15,000 or more actually *fell* from 25 to 23 percent."[5] The report went on to note that "between 1969 and 1976 the median income of black families relative to white families fell from 61 to 59 percent." Moreover, the report observed that racial discrimination was alive and well in employment practices. Possession of a college degree did not guarantee a black person a decent job. In fact, according to the report, white high school dropouts in 1978 had a lower unemployment rate than did black youth with college educations.

These facts made it clear that the rhetoric about "reverse discrimination" was without foundation. Black people had not gained an economic advantage over whites. Nevertheless, blacks continued to be cast as scapegoats for the economic problems of white America.

In 1974 Allan Bakke filed his famous (or infamous) lawsuit charging the University of California with reverse discrimination in its admissions practices. Twenty years after the 1954 Supreme Court desegregation decision the courts were being told that racial minorities had gotten more than their fair share and that white males were now the victims of racial discrimination. The facts revealed, however, that unemployment and poverty in the black community were rising after a period of relative decline in the 1960s and that the proportion of black students going to college was actually declining after more than a decade of substantial gain. In sum, the 1970s witnessed a massive attempt to reverse the entire thrust of the struggles of the 1960s.

The Black Movement and the New Left

Although the black freedom movement was supressed and disrupted, it had an enormous impact on many areas of American life, especially among students of all races. Indeed, the upsurge of social change movements in the 1960s was in no small part due to the spreading influence of the black freedom movement. That loose aggregation of organizations and movements that came to be known as the New Left had its roots in the civil rights and black power movements.

The Student Movement

While the mass movement on the streets was grinding to a halt in the late sixties, the struggle on the college campuses was intensifying. The black studies and anti-Vietnam War movements were mobilizing thousands of college students in protest demonstrations. In California the Black Panthers were forming alliances with Chicano, Asian and white radical students. One of the largest and longest college strikes in history occurred at San Francisco State College in 1968 when black and other students demanded the establishment of a black studies department and open admissions for racial minority students. These alliances catalyzed the spread of militancy to other campuses and communities and the emergence of anti-racist Third World organizations.

Meanwhile, opposition to the Vietnam War had grown to enormous proportions, especially after the 1968 Tet Offensive by the National Liberation Front of South Vietnam. The offensive, in which NLF forces simultaneously attacked many United States bases, made it crystal clear that the United States was losing the war. Students by the hundreds were burning their draft cards and refusing to enter the armed forces. Some of the earliest political draft resistance had been among black students. By the early 1970s thousands of young men, black and white, had refused the draft, fled abroad or gone AWOL from the military. Many of those who remained in the army had become drug addicts. The United States could no longer field an army that was willing and able to fight a racist, imperialist war. The United States war effort was being defeated by the Vietnamese liberation forces and by the unwillingness of young Americans, no matter their race, to blindly follow orders.

Students for a Democratic Society (SDS), which developed into the largest and most influential New Left white student organization, owed a large historical debt to SNCC. SDS evolved from an older but largely ineffectual group known as the Student League for Industrial Democracy, which was part of the old social-democratic left. SDS came into its own just as student sit-in activity in the South was developing. In his book, *SDS,* Kirkpatrick Sale noted that the birth of the civil rights movement gave SDS its initial cause. SDS activists formed campus support groups, fundraising committees and sometimes themselves joined the sit-ins. The sit-in tactic was also adopted by white students demanding political freedom, as during the free speech movement at Berkeley in 1964.

At a deeper level, the radical ideas discussed in SNCC as well as its organizing style profoundly influenced SDS. Clayborne Carson, in his study, *In Struggle: SNCC and the Black Awakening of the 1960s,* made this point emphatically:

> Some observers attributed SNCC's radicalism to the presence of white leftists in the southern struggle; yet SNCC is more accurately seen as a source of insights and inspiration for the New Left. Just as its unique style of unstructured, rebellious activism broke through the ingrained patterns of southern black accommodation, SNCC undermined the pervasive patterns of political and cultural conformity embraced by white college students in Cold War America. SNCC inspired the small band of activists who launched the student rights and anti-war movements of the mid-1960s. Although lacking a developed ideology of its own, the implicit assumptions underlying SNCC's work attracted activists who were unaware of or unconvinced by the strategies of the Old Left.[6]

In 1962, SDS drafted an activist manifesto known as the Port Huron Statement which, among other things, acknowledged that the southern struggle against racism had "compelled" the SDS students to move "from silence to activism." SDS organizers soon launched a program of community organizing in poor urban areas—black, white and racially mixed. Tom Hayden, an SDS founder and co-author of the Port Huron Statement, wanted to find out if the methods SNCC had developed could be applied in the North. Taking a page from the SNCC experience, "participatory democracy" became the guiding political philosophy of SDS.

For several years relations between SNCC and SDS were friendly and mutually supportive. As the struggle in the South became more intense and violent, both organizations were radicalized. Both began to advocate changes in the economic and political structure as prerequisites for ending economic and racial oppression. But with the drift toward radicalism, white liberal political support for SNCC began to fall off and government red-baiting became more frequent. SNCC's response was to promote the notion of independent black political organizing as expressed in the "Black Power" slogan and as attempted in the Lowndes County (Alabama) Freedom Party. Black activists began telling white supporters that they should organize anti-racist campaigns in the white community, the source of racism, rather than working in black communities. Some whites took this idea seriously, but many were alienated by the "Black Power" slogan and abandoned the movement altogether. SDS officially supported SNCC in its new political stance, but the alliance between the two groups was severely shaken and never recovered.

While the issue of independent black organizing proved problematic for the New Left, as it had a century earlier with the abolitionists, both SNCC and SDS continued their work which, ironically, converged in the anti-war movement. Although it would not become obvious for several years, the American intervention in the Vietnam War was to become an unmitigated disaster, dividing the country, raising havoc with the economy and sowing incredible suffering in a small country thousands of miles away.

Since World War II the Vietnamese had been fighting against foreign domination (and domestic collaborationists), first against the Japanese, then the French and finally the Americans. Vowing to halt the spread of communism, the Johnson administration dispatched American combat troops to fight against the insurgents in South Vietnam. SNCC and SDS activists quickly responded to the escalation. In April, 1965, SDS organized and SNCC supported the first large anti-war demonstration in Washington, D.C. Some 25,000 people marched and listened to speeches, one of which was delivered by Bob Moses, a SNCC organizer.

As the war continued to escalate, so did the anti-war movement. Although some in the civil rights movement thought there was a logical connection between civil rights and anti-war work, others thought that anti-war work was diversionary, that it deflected energy away from anti-racist community organizing. Robert Browne, a black college professor and anti-war activist, summarized the reasons for linking the two movements. Writing in *Freedomways* in late 1965, Browne listed them:

1. The recognition that the civil rights movement represents the moral conscience of America and therefore naturally belongs in the vanguard of the Vietnam protest, felt now to be the number one moral issue confronting American society.
2. The argument that the billions of dollars being diverted to the Vietnam war represent funds which might otherwise be available for giving substance to the programs necessary for raising the Negro to a level of real equality in American life.
3. The belief that the civil rights objectives are unachievable under the present organization of American society and therefore must necessarily be fought for as part of a large effort to remake American society, including its foreign policy.
4. The view that the Vietnam war is intimately involved in the American racist attitudes generally, and therefore falls naturally within the range of American Negroes' direct sphere of interest.[7]

SNCC, too, was affected by the debate over priorities within the civil rights movement, but, after some initial equivocation, SNCC threw itself into the fray, taking the lead in supporting the most radical form of anti-war activity—draft resistance. In January, 1966, SNCC worker Sammy Younge, Jr., was murdered in Tuskegee, Alabama, when he attempted to use the "white" restroom at a gas station. This incident prompted the release of SNCC's anti-war statement, which had been under discussion in the organization. "Samuel Younge was murdered because U.S. law is not being enforced," the statement read. "Vietnamese are being murdered because the United States is pursuing an aggressive policy in violation of international law. The U.S. is no respector of persons or law when such persons or laws run counter to its needs and desires." The statement continued:

> We are in sympathy with and support the men in this country who are unwilling to respond to the military draft which could compel them to contribute their lives to U.S. aggression in the name of the "freedom" we find so false in this country.

The statement concluded that "work in the civil rights movement and with other human relations organizations is a valid alternative to the draft. We urge all Americans to seek that alternative, knowing full well that it may cost them their lives—as painfully as in Vietnam."[8]

This statement represented the first step toward the all-out draft resistance stand SNCC was to adopt, culminating in the formation of a National Black Anti-War–Anti-Draft Union.

Meanwhile, SDS was also struggling with the question of draft resistance. After initially dragging its feet, the organization in December, 1966, came out in favor of draft resistance. In a resolution SDS proposed to organize unions of draft resisters: "The members of these unions will be united by the common principle that under no circumstances will they allow themselves to be drafted."[9]

Inspired by the public positions of SNCC and SDS, literally thousands of young men, black and white, refused to submit to the draft. Some protested publicly; others simply slipped away quietly to Canada or went underground. Moreover, resistance to the war among American GIs also reached dramatic proportions, as reflected in instances of "fragging" in which officers were attacked by enlisted men.

With the Tet offensive in 1968, remaining American illusions about winning the war were shattered. Anti-war sentiment became widespread and huge demonstrations against the war became a regular feature of the American scene. Public opinion polls revealed ever-increasing numbers of Americans believed the war to be a "mistake." But as Clyde Taylor commented in *Vietnam and Black America,* black people were

> in a position to know better, to see through the rationale of the war as a "mistake" of U.S. national policy makers. In a position to see how such "mistakes" as Vietnam flow effortlessly out of the character of Americanism. To see how a "mess" in the parlance of American public discussions works out to mean an aggressive, unprincipled venture against other people that turned out not to be profitable. And during the Vietnam years, which were also the years of black people's most resolute confrontation with American injustice, black people were in a position to observe American society being equally "mistaken" at both ends of the planet.[10]

The New Left fell apart with the ending of the Vietnam war. Its mass base of support among college students disappeared. The New Left was also a target for the FBI's COINTELPRO disruption program. SDS split into conficting factions and disintegrated and SNCC was destroyed by government repression. Nevertheless, these two organizations left a lasting imprint on the political consciousness of a generation of Americans.

The Women's Liberation Movement

The black freedom movement inspired not only the activism of the New Left, but also the growth in consciousness among women activists that was to culminate in the women's liberation movement. Writing in *Personal Politics: The Roots of Women's Liberation in the Civil Rights Movement and the New Left,* Sara Evans asserted that through "working for racial justice, [white women] gained experience in organizing and collective action, an ideology that described and condemned oppression analogous to their own, and a belief in human 'rights' that could justify them in claiming equality for themselves.[11]

Ann Popkin, an early organizer in the women's liberation movement, recounted that her first political experience involved walking on a picket line opposing racial discrimination in housing. Like many of the later feminists activists, she worked in the South (the Mississippi summer of 1964) and soon came to feel that "the rhetoric of equality was not borne out in movement activity."[12] Most of the public leaders of the movement were men, although it was the day-to-day routine drudge work, usually performed by women, that kept the movement going.

It was a black woman in SNCC, Ruby Doris Smith, who motivated the first public statement about the role of women in the movement. Long active in the civil rights movement, Ruby Doris Smith was not a person to suffer an indignity without protest. She and other women were angered by the relegation of women in the organization to routine office chores and their exclusion from the decision-making process. At a SNCC staff meeting in 1964 the women presented their views in a position paper. After citing several examples of sexual discrimination in SNCC, the paper continued by drawing an analogy between racism and sexism:

The average white person finds it difficult to understand why the Negro resents being called "boy," or being thought of as "musical" and "athletic," because the average white person doesn't realize that he assumes he is superior. And naturally he doesn't understand the problems of paternalism. So too the average SNCC worker finds it difficult to discuss the woman problem because of the assumption of male superiority. Assumptions of male superiority are as widespread and deep rooted and every much as crippling to the woman as the assumptions of white supremacy are to the Negro.[13]

The statement was not signed and there is some uncertainty as to whether it was authored solely by Ruby Doris Smith or by an interracial group of women under Smith's leadership. In any case, it was largely dismissed by the male leadership of SNCC. Stokely Carmichael insulted the women by replying, "The only position for women in SNCC is prone."[14]

Many of the white women who were involved in SNCC were also active in the New Left, particularly SDS. In 1965 at an SDS meeting some of these women attempted to raise the questions about sexism that had been raised in SNCC, but it was not until 1967 when white women activists began forming small groups that the women's liberation movement came into its own.

The movement came to national attention in 1968 at the annual Miss America Pageant in Atlantic City. A group of feminists organized a guerrilla theater action to protest the "boob girlie show" which they considered demeaning to women. Branded "bra burners," the protestors were ridiculed by the mass media.

Nevertheless, the movement continued to spread as white women organized consciousness-raising groups across the country. These groups provided what Pam Allen, an organizer of several of them, called "free space," a setting in which women could share their deepest feelings and experiences as women.

From consciousness-raising the movement soon turned to activism. Women began organizing around such issues as abortion rights, rape, child care, equality in the workplace, support for gay rights and the Equal Rights Amendment, which, if passed would outlaw sex discrimination.

Although the women's liberation movement had its roots in the civil rights struggle, black women tended to be critical of it. Some of them accused the white women of being racist and narrowly middle class in their concerns. Frances Beal, an organizer of a third world women's group in New York, criticized certain white feminists for being divisive in putting forward the idea that men are the enemies of women.[15] Angela Davis suggested that the anti-rape movement encouraged the racist myth of the black rapist and adopted a "posture of indifference toward the frame-up rape charge as an incitement to racist aggression."[16] Even more ex-plosive was the charge that white women's liberationists were recruiting black women in order to "get next to black men."

Many black men and women dismissed the women's liberation movement as trivial. But in the late 1960s a group of black women in Mount Vernon, New York, began writing about sexual oppres-sion from a race and class perspective. "Poor black women in the U.S. have to fight back out of our own experience of oppression," the women wrote in an open letter to the black power movement criticizing its opposition to birth control. They continued:

> But we don't think you're going to understand us because you are a bunch of little middle class people and we are poor black women. The middle class never understands the poor because they always need to use them as you want to use poor black women's children to gain power for yourself. You'll run the black community with your kind of black power—You on top! The poor understand class struggle![17]

In 1979 the sexism issue dramatically reemerged in the black movement with the publication of Michelle Wallace's *Black Macho and the Myth of the Superwoman,* which accused black men of being manipulators and exploiters of black women. The book pro-voked a heated debate in black organizations and in black publica-tions such as *The Black Scholar.* Although still largely unresolved, this debate underscored the extent to which relations between the sexes in the black community had been affected by changes in the economy, family structure and sex roles generally.

Black women still kept the women's liberation movement at arm's length, but there was a growing recognition among black women of the validity of some of the issues raised by the movement, particularly economic issues, the problem of child care and the ques-tion of exploitation of women by men. Seeking to distinguish themselves from the white feminists, some black women, such as novelist and essayist Alice Walker, chose to describe themselves as ''womanists''—''women who love other women, yes, but women who also have concern, in a culture that oppresses all black people, for their fathers, brothers and sons, no matter how they feel about them as men.''[18]

Third World Movements in the U.S.

The new consciousness forged in the black freedom movement affected not only young whites, but people of all races. In the late 1960s new political struggles and group pride movements emerged among Indians, Chicanos, Puerto Ricans and Asian-Americans. The country was startled by a series of events: The rise of the farmworkers movement and Chicano student militancy, the Indian seizure of Alcatraz Island in San Francisco Bay, the upsurge of Puerto Rican nationalist movements, the sudden radicalism of previously quiescent Asian groups. The flames of freedom, fanned by the black freedom movement, were ablaze in the hearts of all oppressed peoples.

Occasionally these movements converged, as in the Poor People's Campagin, the student strike at San Francisco State College, and the growth of multi-racial organizations like the Third World Women's Alliance. Indeed, the concept of ''third world'' was employed to express the underlying unity of these movements. Just as third world peoples in Africa, Asia and the Americas had been the victims of colonialism and racism, so did the descendants of these peoples living in the United States share a common heritage of racial oppression. And a common heritage of oppression, it was argued, created the basis for a common struggle against it.

While the politics of third worldism was optimistic, it did not always allow for the real cultural and historical differences that distinguished various groups. To be sure, all these groups were struggling against white racial domination—politically, economically and culturally—but this did not mean that all shared identical goals. The unique character of the history and culture of each group defined that group's values and goals. A major concern of American Indians, for example, is reasserting their treaty rights and reclaiming lost lands. Bilingual, bicultural education is a central issue for Chicanos. At the heart of the Puerto Rican movement is the question of the political status and future of Puerto Rico.

These and other historical and cultural differences have sometimes engendered conflict between various third world movements. Suspicion and hostility have undermined cooperation. The result has blunted the third world thrust and fragmented the struggle against white racism. Whether this problem will be overcome depends on the emergence of an anti-racist leadership that can build alliances while also respecting and upholding the legitimate special concerns of each group. As with other progressive movements in American society, the task of the third world movements is to find in historical and cultural diversity the basis for political unity in struggle.

The 1980s

With the arrival of the decade of the 1980s the conflicts and contradictions of this society became even sharper. Ronald Reagan's rise to power brought a clear swing to the right in American government. Faced with a growing economic crisis, the political rulers of the country have abandoned the old welfare state policies that had characterized the federal government since the New Deal. The Reagan administration has replaced the New Deal policies with reactionary and repressive ones in an all-out effort to shore up big business at home and enhance U.S. imperialism abroad. Black people, indeed working people of all races, have been targeted as the chief victims of Reagan's policies. As soon as he took office in 1981 Reagan announced sweeping plans for cutbacks in programs that provided needed human services, including Medicaid, food stamps, aid to education, the Comprehensive Employment Training Act (CETA), child support programs, unemployment insurance and affirmative action programs. At the same time he pushed through tax cuts for the big corporations and tax breaks for individuals—of benefit mainly to the wealthy.

Historian Manning Marable put his finger on the significance of Reagan's program: "Reagonomics should be understood as a conservative political response to the organic crisis of capital accumulation. The period of American capitalist hegemony over the world's human and material resources, from 1945 to 1973, has come to an unceremonious end. The fiscal crisis of the state and many industries now only generates permanent inflation, high unemployment and social chaos. What is termed Reagonomics is actually a coherent political strategy to conserve the economic power and privilege of the dominant capitalist class while seeking to revitalize the economy at the expense of blacks, latinos, the working class and the poor."[19]

Internationally, Reagan has pursued a policy of provocation and intervention against progressive Third World countries, such as Cuba and Angola, while politically aligning the United States with openly reactionary and racist governments such as South Africa. The objective is to reestablish America's military and political dominance in the Third World, but such militarist policies might well backfire and alienate many governments, including some of America's European allies. Moreover, as became evident at the Cancun conference in Mexico, the Reagan administration is firmly opposed to building a new international economic order that would provide for a more equitable distribution of the world's wealth. As long as the American government holds to this position, it will only increase the frustration and hostility of Third World countries whose human and material resources have been drained to support American opulence.

The outcome of Reagan's domestic policies is also uncertain. Not only have blacks and other racial minorities been hurt by Reagan's program, but so have millions of whites—especially the elderly, the unemployed, women, and the poor. In September, 1981, there were major demonstrations against Reagan's policies in Washington and other cities. Despite himself, Reagan may be doing more to unite and organize opposition to government policies than anything since the civil rights movement.

Conclusion

The 1960s and 1970s witnessed an outburst of social activism unlike anything seen since the 1930s. Like the struggles of the 1930s, recent social movements occurred in the context of economic expansion followed by stagnation and decline and the actuality or threat of war. In the 1930s America's rulers responded with concessions in the form of social reforms and accomplished economic recovery through war-induced expansion. As a result of World War II the United States achieved political and economic dominance over both the underdeveloped and the developed industrial countries of the capitalist world.

Today, however, American hegemony is a thing of the past. The U.S. has fought a consistently losing battle against the spread of national liberation and socialist movements. Despite occasional counter-revolutionary setbacks as in Guatemala in 1954 and in Chile in 1973, a general trend is apparent in the revolutionary victories in China, Cuba, Vietnam, Angola, Guinea-Bissau, Mozambique, Nicaragua and other third world countries. Moreover, America's economic domination of Europe and Japan has eroded as these "allies" become increasingly scrappy economic and political competitors.

America's economic and political crises have undermined the old labor-liberal-minorities coalition formed during the New Deal. A growing rightward drift in national politics is producing new coalitions, with militarist provocation becoming the government's foreign policy stance.

The recent development of an anti-nuclear–anti-war movement in the United States and Europe has had some effect in countering the drift toward war. The ulimate success of this movement, however, will depend in part on its ability to incorporate working class and third world peoples in the United States and abroad, and to develop an anti-racist and anti-imperialist perspective.

The rightward and racist shift in national politics presents a major challenge to social reformers. With the labor movement on the defensive and political liberals nearly routed, progressive social reformers have been forced to reconsider their strategies. In the black freedom movement, after a period of quiescence, activist organizations are again developing, such as the Black United Front, the National Black United Fund, the embryonic National Black Independent Political Party, and progressive professional organizations such as the National Conference of Black Lawyers. Organizationally, the black freedom movement, and social reformism in general, have become characterized by a greater division of labor and professionalization. While these developments make it possible for important social change work to be done in the areas of human services and legal rights, a reawakening of the mass movements is essential to defend the gains of past struggles and create the social momentum for forward movement.

This review of the development of recent social movements has underlined the seminal role of the black freedom struggle in the 1960s. The ideological impact of the black freedom movement on the consciousness of Americans was widespread. Many were inspired to join the movement against racism or to take up struggles among other constituencies. Among college students the ''silent generation'' of the 1950s was replaced by the activists of the 1960s. A new spirit of rebellion flowered among racial minorities, women of all races, prisoners, gays and others. Old patterns of accommodation were rejected and resistance was embraced.

Not only did the black freedom movement usher in a new period of social activism, it also showed the importance of broadly based, mass struggles. Important reforms were won by the mass movements, most notably the end of legally sanctioned segregation and discrimination against racial minorities and women and the American withdrawal from Vietnam. To be sure, the success of liberation forces in South Vietnam and other third world countries were major contributors to these victories, but without the popular pressure generated by the mass movements, the U.S. government might well have responded in a totally reactionary manner rather than making progressive concessions. Mass movements do bring about change, although not necessarily revolutionary change.

Without basic changes in the nation's political economy, however, the reforms gained will be undermined once the pressure created by the mass movements has abated. This was certainly the trend in the late 1970s and continues in the 1980s, as evidenced, for example, by the systematic dismantling of affirmative action programs. In a period of economic expansion such as in the mid-1960s, the government could be prodded to make some concessions to the civil rights movement, but during a time of economic crisis class contradictions become sharper with the result that the government retrenches and openly attacks the living standards of all working people, especially blacks and other racial minorities.

In the 1980s, therefore, an attempt to rejuvenate the civil rights movement alone will not be sufficient. The 1980s are revealing that the abolition of racism is, in the end, inseparable from the necessity of ending the exploitation of the labor of men and women and achieving a just peace between nations.

NOTES

1. Quoted in George Breitman, *The Last Year of Malcolm X* (New York: Merit Publishers, 1967), pp. 35–36.
2. George Breitman (ed.), *Malcolm X Speaks* (New York: Grove Press, 1966), p. 218
3. *Ibid,* pp. 75–6.
4. For a detailed discussion see Cathy Perkus (ed.), *COINTELPRO: The FBI's Secret War on Political Freedom* (New York: Monad Press, 1975).
5. Robert B. Hill, *The Illusion of Black Progress* (Washington: National Urban League Research Department, 1978), p. 27.
6. Clayborne Carson, *In Struggle: SNCC and the Black Awakening of the 1960s* (Cambridge: Harvard University Press, 1981), p. 175.
7. Clyde Taylor (ed.) *Vietnam and Black America* (New York: Anchor Books, 1973), p. 70.
8. Quoted in Robert L. Allen, *Black Awakening in Capitalist America* (New York: Anchor Books, 1970). p. 46.
9. Kirkpatrick Sale, *SDS* (New York: Vintage Books, 1974), p. 315.
10. Taylor, *Vietnam and Black America,* p. xviii.
11. Sara Evans, *Personal Politics: The Roots of Women's Liberation in the Civil Rights Movement and the New Left* (New York: Knopf, 1979), p. 24.
12. Ann Popkin, "The Personal is Political," in Dick Cluster (ed.), *They*

Should Have Served That Cup of Coffee: Seven Radicals Remember the 1960s (Boston: South End Press, 1979), pp. 187–8.

13. Evans, *Personal Politics,* p. 234.
14. *Ibid.*
15. Frances Beal, "Slave of a Slave No More: Black Women in Struggle," *The Black Scholar,* March, 1975.
16. Angela Davis, "Rape, Racism and the Capitalist Setting," *The Black Scholar,* April, 1978, p. 25.
17. Quoted in Allen, *Black Awakening,* pp. 169–70.
18. Alice Walker, *The Black Scholar,* November-December, 1981, p. 80.
19. Manning Marable, "Reaganism, Racism and Reaction: Black Political Realignment in the 1980s," *The Black Scholar,* forthcoming.

Index